Questions & Answers

FAMILY LAW

Questions & Answers

FAMILY LAW

Seventh edition

Ruth Gaffney-Rhys
Reader in Law, University of Wales, Newport

with Chris Barton
Visiting Professor of Family Law,
Staffordshire University Law School

Mary Hibbs
Former Solicitor and Senior Lecturer in Law,
Staffordshire University Law School

Penny Booth
Freelance Law Tutor, Honorary Research Fellow,
Centre for the Study of the Child, the Family and the Law,
University of Liverpool, and Former Professor of Child and
Family Law, Staffordshire University Law School

2013 and 2014

OXFORD
UNIVERSITY PRESS

OXFORD

UNIVERSITY PRESS

Great Clarendon Street, Oxford, OX2 6DP,
United Kingdom

Oxford University Press is a department of the University of Oxford.
It furthers the University's objective of excellence in research, scholarship,
and education by publishing worldwide. Oxford is a registered trade mark of
Oxford University Press in the UK and in certain other countries

© Ruth Gaffney-Rhys, Chris Barton, Mary Hibbs, and Penny Booth 2013

The moral rights of the authors have been asserted

Fourth edition 2004
Fifth edition 2007
Sixth edition 2011

Impression: 2

Public sector information reproduced under Open Government Licence v1.0
(http://www.nationalarchives.gov.uk/doc/open-government-licence/open-government-licence.htm)

Crown Copyright material reproduced with the permission of the
Controller, HMSO (under the terms of the Click Use licence)

British Library Cataloguing in Publication Data
Data available

ISBN 978-0-19-966194-7

Printed in Great Britain by
Ashford Colour Press Ltd, Gosport, Hampshire

CONTENTS

Key features

The Q&A series provides full coverage of key subjects in a clear and logical way.

This book contains the following features:

- Questions
- Commentary
- Bullet-pointed answer plans
- Examiner's tips
- Suggested answers
- Further reading suggestions

 online resource centre

www.oxfordtextbooks.co.uk/orc/qanda/

Titles in the Q&A series are supported by additional online materials to aid study and revision.

Online resources for this title are hosted at the URL above, which is open access and free to use.

PREFACE

The first edition of this book was published in 1994, shortly after the Children Act 1989 and the Child Support Act 1991 came into force. Since then we have witnessed several significant changes, such as the introduction of civil partnerships, the recognition of gender reassignment, the reform of adoption law and improved protection for the victims of domestic violence. Family law is so fast-moving that much has happened since the sixth edition of this book, including a review of the family justice system, the introduction of legislation to restrict the availability of legal aid and a proposal to allow same-sex marriage. Although the content of family law modules is modified to reflect these developments, family law students continue to be assessed in the same way, i.e. by examination or by examination and coursework. Furthermore, the style of the examination and assignment questions has not altered, as family law students are still expected to tackle essay and problem questions. This book is intended to help students facing such assessments and should be supplemented by the further reading identified at the end of each chapter.

Ruth Gaffney-Rhys
Summer 2012

- New questions on the use of mediation in divorce proceedings, the rights and responsibilities of fathers and surrogacy.

- Discussion of recent case law such as *Radmacher (formerly Granatino) (Respondent) v Granatino (Appellant)* [2010] UKSC 42 (on prenuptial contracts), *Jones (Appellant) v Kernott (Respondent)* [2011] UKSC 53 (on beneficial interests in property), *Re K (Children)* [2011] EWCA Civ 973 (on relocation outside of the jurisdiction) and *Re S (A Child)* [2012] UKSC 10 (on child abduction).

- Discussion of new legislation including: the Legal Aid, Sentencing and Punishment of Offenders Act 2012 (not in force at the time of writing) and Practice Direction 3A – Pre-Application Protocol for Mediation Information and Assessment (which came into force in April 2011).

- Discussion of recent decisions of the European Court of Human Rights, e.g. *Schalke and Kopf v Austria* [2010] ECHR 995 (on same-sex marriage).

- Discussion of consultation documents and proposals, e.g. *Equal Civil Marriage: A Consultation* (2012), *Strengthening Families, Promoting Responsibility: The Future of Child Maintenance* (2011), *Forced Marriage Consultation* (2011) and the Family Justice Review Final Report (2011).

- Recent statistics, e.g. the Judicial and Court Statistics 2011 (published in 2012).

- Updated 'Further reading' lists.

- An 'Examiner's tip' for every question, which suggests how students can gain extra marks and avoid pitfalls.

- Additional diagrams and tables.

TABLE OF CASES

TABLE OF UK LEGISLATION

Bills

TABLE OF SECONDARY LEGISLATION

TABLE OF INTERNATIONAL LEGISLATION

1 Introduction: technique for exams and coursework

Most students enjoy family law—they are likely to be finalists studying it from choice—but hardly anyone enjoys being assessed. This book shows candidates how to display their learning (and/or how to disguise their ignorance). Although the means of converting a year's study into good marks can be mastered far more easily than the year's study itself, even senior students can be surprisingly reluctant to devote time to it. So even though this opening chapter is particularly valuable to them, it has been kept short.

This chapter starts with three lists of exam hints. Where relevant, the assumption is that the exam is to be set internally. The first list consists of preparation advice whilst the second covers the exam itself. Some of the points made in these two lists are obviously applicable to any exam, law or otherwise. Even third-year students may gain from the first two lists, if only by way of a refresher course. The third list is exclusively concerned with *family law* exams.

Before embarking on these lists, you should take note of the following advice about coursework, now commonly a part of the assessment process. The advice is that the *minimum* the markers want in return for the extra time and the ability to consult the books and each other which coursework affords, is that you *do the basics properly*. (See the postscript to this chapter at pp. 6–7, **Postscript—coursework**.)

Dos and don'ts BEFORE exams

(a) Get the time and place right; check that noticeboard (and your emails) again and do not rely on your classmates (for this or for anything else).

(b) Know the form; i.e. duration, degree of choice, any reading time. Is the exam in parts? Is the exam 'open book'? 'Seen'? Is anything compulsory? Are marks for all questions equal?

(c) Don't believe what your classmates say about how little work they are doing. There is no substitute for thorough learning: it is the only way you can approach an exam with (justifiable) confidence.

(d) Look at past papers. Some examiners actually recycle material, attempting to salve their consciences by changing dates and names etc. Be particularly suspicious if there are no past papers in the library or on the net. That apart, problems, in particular, are a bit like crossword puzzle clues in that you become familiar with the examiners' style.

(e) Take note of the examiners' (and the externals') views, particularly if published. Revision classes are likely to be rich in implicit—or even express—hints.

(f) Work out the time at which you should be starting the second and subsequent questions. If the arithmetic is complicated, e.g. the exam starts at 9.15, with ten minutes' reading time with five questions to do in three hours, then it is easy to lose track of time. Remember to allow for reading time in this.

(g) The last topic taught is a good bet; similarly, anything new, e.g. Law Commission recommendations etc.

(h) Claim any allowance to which you may be entitled, e.g. extra time, amanuensis, word-processor, private room, etc.

(i) If the exam is open book, make sure you have everything you are allowed and know your way around it. Check how best to deploy it all within the limited confines of an exam hall desk. Remember that the examiners will want something extra from you in return for their benevolence (more so, of course, if they have also given advance notice of the questions). Do not forget that, as in all exams, you are required to answer the question set, and that an open book (or 'seen') exam is particularly unlikely to be of the 'Tell me all about ...' variety, so you will not be able to answer simply by 'lifting' from the book.

(j) Prepare a short introductory statement for each topic; definition(s); place within the subject as a whole; an out-of-the-way quote from the wilds of the further reading; and some thought of your own. On the day, however, do remember to tailor it to the actual question, of course.

(k) If you have, or you think you have, weaknesses in your exam technique, go to your college's student counsellors. They are free, accessible and private. There is no shame involved and you cannot lose; they tend to know a lot about exam worries, rational and otherwise.

Dos and don'ts DURING exams

Before you start writing

(l) Check the rubric, despite point (b).

(m) Read the whole paper with the object of deciding which questions you can, and ideally will, do. (This applies whether or not there is any formal 'reading time', but if there is, then scribble notes on the paper itself, if permitted.) Make sure you have read all the paper—turn the page over!

(n) Achieve this object (i.e. point (m)) by deciding which areas of the subject are invoked by which questions.

(o) In doing this, you might read the essay questions, or part-questions, first. That way—essay questions having less bulk and less potential for concealment than problems—early inroads may be made more quickly. Then look at the problems, starting with those which are the other part(s) of the half-essay questions, and remember that a two-part question may involve different topic(s) in each part. Remember also that all this may take some time, and involve reading several sides of A4 paper.

(p) The golden rule, particularly with problems, is not to panic if the penny doesn't drop on first reading—read it again and the ideas should start to come. If they do not, take your law into the question, i.e. check off the topics covered in the course. If in doubt, do not do it—always assuming you can do the required number without it.

(q) Ready to start? Think (see point (j)) and note the time (see point (f)). Do not start before you are ready just because everyone else appears to be scribbling furiously.

Answering: pointers common to both essays and problems

(r) Use a conventional essay style with paragraphs and a beginning, middle and end: *not* note form other than where you are desperate for time, i.e. at the end of the last question.

(s) Spelling and general literariness will pay, so at the very least make sure you can spell 'Matrimonial Causes' and 'Cretney' and the like. (Do not call it 'the Children's Act' and, on a related issue, start your preparation for the resit now, if you have referred to extra-marital cohabitation as 'common law marriage'.) If you have 'good cause' for any writing or spelling difficulties, then you should already have acted on point (h); if not see points (ee) and (ff) which follow.

(t) Use point (j).

(u) Cite authority for your propositions. As ever in law exams, the more relevant authority you cite properly, the better your answer. So far as cases are concerned, the principle and the facts are the most important; names if you can remember them; with dates a poor fourth (unless they are significant, e.g. for modernity). Underline, or otherwise emphasize, the name. This is not merely for cosmetic reasons: it is the handwritten equivalent of the italics used in print. If you cannot remember the name, use some such phrase as 'in a decided case'. In child law, many cases are known by a single capital letter.

(v) Spell out the name of a statute the first time you use it ('**Family Law Act 1996**', but 'FLA' thereafter)—as a finalist, you will know too much to want to pad out your answers unnecessarily. Try to recall the section numbers if you can, particularly the key ones (e.g. **s. 8, Children Act 1989** orders); more so if it is open book.

Answering: essays

(w) As a very general principle, essays are easier than problems in that there is less scope to display technique (see points (z)–(dd) which follow); it follows (equally generally) that the same amount of knowledge may be deployed to greater effect in a problem.

(x) Use your knowledge in the manner required of you, i.e. if the question is: '**The Adoption and Children Act 2002** represents a missed opportunity for unmarried fathers and their children', then there are few marks to be had for discussing the Act generally. Do not just describe the material concerned—judge it in the way asked of you. Answer the question set, not the question you wish had been set.

Ground your analysis in the academic materials you have been studying, and remember that if the essay attributes a view to someone or something prominent, be it *Bromley's Family Law* or the Law Commission, there is likely to be something to be said for it.

(y) Say what you are going to say, say it, and say what you have said. This is easy enough in coursework, but do not panic in the exam if, halfway through an answer, you change your mind. The examiners see many such changes of direction.

Answering: problems

(z) ISAC!—Identify (the relevant area of law). State (the relevant law). Apply (the law to the facts of the problem). Conclude.

(aa) Note the question, i.e. what you are being asked to do with the data. Often, it will be to advise one or more of the parties; e.g. would she succeed in her application for/resistance to: a residence order, financial relief or occupation order? The answer may well be qualified—examiners like their creations to be evenly balanced. The point of law may be unclear, or its application to the declared facts debatable. (Implicitly praise the question for being so darned clever.) So debate the issues—do not just raise them.

(bb) Make sure that you have grasped the legal significance of all the data. There will be little in the way of superfluous material. If your initial analysis leaves parts of the story untouched, read them again. You could use a highlighting pen for this purpose, thus giving you a cumulative visual check.

The examiners started by thinking, 'Q. 3(a). We will make it a nullity problem…er…duress, lot of cases there…non-consummation, ditto…good, three-year bar for the first, but not the second…so the marriage can be coming up to three years old and we will make the non-consummation part the less likely to work…'. If you decode the story and start by telling the examiners where they started, they will be impressed from the outset and expect to read what should be there.

(cc) Deal with each area in turn, after you have set the scene (see points (j) and (bb)). So far as choice of sequence is concerned, there are a number of possibilities. Use any one of them, but make sure you announce it (never give the examiners the chance to miss how clever you—and they—are). Two easy alternatives are, respectively, the order in which: (i) the facts appear in the question; or (ii) the relevant law appears in the statute. Another way, particularly if you are running out of time, is in descending order of volume of material, so you deal first with those points which are worth the most marks. Perhaps the best sequence—and hardest (but see point (y))—is in ascending order of importance, so that each point carries an increasingly heavier punch.

(dd) If you are 'defending', one weak area in the other's case may do the trick overall, although the story will never be structured so as to permit you to kill the whole thing off by dealing with one item only. When you are 'attacking', you will need to be satisfied, on balance, with all the links in your chain.

After the exam

It is much better (and ultimately easier, probably) to have done the work, rather than to have recourse to these next two, however:

(ee) File your medical certificate/statement of extenuating circumstances before the deadline. Also see your personal tutor and student counsellor, if you have not done so pre-emptively (see points (h) and (s)).

(ff) Appeal, where appropriate.

Family law exams in particular

(gg) Be modern. The bad news about family law for teachers and practitioners, i.e. that it changes more in a month than jurisprudence does in a decade, can be turned to your advantage. An hour with the most recent Family Law Reports (and/or Family Law journal) during the revision period might repay you with a case for a question.

(hh) Be aware of the potential for mixed-topic questions. In the good old 'real world' the client may well want a divorce, ancillary relief and a residence order as well as immediate protection from violence; it is sometimes thus in the exam as well. Consider the significance of this when you are considering what topics to drop during revision—with a bit of luck, you can hawk beneficial interests round three exams, i.e. land law, equity and trusts—and family law.

(ii) Remember that different topics attach different degrees of priority to the welfare (of children) principle—e.g. occupation orders, financial relief and **s. 1 of the Children Act (CA) 1989**. Know chapter and verse in each case.

(jj) Be sensitive as to whether the partnership is marital, registered or neither.

(kk) Be ready to make choices between/amongst a number of possible courts and remedies, e.g. divorce or magistrates' court, say.

(ll) Be ready to use some statistics, e.g. numbers of divorces and the children involved; one-parent families; wedding/registration rates; pre-marital cohabitation rates;

number of same-sex couples; number of fixed-term financial relief orders made etc. Essays (law reform etc.) can make particular use of this and other social data, but you can slip them into problems in half a sentence.

(mm) Note dates and times, e.g. when the parties were wed/registered, how long they have lived apart, how old the children are. Virtually all family law problems contain data which is time-significant. The length of the relationship may involve bars in nullity; how much of it was merely pre-marital might still affect financial relief. The age of children can always be used; e.g. the weight to be attached to their views, whether they can be given leave to apply for a **CA 1989, s. 8** order or be treated as '*Gillick* [spelling] competent'.

(nn) Be right-on! Family lawyers, at least those who teach, tend to an attitude of 'social responsibility'. Get a copy of the Resolution (formerly the Solicitors Family Law Association) Code of Practice (see www.resolution.org.uk) and trot out its contents as appropriate.

(oo) Europe and the UN. You should be ready and able to slip appropriate Articles from the **European Convention on Human Rights (ECHR) 1950** or **the United Nations Convention on the Rights of the Child (UNCRC) 1989** into your assessments. Here is a checklist of some of the Articles, and their accompanying rights, which bear repeated playing. **ECHR 1950: 6** (a fair hearing); **8** (respect for private and family life); **12** (marry and found a family); **14** (prohibition of discrimination); and **Article 5 of the 7th Protocol** (equality of rights of spouses). Almost by definition, homes can be found in the answer to almost any child law question for at least one Article from the **UNCRC**. A core selection might include: **3** (child's best interests); **5** (parental guidance appropriate to child's evolving capacities); **9** (right to contact with both parents); **12** (child's opinion to be taken into account); **18** (joint parental responsibility); **19** (state obligation of protection from abuse) and **21** (child's best interests in adoption). Be sure you know the differing weights attached to each Convention by our domestic law.

Postscript—coursework

A lawyer who 'did it for real' the way it is done in exams might well be guilty of professional negligence: i.e. a number of inadequately summarized matters (probably chosen for their difficulty) being dealt with in handwriting in a ridiculously short time without reference or consultation.

Coursework—now often used as a mid-year assessment device contributing up to 50 per cent of the total marks available—examines skills which cannot otherwise be tested properly, or sometimes even at all. It is a medium by which a person's capacity for research and reflection can properly be measured at appropriate length. It encourages recourse to word-processing and allows for peer discussion without prejudice to individual responsibility. It provides an opportunity for self-managed time and to anticipate (other) postgraduate skills. In particular—and you may care to remember this—it removes pretty well every excuse for getting the basics wrong.

Not surprisingly, most students get more marks in coursework than they do in the exam. On which point, do check the weighting between the two, and measure your commitment accordingly. Your rapture on reaching a coveted First in an assignment should be modified if it contributes a mere 25 per cent of the total, although such niggardliness should also be reflected in the quantity (not quality) required of you. In a modern Law School all such information, including the coursework questions themselves and what you get your marks for, should be contained in the Module Study Guides distributed in the first lecture: and be permanently available—and updated—on the internet. Maximize your exploitation of such rubrics, and your advance knowledge of the question. Let them both marinate in your consciousness as the course unfolds, and as you make the connections between your growing knowledge and what is asked of you. If you discuss it with your classmates, avoid collusive plagiarism, of which more later. Tailor your tutorial preparation with the coursework in mind.

High marks in word-limit coursework, and this also applies to exams, where it is much harder to do, are achieved by demonstrating a depth of understanding available only to those who have mastered the rudiments—which such people may therefore safely go light on. (To put it another way, missing the opportunity to go beyond the student texts will limit the rewards available.) The three steps involved in this may be stated very simply. First, raid the primary sources for stuff not in the main texts. Quotations from judgments are an easy example. Secondly, ransack the relevant academia—journals and books. Electronically, the titles are quickly found, at which point (with the help of the abstracts and conclusions) gut them quickly, fishing out a relevant quote. Thirdly, keep pondering: what does the question *mean*? and what do *you* think about it?, remembering that the more you read, the more you'll get out of yourself. One specific tip: if the question contains a quotation, then look it up, milk the whole of the material and see if you can find any response to it elsewhere.

This is a good point at which to discuss plagiarism, i.e. passing off other people's work as your own, be it your classmate's (whether he or she knows it or not) or someone more august. If the marker detects plagiarism you are likely to face a disciplinary hearing for academic dishonesty. So if you find some good stuff in the books or on the net, use it happily—just attribute it. Paying some dubious supplier, or even sweet-talking your aunt the judge, to do the whole thing? On your own head be it if you get caught: resit limited to a Third and no reference to the Law Society are just two of the likely outcomes. Many places are getting wise to such ploys and use secret countering devices, although anonymous tip-offs from—understandably resentful—classmates remain a prolific source.

Conclusion

The answers in this textbook are 'suggested', rather than 'model'. In an effort to supply more information, some are rather longer than one might be able to handwrite under examination conditions. However, they may be shorter than the word limit set for a piece of coursework.

Further reading

Burton, F. (2012) *Family Law* (Abingdon: Routledge–Taylor and Francis).

Finch, E. and Fafinski, S. (2011) *Legal Skills*, 3rd edn (Oxford: Oxford University Press).

Harris-Short, S. and Miles, J. (2011) *Family Law: Text, Cases, and Materials*, 2nd edn (Oxford: Oxford University Press).

Heenan, S. and Heenan, A. (2012) *Family Law: Concentrate* (Oxford: Oxford University Press).

Herring, J. (2011) *Family Law*, 5th edn (London: Longman).

Lowe, N., and Douglas, G. (2006) *Bromley's Family Law*, 10th edn (Oxford: Oxford University Press).

Masson, J., Bailey-Harris, R. and Probert, R. (2008) *Cretney's Principles of Family Law*, 8th edn (London: Sweet & Maxwell).

Ministry of Justice (2012) Judicial and Court Statistics.

Oldham, M. (2012) *Blackstone's Statutes on Family Law 2012–2013*, 21st edn (Oxford: Oxford University Press).

Probert, R. (2009) *Cretney and Probert's Family Law*, 7th edn (London: Sweet & Maxwell).

2 Family law: cohabitation and marriage

Introduction

Family law students are increasingly expected to be able to discuss the meaning of the 'family' and the social policies that drive legal reform in this area. Examinations and assignments often pose all-embracing questions such as 'The law is primarily interested in the nuclear family. Discuss', which enable candidates to demonstrate broad knowledge of the law and current social issues. The first question in this chapter falls into this category. The second question considers marriage, in particular forced marriage, which has become popular amongst examiners since the **Forced Marriage (Civil Protection) Act 2007** came into effect. Questions on the 'right to marry' will also frequently appear in family law assessments, as it is an opportunity to examine the impact of **Art. 12 of the European Convention on Human Rights 1950** and has generated some interesting case law. For example, in *Schalke and Kopf v Austria* [2010] ECHR 995 the European Court of Human Rights confirmed that contracting states are not required to allow same-sex marriage.

The final question concerns extra-marital cohabitation and asks students whether they approve of the legal differences between such relationships and marriage. It clearly requires candidates to display wide-ranging knowledge of the law relating to property, domestic violence, children and death. However, the distinction between married and unmarried couples will also appear in questions that focus on one of these topics alone. For example, part (b) of the first question in **Chapter 5**, which considers domestic violence, asks how the answer would differ if the parties had never married.

Question 1

In which members of the family is family law interested?

 Commentary

Although this question is apparently descriptive in scope, it provides room for debate as to what constitutes 'family' and as to the meaning of 'interest' in this context. Elementary contextual knowledge, such as the meaning of 'nuclear' and 'extended', can be pressed into service, as can anthropological definitions of the family unit. This answer aims to show how the student with a good overall knowledge of the subject can scan that knowledge to good effect.

 Answer plan

- The most important members are the nuclear family—on division.
- The most important of those are partners, parents and children.
- Some differences between marriage and registration but not between 'different' and 'same' sex cohabitations.
- Grandparents, step-parents and in-laws.
- Net most widespread on death!

 Examiner's tip

Try to include reference to **Art. 8 of the European Convention on Human Rights** and the European Court's definition of the family.

 Suggested answer

Had the question asked about the family members with which the law is most *frequently* concerned, it would not be necessary to venture far beyond the nuclear family, marital or otherwise. Domestic partners (married, unmarried and now registered) and children (marital and non-marital) take up most, if not all, of the time of the family lawyer. Of those, the extra-marital group had little legal significance, particularly so far as the adult partners were concerned, until the early 1970s (e.g. the fate of the family home in *Cooke v Head* **[1972] 1 WLR 518**). Had the question been about *when* the law is most interested, it would have been necessary to limit the enquiry to the division, or at least the straining, of relationships. It should be noted at the outset that the very word '"family" . . . must be given its popular meaning at the time relevant to the decision in the particular case' (*Dyson Holdings v Fox* [1975] 2 All ER 1030, 1035–6 *per* James LJ). At the end of the millennium the House of Lords held that a homosexual couple could constitute a 'family' for the purposes of tenancy succession under the **Rent Act 1977** (*Fitzpatrick v Sterling Housing Association* [2000] 1 FCR 21). **Section 62(3) of the Family Law Act 1996 (FLA 1996)** had already included within its definition of 'associated persons' those who 'live or have lived in the same household', thus permitting a same-sex partner to obtain a 'non-molestation' order. The **Gender Recognition Act 2004**, the **Civil Partnership Act 2004** and the **Domestic Violence, Crime and Victims Act 2004** all extended the domain of 'family' law. The first introduced 'gender recognition certificates' which grant the bearer 'acquired' gender status, the second affords quasi-marital status to registered same-sex couples and the third extended the definition of 'associated persons' (**FLA 1996**) to 'intimate personal relationships', i.e. those which have never involved marriage, cohabitation or even engagement. The incorporation into English law of the **European Convention on Human Rights 1950** by the **Human Rights Act 1998** has considerable potential here, as **Art. 8** requires respect for family life. For example, in *Re R (A Child) (IVF: Paternity of Child)* [2005] UKHL 33 it was held that whilst genetic fatherhood does not always produce family life, social parenthood may. The European Court of Human Rights may declare that a relationship falls within the definition of 'family life' for the purpose of **Art. 8** when English law does not recognize it (see *X, Y and Z v UK* [1997] 2 FLR 892) and vice versa.

We may at least start with the law's acknowledgement of the seven 'primary' relatives (mother, father, sister and brother from the 'family of orientation', and partner, son and daughter from the 'family of procreation'). It seems that the latter group attracts the most, and the most-invoked, law. So far as financial support for the children is concerned, it now makes very little difference whether the parents are married or not. With regard to child support legislation, the **Child Support Act 1991** (reformed by the **Child Maintenance and Other Payments Act 2008**) requires a 'non-resident parent' (**s. 1(2)**) to meet her or his 'responsibility to maintain' if she/he is 'in law the mother or father of the child' (**s. 54**). The non-marital father is, however, not equated with his married counterpart in so far as the prima facie vesting of parental responsibility is concerned. **Section 2(1) of the Children Act (CA) 1989** treats the married father in the same way as his wife, i.e. automatic parental responsibility, but the father who is not married to the mother needs a court order, the mother's agreement or needs to have jointly registered the birth (**s. 4** as amended by the **Adoption and Children Act 2002**). Joint registration is likely to become more common if the draft Registration of Births (Parents Not Married and Not Acting Together) Regulations 2010 come into force, as this legislation will require both parents to register their details, unless exceptional circumstances apply. Most importantly, if the child's upbringing becomes a matter for the court, then 'its' welfare becomes 'the paramount consideration' under **s. 1(1) of the CA 1989**, a criterion which may bring into play adults from outside the family.

So far as the unmarried partners themselves are concerned, there is no duty to maintain, no divorce and no financial relief, despite popular misunderstandings about the wrongly named 'common law marriage'. At the other extreme, the position of cohabitants sometimes approaches assimilation with that of spouses, for example **s. 2(2) of the Law Reform (Succession) Act 1995** amended the **Inheritance (Provision for Family and Dependants) Act 1975** to permit claims by a surviving cohabitant, provided the cohabitation lasted for a continuous period of at least two years immediately before the deceased's death (**s. 1(1A) of the 1975 Act**). (Even then, a surviving cohabitant is less well placed than a spouse in that the former's financial provision is limited to an amount sufficient for his or her 'maintenance' (**s. 1(2)(b)**).) Under the **Civil Partnership Act 2004**, there is no legal distinction to be made between unmarried different-sex cohabitants and their unregistered same-sex equivalents. (On the other hand, there are a number of differences between marriage and registration, for example the opening ceremonies, and the grounds for nullity and divorce.) So far as cohabitation is concerned, the Law Commission recommended that there be an opt-out scheme involving discretionary remedies for 'eligible' unwed/unregistered couples (Law Com Consultation Paper No. 179, 2006) but this was not acted upon. The Law Commission has also recommended improving the rights of a cohabitant in the event of the partner's intestacy (Law Com No. 191, 2009 and No. 331, 2011) but legislation has not been introduced to implement the recommendations.

In terms of the 'family of orientation', does the law retain any interest after the child comes of age at 18 (**s. 1, Family Law Reform Act 1969**)? Precious little continuing duty is owed by the parents; indeed, on divorce the court's duty under **s. 41 of the Matrimonial Causes Act 1973** to consider whether its **Children Act 1989** powers should be exercised is limited to children of the family under 16, unless the court directs otherwise (**s. 41(3)(b)**). The corollary is that until such time as the state offloads responsibility for the elderly, adult children owe little if any legal duty to their parents. It is in the area of succession, particularly the intestate variety, that the law is most concerned with adult parent–child relationships. Siblings and the extended family are also involved, as seen later.

This leads onto the 33 'secondary' relatives as the sociologists call them. One can start with grandparents, who might well be given leave to apply for a **s. 8 CA 1989** order under **s. 10(1)(a)(ii)**—as in *Re W (Contact Application by Grandparent)* [1997] 1 FLR 793. Similarly, in *Re C (Family Placement)* [2009] EWCA Civ 72 a residence order was made in favour of a grandmother in preference to a care order.

Even more branches of the family tree are encountered by way of the incest taboo and the prohibited degrees of consanguinity and affinity. Under **Sch. 1 to the Marriage Act 1949**, the prohibited degrees of consanguinity cover parents, grandparents, children, grandchildren, brothers, sisters, half-brothers, half-sisters, uncles, aunts, nephews and nieces—a list which **ss. 64 and 65 of the Sexual Offences Act 2003** duplicate in its entirety for the purposes of criminalizing adult familial carnal knowledge. Apart from these consanguinity bars there still remains, even today, the possibility that a marriage contracted between certain affines would be invalid. Following the **Marriage (Prohib-**

ited Degrees of Relationship) Act (M(PDofR)A) 1986 marriage between step-relatives is permitted if (a) both parties are 21 or over and (b) the stepchild had never been a child of the step-parent's family at any time whilst the stepchild was under 18. The policy is that marriage should not be permitted where one of the parties has effectively acted as the other's mother or father during the stepchild's childhood, yet sexual inter-course and cohabitation remain available, of course. The **M(PDofR)A** also permitted marriage between in-laws if both parties were over 21 and both former spouses were deceased. However, these requirements were removed by the **Marriage Act 1949 (Remedial) Order 2007** following the decision of the European Court of Human Rights in *B and L v UK* **[2006] 1 FLR 35**, which held that the law violated **Art. 12** (the right to marry) of the **European Convention for the Protection of Human Rights and Fundamental Freedoms 1950**. The Court's reasoning was that the bar did not prevent such couples from either having sex, or cohabiting with, one another, and that it could in any case be circumvented by a private Act of Parliament.

Incidentally, under the **Adoption and Children Act 2002** (inserting **s. 4A** into the **CA 1989**) a *married* step-parent is able to obtain parental responsibility. The parent-spouse will need to have 'parental responsibility' (PR), and to consent, as will the other parent with PR. Failing that, the step-parent may apply for a court order.

Perhaps the legal net is at its most widespread on death. Should the deceased leave no surviving spouse or issue then, under the **Administration of Estates Act 1925**, all goes to the parent (in equal shares if they both survive), then brothers and sisters of the whole blood (the issue of any predeceased siblings taking their share), then brothers and sisters of the half blood, then grandparents equally, then (finally) uncles and aunts, with their issue taking their predeceased parents' share(s) on the statutory trusts. It is clear from this list that cohabitants, step-relations and in-laws cannot inherit under the law of intestacy. As explained earlier, in terms of unmarried partners, the Law Commission has proposed reform (Law Com No. 191, 2009 and No. 331, 2011).

To conclude, it is apparent that different areas of family law recognize different relationships, because the rationale of those laws varies. The **Marriage Act 1949** (as amended) recognizes step-relations because there is a need to protect children from exploitation by their step-parents or step-grandparents. In contrast, the **Administration of Estates Act 1925** refers to many secondary relations (but not cohabitants, step-relatives or in-laws) because the purpose of the legislation is to ensure property is passed to blood relatives (if the deceased left no will and no spouse). Different areas of family law are thus 'interested' in different family members.

? Question 2

How does the law protect adults at risk of being forced to marry?

Commentary

Until recently, the issue of forced marriage had not frequently appeared in family law examinations. However, such questions have become more common following the adoption of the **Forced Marriage (Civil Protection) Act 2007**, which came into force in November 2008. This question requires students to consider the statutory and inherent powers of the family courts to prevent forced marriages from taking place. If it had not specifically referred to 'adults', candidates could also have discussed wardship and the provisions of the **Children Act 1989**, that can be used to prevent a child from being forced into marriage. It is not necessary to discuss the law of nullity as the question refers to adults at risk of being forced to marry rather than persons who have married as a consequence of duress.

 Answer plan

Non-specific protection	Specific protection
Inherent jurisdiction of the High Court—**Re SK [2005]**	**Forced Marriage (Civil Protection Act) 2007**
Non-molestation orders—**FLA 1996**	Inserted 19 provisions into the **FLA 1996**
Injunctions—**Protection from Harassment Act 1997**	Forced marriage protection order—**s. 63A FLA 1996**—civil order
Criminal law—assault, kidnap etc.	Breach of an order constitutes contempt—**s. 63(O) FLA 1996**

 Examiner's tip

Demonstrate the currency of your knowledge by including recent proposals to criminalize forced marriage.

 Suggested answer

The Consultation Paper *Forced Marriage: A Wrong Not a Right* (FCO/Home Office, 2005) defined a forced marriage as one 'conducted without the valid consent of one or both parties where duress is a factor' (p. 1). It must be distinguished from an arranged marriage, which is one where the families of one or both parties take a leading role in choosing the spouse, but the bride and groom provide free and full consent. The Forced

Marriage Unit (which is run by the Foreign and Commonwealth Office and the Home Office) was established to provide assistance for those at risk of being forced to marry in the UK and overseas. In 2010 the Unit gave advice in 1,735 cases, compared with 1,682 in 2009. However, it should be noted that many victims of forced marriage do not actually report the matter (www.fco.gov.uk/en/travel-and-living-abroad/when-things-go-wrong/forced-marriage/).

The family courts can grant a range of civil remedies to protect an adult at risk of being forced into a marriage. First, the High Court can utilize its inherent jurisdiction, which means the automatic, non-statutory powers that the court can exercise on behalf of the Crown. The Crown, as *'parens patriae'* or father of the nation, has a special duty to protect its subjects, particularly those who cannot protect themselves, such as children and vulnerable adults. The High Court has employed its inherent jurisdiction to protect adults (and children) at risk of forced marriage. For example, in *Re SK (Proposed Plaintiff) (An Adult by Way of her Litigation Friend)* [2005] 2 FLR 230 a solicitor was asked by the Foreign and Commonwealth Office to initiate proceedings in relation to an adult female (SK) who was believed to have been taken to Bangladesh for the purpose of a forced marriage. The court granted an order requiring SK's family to disclose her whereabouts and to allow SK to attend the British High Commission to be interviewed. The order also prohibited SK's parents from causing her to undergo a marriage ceremony and from threatening, harassing or using violence towards her. Following the order, SK was interviewed by a British Consular Officer and returned to the UK. In *M v B, A and S (by the Official Solicitor)* [2006] 1 FLR 117 the High Court exercised its inherent jurisdiction to protect a 23-year-old female with a severe learning disability (S) from being forced to marry. The order prohibited the family from taking any steps to arrange a marriage for S without the leave of the court and required them to surrender S's passport as there was a risk that she would be taken to Pakistan to be married. These cases demonstrate that High Court judges are prepared to use their inherent powers to prevent forced marriages from taking place. The fact that an application can be made by a third party acting as a litigation friend is also significant, as the victim may be unable to initiate proceedings him or herself.

An individual who is being pressurized into marriage may also be able to apply for a non-molestation order under the **Family Law Act 1996 (FLA 1996)** or an injunction under the **Protection from Harassment Act 1997**. A non-molestation order is an order prohibiting one party from molesting the other (**s. 42 FLA 1996**). Molestation is not defined in the Act but includes 'any form of serious pestering or harassment' (*Family Law: Domestic Violence and Occupation of the Family Home* (Law Com No. 207, 1992), para. 3.1). The courts can make an order against an 'associated person', which is defined in **s. 62(3)** and includes relatives of the victim. A non-molestation order could therefore be made against individuals who pressurize a family member to marry. **Section 3(3) of the Protection from Harassment Act 1997** enables an individual to apply for an injunction to prevent harassment. Harassment encompasses physical violence and 'alarming a person or causing the person distress' (**s. 7(2)**), however, it is only committed if conduct occurs on at least two occasions. The perpetrators of a forced marriage will commit harassment if they place pressure on the victim over a period of time, but not if they make one single attempt at forcing someone to marry. Although a person at risk of forced marriage may have the right to apply for a non-molestation order or injunction, in practice he or she may be reluctant to initiate proceedings against family members. Similarly, the activities associated with forced marriage may involve the commission of a criminal offence (e.g. assault and kidnap), but as most victims do not want their relatives to be prosecuted, they may be unwilling to contact the police for protection (*Forced Marriage: A Wrong Not a Right*, para. 2.1).

These laws were not created with forced marriage in mind and do not therefore make it clear that pressurizing someone into a marriage is unacceptable. Parliament thus enacted the **Forced Marriage (Civil Protection) Act 2007** in order to make this explicit and to provide more practical remedies. The Act inserted 19 provisions into the **FLA 1996** and therefore amalgamated the new provisions on forced marriage and those that already existed to protect the victims of domestic violence. **Section 63A of the FLA 1996** provides that the High Court and the county court can make an order for the purpose of protecting a person from being forced into a marriage or for the purpose of protecting a person who has been forced into a marriage. Force includes coercion 'by threats or other psychological means' (**s. 63A(6)**), which reflects the fact that threats of social exclusion are common in forced marriage cases. (See, for example, *Hirani v Hirani* [1983] 4 FLR 232.) The conduct that forces (or attempts to force) an individual to marry may be directed at the victim him or herself, the perpetrator him or herself or another person (**s. 64A(5)**). This provision was included because the perpetrators of forced marriage may threaten to harm themselves or other family members rather than the victim. For example, in *NS v MI* **[2007] 1 FLR 444** the victim's parents threatened to kill themselves if NS did not marry NI. **Section 63C(2) of** the Act provides that an application can be made by the person to be protected or a relevant third party without the need for leave of the court. The **Family Law Act 1996 (Forced Marriage) (Relevant Third Party) Order 2009** designates local authorities as relevant third parties, which is unsurprising given their expertise in child abuse cases and the protection of vulnerable adults. Any other interested person, for example friends, teachers and relatives, will require leave to apply for an order. It is essential that third parties can make an application because the victim may be too vulnerable to act for him or herself, unwilling to instigate proceedings for fear of reprisals or physically unable to make an application if he or she is being held against his or her will (as *Re SK* demonstrates).

The order can be made against those who force, attempt to force or may force a person to marry (**s. 63B(2)**) and those who encourage or assist them (**s. 63B(3)**). Where necessary, the application can be made without notice (**s. 63(D)**). The order itself may contain 'any such prohibitions, restrictions or requirements and such other terms as the court considers appropriate' (**s. 63B(1)**). For example, an order might prohibit the respondents from organizing a marriage for the victim and oblige them to surrender the victim's passport to the court. If the victim has been removed from the jurisdiction, the order can require the respondent to allow the victim to attend the British High Commission. This obligation was imposed by the High Court in the much publicized case of Dr Humayra Abedin, who was held captive by her family in Bangladesh. Following the order, Dr Abedin was released into the custody of the British High Commission and returned to the UK. The contents of a forced marriage protection order thus resemble the orders made by the High Court when exercising its inherent jurisdiction. However, the **2007 Act** improves access to justice as the county courts can also make protection orders and, in time, jurisdiction will be extended to the Magistrates' Family Proceedings Court. By the end of 2011, 414 orders had been issued by the courts (Judicial and Court Statistics, 2012).

Failure to comply with a protection order constitutes contempt of court, which is punishable by up to two years in prison (**s. 63(O)**). This is designed to ensure that orders are taken seriously, but should not deter those at risk from coming forward, as their relatives will not automatically be prosecuted. However, the Government has since announced that it intends to make breach of a forced marriage civil protection order a specific criminal offence and proposes to create a specific offence of forcing someone to marry (*Forced Marriage Consultation* (Home Office, 2011) and *Summary of Responses* (Home Office, 2012)) in order to emphasize the severity of forced marriage. The Government does, however, recognize that this alone will be insufficient to protect the victims or potential victims of forced marriage and as a consequence intends to launch a three-year programme aimed at prevention and support for victims (Home Office, 2012).

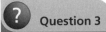

? Question 3

Do you approve of the legal differences between marriage and cohabitation?

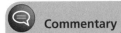

Commentary

Family law courses are likely to keep a running total of the score between the two forms of partnership, and the examination candidate is likely to have to economize, rather than maximize, in order to do well. It has become a 'scan and summarize question'. In an exam, it will not be possible to deal with every relevant incident, but your examples should be representative. Roam over the entire subject, for example violence, the home, property, money, succession and children. Perhaps this is best done chronologically, working through the history of the partnership from its inception onwards. Do use some statistics.

Answer plan

- Statistics—decline in weddings, increased cohabitation.
- Forms of cohabitation and reasons for cohabitation.
- Financial agreements.
- Property rights.
- Domestic violence.
- Children.

Examiner's tip

This question is a good example of the need for analysis. You are not asked just for a statement of the differences but for a value judgment about them.

Suggested answer

There has been a long-term decline in weddings over the last 40 years, from 480,285 in 1972 to 231,490 in 2009 (ONS, 2011). In contrast, the Office for National Statistics reported that there were 2.3 million cohabiting couples in the UK in 2008 and has estimated that this figure will rise to 3.8 million in 2033 (ONS, 2011). Perhaps these developments are to do with the fact that many people believe that informal pairing produces marriage-like status and that such relationships have become socially acceptable. As the number of cohabiting couples has grown and social acceptance of them has increased, so too has their legal recognition. It should be noted that unregistered same-sex couples must be treated in the same way as heterosexual cohabitants (see ***Ghaidan v Godin-Mendoza* [2004] 2 FLR 600**): reference to cohabitants in this essay thus includes heterosexual and homosexual couples. Similarly, civil partners (with a few exceptions) have the same rights as spouses under the **Civil Partnership Act 2004** and, as a result, this answer will not specifically discuss civil partners.

It may be helpful, in deciding whether to 'approve' of the 'legal differences', to consider the likely reasons for this lifestyle. Cohabitants might be categorized as: 'informed' (avoiding responsibility), 'uninformed' (living in ignorance), 'reluctant' (one wishes to marry but the other does not) and 'forced' (one or both married to someone else, or of the same sex)—see *Cohabitation—The Case for Clear Law* (Law Society, 2002). It should not be forgotten that living together can be achieved at will, and without expense, and that the declining social disapproval has been increasingly self-fulfilling. Times have changed: cohabitation is a socially acceptable alternative to marriage, rather than a mere prelude to it.

The legal differentials can be considered under a number of heads, for example choice of partners, during the functioning relationship, after death, the failing relationship, ending it and afterwards.

At the start of the relationship, the parties may enter into a domestic partnership agreement, the status of which has been considered by the courts in recent years. In so far as a 'pre-marital contract' might purport to deal with the post-marital financial arrangements, it cannot be guaranteed as binding, because the parties may not contract out of the divorce court's powers of financial relief under the **Matrimonial Causes Act (MCA) 1973.** However, a court hearing an application for financial relief must consider the agreement, as it is required to have regard to 'all the circumstances' under **s. 25** (see *K v K (Ancillary Relief: Prenuptial Agreement)* [2003] 1 FLR 120). In *Radmacher v Radmacher (formerly Granatino)* [2010] UKSC 42, the Supreme Court set out the factors that a court should consider when deciding how much weight to attach to a pre-nuptial contract. The Law Commission is also examining this issue and so we may see legislative reform in the future (*Consultation on Marital Property Agreements* (Law Com No. 198, 2011)). So far as cohabitation contracts are concerned, it is clear from *Sutton v Mishcon de Reya and Gawor and Co.* [2004] EWHC 3166, that they are binding provided there is a manifested intent to create legal relations, there is no promise of payment for sexual services and none of the vitiating factors apply. In 2006 the Law Commission recommended legislation to provide, for the avoidance of doubt, that cohabitation contracts for financial and property matters are not contrary to public policy (para. 10.9). Perhaps couples who hanker for pre-emptive private ordering are better served by cohabitation, rather than pre-marital, contracts, given that the former involve a comparatively blank legal canvass.

Where differences do still exist, the more stringent law, if any, is to be found in marriage. A refusal of sex, or infidelity, may give rise to matrimonial causes or domestic proceedings, whereas no such rights or duties arise from a 'mere' cohabitation, no matter how long-standing. Given that cohabiting couples can technically terminate their relationship by ceasing to cohabit, such differences are to be expected.

Generally, the question of who owns the home is a matter of standard principles of contract, conveyancing, equity and trusts which do not make a distinction between married and unmarried couples (*Pettit v Pettit* [1970] AC 777; *Gissing v Gissing* [1971] AC 886). In cases concerning insolvency, the partner of the bankrupt must rely on his or her property rights and no distinction is made between married and unmarried couples. However, spouses and cohabitants with children are afforded slightly better protection if the creditor applies to sell the property under the **Trusts of Land and Appointment of Trustees Act 1996.** But if a couple separates, a spouse has the safety net of the courts' discretionary powers of property adjustment under **the MCA 1973** whereas a cohabitant does not. There are thus hard cases like *Burns v Burns* [1984] **FLR 216** (19-year cohabitation, the woman took the man's name and gave up her job to look after him), and *Lloyds Bank plc v Rosset* [1990] **2 FLR 155** (wife's supervision of renovation), where the court refused to draw the inference from the woman's indirect contribution that the beneficial interest be shared. In *Stack v Dowden* [2007] **1 FLR**

1858 Baroness Hale and Lord Walker both indicated that, in relation to matrimonial or quasi-matrimonial property, the narrow approach adopted in *Rosset* was outdated. Despite this, it remains difficult for a cohabitant to claim a beneficial interest in property that is registered in the sole name of her partner, as *James v Thomas* [2007] **EWCA Civ 1212**, which was decided after *Stack v Dowden*, demonstrates. Whether this should be changed is the subject of much debate. On the one hand, it can be argued that an individual who has chosen to remain unmarried should not have the consequences of marriage forced upon him. On the other hand, a cohabitant who has given up work to look after the home and children deserves protection and if she is unable to make a claim against her former partner, she may be reliant on the state for support.

Death provides a variety of legal responses. As explained in the **Suggested answer to Question 1,** cohabitants have no rights on intestacy under the **Administration of Estates Act 1925** as amended. The Law Commission has recommended that a surviving cohabitant should in certain circumstances share the deceased partner's estate without having to go to court (2009) but this has not yet been acted upon. In addition, a cohabitant's rights differ from those of a spouse under the **Inheritance (Provision for Family and Dependants) Act 1975** as the former can only qualify as of right if he or she had been living with the deceased at the time of the death and for at least two years beforehand. It is thus clear that a cohabitant has to prove that the relationship is durable, whereas a spouse does not, as the latter has proved his or her commitment by forming the marriage.

During the failure of the relationship, rights of protection from violence and of occupation in the home are, again, available to both sorts of partner under **Part IV of the Family Law Act 1996.** The **Domestic Violence, Crime and Victims Act 2004** repealed **s. 41,** which required the court, when considering an application for an occupation order by a non-entitled (i.e. non-owning) cohabitant, 'to have regard to the fact that the parties have not given each other the commitment involved in marriage.' The definition of 'cohabitants' now includes same-sex pairs, thereby enabling the one to make an 'occupation' application under **s. 36 of the 1996 Act** (i.e. where only the other has an interest in the property). It is clearly appropriate to provide protection from domestic violence to as many people as possible, regardless of the form or duration of their relationship.

Many people would say that legal differences require the greatest scrutiny where they concern a person's capacity as a parent; children have no say about the nature of their parents' relationship. **Section 1(1) and (2) of the Children Act 1989** grants prima facie 'parental responsibility' (PR) for marital children to each parent, but to the mother only if the parents are unmarried. In not granting prima facie 'responsibility' to the father who is not married to the mother, irrespective of whether he is a rapist (as a husband could equally well be), a one-night stander, or a better man/partner/father than the average husband, the law may well be depriving large numbers of children of a vital right. A putative father may obtain PR under **s. 4** by court order, by agreement with the mother (the latter is made in a prescribed form and filed in the Principal Registry of the Family Division) or, following the **Adoption and Children Act 2002,** by joint registration of the birth. In 2010, over 87 per cent of births outside marriage were registered by both parents which means that the vast majority of fathers in a cohabiting relationship now have parental responsibility for their children (ONS, 2011). As explained in the **Suggested answer to Question 1**, joint registration will become more common (and as a consequence more fathers will acquire PR) if the draft Registration of Births (Parents Not Married and Not Acting Together) Regulations 2010 come into force.

In moving to the ending of the partnership, we remain in the area of child law. The **Child Support Act 1991** (as amended) requires each parent of qualifying children to maintain them and is therefore even-handed between marrieds and others. **Section 15 of the Children Act 1989** provides almost the same opportunities of financial relief for non-marital children as does **Part 2 of the MCA 1973** for spouses and children on divorce. Where divorcing parents have 'children of the family', then, under **s. 41(2) of the MCA 1973** the court may, exceptionally, delay the decree absolute if **Children Act 1989** orders are contemplated, whereas unmarried couples with children can separate without restriction.

This survey demonstrates that the law oscillates between no recognition of cohabitation (e.g. no divorce), and in other contexts, near equation with marriage. Some argue that this selective policy is probably appropriate in that the parties must be taken to have rejected the trappings of marriage in their decision not to wed. Yet surveys suggest that people's perceptions of the legal consequences, accurate or not, play little part in their decisions as to family form. This approach is surely inappropriate, however, so far as their children are concerned; many people are coming round to the view that it is family function not form that should be recognized, and that even as regards the adults, some monitoring is necessary in order to avoid injustice to, for example women who have mixed their labour in the family home.

In 2006, the Law Commission (see earlier) provisionally proposed that there should be an opt-out scheme involving discretionary remedies for 'eligible' unwed/unregistered couples. The Law Commission's proposals formed the basis of the **Cohabitation Bill** that was presented to Parliament in 2008. Unfortunately the Bill did not successfully proceed through the Houses and, following the change of government, is unlikely to be resurrected.

Further reading

Bamford, N. (2011) 'Families but Not (Yet) Marriages? Same-Sex Partners and the Developing European Convention "Margin of Appreciation"'. 23(1) CFLQ 128–43.

Barker, N. (2012) 'Civil Partnerships: An Alternative to Marriage? *Ferguson and others v UK*'. Fam Law 548.

Gaffney-Rhys, R. (2009) 'The Implementation of the Forced Marriage (Civil Protection) Act 2007'. 31(3) Journal of Social Welfare and Family Law 246–56.

Government Equalities Office (2012) *Equal Civil Marriage: A Consultation*.

Home Office (2011) *Forced Marriage Consultation*.

Home Office (2012) *Forced Marriage—A Consultation: Summary of Responses*.

Leigh, S. and Barry, D. (2011) 'Cohabitation: Compare and Contrast the Australian System'. Fam Law 404.

Probert, R. (2011) 'The Evolution of the Common Law Marriage Myth'. Fam Law 283.

Strickland, P. (2012) 'Forced Marriage'. Standard Note. SN/HA/1003. 23/3/2012/ Home Affairs Section. House of Commons Library.

Websites

www.fco.gov.uk/en/travel-and-living-abroad/when-things-go-wrong/forced-marriage

www.lawontheweb.co.uk/Family_Law/Cohabitation

3

Nullity

Introduction

Nullity is a good option for the exam as it is a comparatively brief, settled and compact subject. It is also popular with examiners, because it lends itself to made-up stories of doubtful outcome which test analytical skills and to essay questions due to its conceptual significance. It contains established case law within a statutory setting, and has a number of grounds and defences to interrelate.

Beware of confusing the nullity question with the divorce question, or of overlooking a divorce aspect. They both involve failed marriages from which at least one party wishes to be freed by the court, but nullity is concerned with marriages that are legally blemished from the outset whereas divorce is not. That is why books often deal with it near the start of the subject, with weddings and capacity, rather than with divorce. The really spectacular flaws, which give rise to the void *ab initio* grounds such as incapacity and informality, are specified in **s. 11 of the Matrimonial Causes Act (MCA) 1973**. They are unlikely to fill a question on their own because they have attracted less case law, are virtually bereft of bars and do not require a decree. A nullity question is therefore likely to require a discussion of voidable marriage, the grounds for which are contained in **s. 12 MCA**. Candidates should also be aware of **ss. 48 and 49 of the Civil Partnership Act 2004 which** generally mirrors **ss. 11 and 12 MCA 1973**. The key difference between the provisions is that a partnership cannot be set aside on the ground of non-consummation. Students should therefore be prepared to tackle a question that considers non-consummation of marriage and then proceeds to ask whether the answer would be different if the parties had been civil partners.

Question 1

Several years ago, Robin married Pauline, his ex-wife's mother, but quickly realized that she was too old for him and left her. His ex-wife, Jane is still alive.

Two years ago he met and fell in love with Heidi, an Austrian woman who had just arrived in the UK and spoke little English. Robin persuaded her to go through a ceremony of marriage at a register office, but Heidi thought it was merely a ceremony of betrothal.

Because of an hereditary illness, it would be unwise for Robin to have children, yet Heidi refuses to use any form of contraception as to do so would be contrary to her religious beliefs. Consequently the marriage has never been consummated.

Now, Robin has recently met Alice and intends to marry her next month despite the fact that she was born male and has undergone a 'sex-change' operation.

Discuss the validity of Robin's marriages to Pauline and Heidi and advise him with regard to his intended union with Alice.

Commentary

As a well-prepared student, you will have heard the data screaming 'nullity' at you even before the word 'validity' in the instruction gave the game away. From the data, you should deduce that the basic marks lie in prohibited degrees, lack of consent, non-consummation and transsexual marriage. To achieve the maximum marks you will also need to link the separate issues into an overall analysis. For example, if Pauline's marriage is void *ab initio* it is unnecessary (although it may be desirable) to obtain a decree to dispose of it. It is then necessary to consider if Heidi's marriage is voidable. But if Pauline's marriage is valid, then Heidi's must be void and again a decree of nullity is not required. Finally, it should be realized that the question is riddled with uncertainty, thus providing potential, in a problem question, for marks.

Answer plan

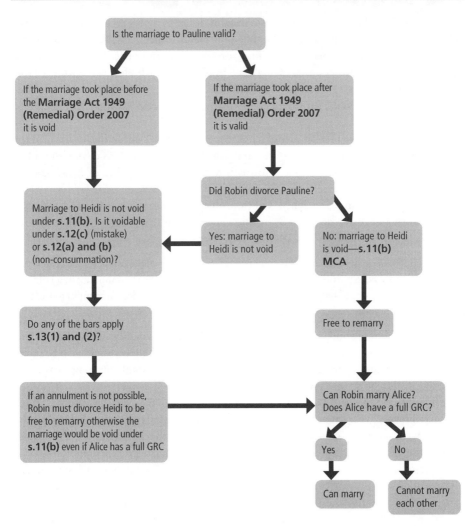

Is the marriage to Pauline valid?

If the marriage took place before the **Marriage Act 1949 (Remedial) Order 2007** it is void

If the marriage took place after **Marriage Act 1949 (Remedial) Order 2007** it is valid

Did Robin divorce Pauline?

Marriage to Heidi is not void under **s.11(b).** Is it voidable under **s.12(c)** (mistake) or **s.12(a) and (b)** (non-consummation)?

Yes: marriage to Heidi is not void

No: marriage to Heidi is void—**s.11(b) MCA**

Do any of the bars apply **s.13(1) and (2)**?

Free to remarry

If an annulment is not possible, Robin must divorce Heidi to be free to remarry otherwise the marriage would be void under **s.11(b)** even if Alice has a full GRC

Can Robin marry Alice? Does Alice have a full GRC?

Yes

No

Can marry

Cannot marry each other

Examiner's tip

Ensure that you understand the difference between a marriage that is void *ab initio*, which does not require a decree to end it and a voidable marriage which does require annulment from the court.

The difficulties which beset Robin arise from his desire to marry Alice despite his existing unions, if such they are, with Pauline and Heidi respectively. Clearly the matter must involve either annulment (the voiding of a marriage for innate legal invalidity) or dissolution (termination of a valid marriage by a divorce order following irretrievable breakdown). There is a functional connection in that a 'decree' of nullity and a divorce 'order' will each 'open the gate' to ancillary financial relief and to orders with regard to children.

This question clearly focuses on nullity as it specifically asks about the 'validity' of the unions. **Sections 11–16 of the Matrimonial Causes Act (MCA) 1973** deal with nullity. They consolidate the substantive reforms instituted by the **Nullity of Marriage Act 1971.**

Before embarking upon an analysis of the nullity provisions, it is necessary to draw a distinction between marriages void *ab initio* (void) and those which are merely voidable. In *De Reneville v De Reneville* **[1948] P 100,** Lord Greene MR said:

> A void marriage is one that will be regarded...as never having taken place and can be so treated by both parties to it without the necessity of any decree annulling it: a voidable marriage is one that will be regarded as...valid...until a decree annulling it has been pronounced...

The current void grounds are enumerated in **s. 11** and the voidable ones in **s. 12.** The latter set is variously subject to a series of bars specified in **s. 13.** It should also be noted at the outset that, by virtue of **s. 16,** a decree annulling a voidable marriage leaves the marriage valid 'up to that time'.

It is necessary to begin by discussing the validity of the marriage to Pauline, which occurred several years ago, because if this marriage is either valid or voidable then the Heidi marriage will be void *ab initio* without need for further examination. The answer lies in the 'prohibited degrees of relationship'. English marriage is 'exogamous', i.e. a partner must be chosen from outside a specified group. That group includes affines, based upon the theological idea that as husband and wife were one, marriage to a sister-in-law was as incestuous as marriage to a sister. The number of prohibited relationships based on affinity has been steadily reduced by statute. The **Marriage (Prohibited Degrees of Relationship) Act 1986** provided that a man could marry his former mother- or daughter-in-law if both parties had reached the age of 21 and the former spouses of both parties were deceased. These requirements were abolished by the **Marriage Act 1949 (Remedial) Order 2007** following the decision of the European Court of Human Rights in *B and L v UK* **[2006] 1 FLR 35,** which declared that they violated the right to marry contained in **Art. 12** of the Convention. The Order came into force on 1 March 2007. If the marriage between Robin and Pauline was solemnized after this date, it is valid and requires a decree of divorce to bring it to an end. As Robin has not obtained a divorce, the marriage to Heidi would automatically be void under **s. 11(b)** on the basis that Robin was already lawfully married. If the marriage ceremony took place before this date, the marriage would be void as Robin's ex-wife, Jane, was alive when the ceremony took place, in which case the marriage to Heidi is not void and it is therefore necessary to consider whether it is voidable.

Heidi, 'spoke little English' and believed the register office event to be 'a ceremony of betrothal'. It is therefore possible that the marriage is voidable under **s. 12(c)** on the basis 'that either party…did not validly consent to it,…in consequence… of…mistake.'

It is clear from the decided cases that mistake is operative 'in two cases only' (*Bromley's Family Law*, 10th edn (2006), p. 85). The first, mistake as to person, is clearly unhelpful here. Perhaps the second, mistake as to ceremony, will run. The criterion is strict; the party must have been unaware that he or she was contracting a marriage. A mistake about the legal consequences of matrimony is insufficient, as in *Way v Way* [1950] P 71, where the husband wrongly assumed that his Russian wife would be allowed to leave the Soviet Union and live with him. In *Valier v Valier* (1925) 133 LT 830, the Italian husband had a poor command of English and did not understand the nature of the register office ceremony. He was consequently granted a decree on the basis of lack of consent due to mistake. If that were not enough, Heidi's predicament is further reflected in *Mehta v Mehta* [1945] 2 All ER 690 which involved a mistaken belief that a Hindu marriage ceremony was one of religious conversion. How could Heidi have been aware that she was contracting marriage—the requirement for valid consent—if she thought that she was merely 'contracting' an engagement?

One difficulty arises so far as the bars are concerned. Although this marriage is within the three-year bar applied to **s. 12(c) to (h)** by **s. 13(2)**, it may be that the 'statutory approbation' bar found in **s. 13(1)** (which applies to all voidable grounds) may present more of a problem. This will be examined after considering **s. 12(a) and (b)** to which **s. 13(1)** is also relevant.

Heidi and Robin's marriage has 'never been consummated', however, non-consummation *per se* is not sufficient to mount a petition. It must be due to either 'the incapacity of either party' (**s. 12(a)**) or 'the wilful refusal of the respondent' (**s. 12(b)**). There is no suggestion of incapacity here but can one of them, preferably Robin, petition on the basis of the other's wilful refusal?

In *Baxter v Baxter* [1948] AC 274, the House of Lords held that a wife's refusal to allow intercourse unless her husband used a condom did not qualify. *Bromley's Family Law*, 10th edn, states (p. 82):

> It cannot be a wilful refusal to consummate for one spouse to insist upon the use of contraceptives or, probably, of coitus interruptus.

It is thus clear that Heidi would not be able to petition on the basis of Robin's wilful refusal, but there is no evidence that she is keen to do this anyway. Turning this quote around, it seems that a petition on the basis of Heidi's wilful refusal would also fail. Furthermore, Robin's petition might fail by virtue of **s. 13(1)** in that he might be said to have 'conducted himself in relation to the respondent as to lead (her) reasonably to believe that he would not seek to do so; and that it would be unjust to the respondent to grant the decree.' This would only apply if he had known his rights at the time of such conduct (see **s. 13(1)(a)**).

We may conclude that Heidi would have to petition on the ground of lack of consent due to mistake and if she does not do so, Robin would have to divorce her in order to marry Alice. As the marriage is more than one year old, **s. 3 MCA 1973** will not apply. But remember, if Robin's marriage to Pauline is valid, the marriage to Heidi is void. Robin would therefore have to divorce Pauline, rather than Heidi, in order to marry Alice.

If Robin is free of earlier marriage(s) he and Alice may not have the capacity to marry one another due to Alice's sex-change operation. **Section 11(c) MCA** provides that a marriage is void if the parties are not 'respectively male and female'. Initially, the English courts refused to recognize the post-operative sex of transsexuals. (See *Corbett v Corbett* [1971] P 83 and *J v S-T (formerly J) (Transsexual: Ancillary Relief)* [1997] 1 FLR 402.) However, in 2002 there was a significant development in this area. In two transsexual cases, ***Goodwin v UK*** (**Application No. 28957/95**) [2002] 2 FLR 487 and *I v UK* (**Application No. 25680/94**) [2002] 2 FLR 518, the European Court of Human Rights held unanimously that there had been violation of the right to respect for private and family life and the right to marry and found a family as guaranteed respectively by **Arts 8 and 12 of the European Convention on Human Rights**. Following this, the House of Lords made a declaration of incompatibility under **s. 4 of the Human Rights Act 1998** in *Bellinger v Bellinger* [2003] 1 FLR 1043.

To rectify the incompatibility, the **Gender Recognition Act (GRA) 2004** was enacted on 1 July 2004. The Act provides that a person of either gender who is at least 18 may make an application, to a Gender Recognition Panel (GRP), for a gender recognition certificate (GRC). This is on the basis of living in the other gender, or having changed gender under the law of a country or territory outside the UK (**s. 1(1)**). The GRP must grant the application if satisfied that the applicant:

(a)   has or has had gender dysphoria (i.e. gender dysphoria, gender identity disorder and transsexualism which are said to affect 1 in 10,000 people);

(b)   has lived in the acquired gender throughout the period of two years ending with the date on which the application is made;

(c)   intends to continue to live in the acquired gender until death (**s. 2(1)**).

The applicant must provide the information by way of a statutory declaration and medical evidence in support (**s. 3**). If a GRP grants an application it must issue a GRC to the applicant. A married applicant will receive an interim GRC, which would make the existing marriage voidable (**s. 12(g) MCA 1973** (as amended by **GRA 2004**)). A decree would not be granted on the **s. 12(g)** ground unless proceedings are instituted within six months of the issue of the interim GRC (**s. 13(2A) MCA 1973** as amended by **GRA 2004**).

The court granting the nullity decree under **s. 12(g)** must issue a full GRC. If the marriage ends for any other reason, i.e. divorce, nullity on any other ground or death, the applicant with an interim GRC may apply, within six months of the end of the marriage, for a full GRC. The fact that a person's gender has become the acquired gender will not affect the status of the person as the father or mother of a child.

If the applicant is not married, the certificate is to be a full GRC, on the issue of which the person will be entitled to a new birth certificate reflecting the acquired gender (provided a UK birth register entry already exists for the person) and will be entitled to marry someone of the opposite gender to his or her acquired gender.

If Alice has obtained a full GRC, she thus has the capacity to marry Robin. If the marriage goes ahead, it would be voidable under **s. 12(h)**, but Robin would only be able to petition on this basis if he was not aware that Alice had undergone gender reassignment surgery. As the facts suggest that Robin is aware of Alice's surgery, it is unlikely that the marriage could be set aside. Of course, Robin can only marry Alice if he ends his marriage with Pauline or Heidi.

 Question 2

Should nullity proceedings in marriage be abolished and replaced by divorce?

 Commentary

Even in the heat of the exam, this sort of question can be accurately assimilated at a glance. This one may certainly seem attractive to the weak student who has done enough to write about 'nullity' and 'divorce' for 45 minutes or so. But a good answer will need to deploy some knowledge of history, statistics, proposals and what the writers think about it all. More positively, the issue is comparatively static at the moment, at least by family law standards.

 Answer plan

- Brief history of nullity and divorce.
- Current law.
- Define and explain difference between void and voidable.
- Statistics.
- Effects of decrees.
- Published recommendations for reform.
- Own views/recommendations.

Examiner's tip

If this question is set as an assignment task, research the law in Australia, where voidable marriage has been abolished.

Suggested answer

Since the (first) **Matrimonial Causes Act (MCA) in 1857**, petitions of divorce and nullity have provided the only means whereby the civil court can end a marriage (divorce) or declare it invalid (nullity). To understand this question properly it is necessary to delve even further back into the history of 'family' law.

Until the Reformation, English law followed the canonical law (which considered marriage to be a sacrament) and did not therefore permit divorce, in any modern sense at least. The ecclesiastical courts had exclusive jurisdiction over marriage law and, although they could not dissolve marriages, there was nothing to prevent them from declaring that some impediment had prevented the parties from acquiring the status of husband and wife.

Until the middle of the nineteenth century the only means of divorce was by private Act of Parliament, with an average of two a year, and a total of four only on the wife's petition. Historical and religious influences thus produced radical differences of both concept and forum between the two 'remedies'. The **1857 Act** removed the latter distinction by vesting the existing jurisdiction of the ecclesiastical courts in a new statutory Divorce Court (transferred to the High Court by the **Judicature Acts 1873 and 1875**) and by permitting divorce '*a vinculo matrimonii*' (which permitted the parties to remarry) by judicial process.

Today, of course, both decrees serve much the same social purpose; i.e. to permit the parties to escape failed unions, but annulments are now far outnumbered by dissolutions. Judicial and Court Statistics (2012) show that 119,610 decrees of divorce were made absolute in 2011 as opposed to a mere 206 nullity decrees (Table 2.5). However, the number of divorces has fallen over the past five years while the number for nullity each year remains statistically insignificant by comparison. It should also be noted that the number of weddings has *also* dropped. There was a particularly sharp reduction in nullity petitions following the **Matrimonial and Family Proceedings Act 1984** which reduced the waiting period for divorce from three years to one. Since **the Divorce Reform Act 1969**, virtually all marriages can now be dissolved if one party so desires, whereas previously the petitioner had to prove that the respondent had committed a 'matrimonial offence'. If not, then the only way out (at least in theory) was nullity. In *A v J (Nullity Proceedings)* [1989] FLR 110, 111, Anthony Lincoln J said:

> Nullity proceedings are nowadays rare, though not wholly extinct. It is unfortunate that these had to be fought out...there would have been no difficulty in pronouncing

mutual decrees nisi, dissolving the marriage, if the necessary consent (to a decree) had been forthcoming.

Furthermore, nullity and divorce afford the courts virtually identical powers of financial relief and in relation to children of the family. Quite apart from that, even void marriages now attract many of the legal consequences of marriage. Since 1959, in a principle now enshrined in **s. 1(1) of the Legitimacy Act 1976**, the children of such a marriage will be treated as their parents' legitimate offspring if at the time of conception (or marriage ceremony if later) both or either of the parents reasonably believed the marriage to be valid. Similar recognition is to be found in what is now **s. 1(1)(a) of the Inheritance (Provision for Family and Dependants) Act 1975**, which enables a person who entered a void marriage in good faith with a person since deceased to apply to the court for reasonable provision out of his estate, just as if the applicant were his widow.

So far as the respective decrees are concerned, the effect of a nullity decree on a voidable marriage is now very close to that of divorce on a valid marriage. Since the **Nullity of Marriage Act 1971**, 'the marriage shall, notwithstanding the decree, be treated as if it had existed up to that time' (**s. 16 MCA 1973**).

Can the subsuming of nullity within divorce therefore be represented as the next, and final, step in an inevitable historical development? It seems essential to distinguish between void (*ab initio*) and voidable marriages. There seems to be no lobby in favour of assimilating the first within divorce. Such dramatic, inescapable, flaws are specified in **s. 11 MCA 1973**, i.e. incapacity (age, gender, prohibited degrees, existing marriage) and serious, guilty failures to comply with the required form, must surely be kept separate from the 'mere' dissolving of a subsequently unsuccessful union.

Many see a stronger case for including voidable marriage within divorce (as is now the case in Australia under the **Family Law Act 1975**) even though the Law Commission, admittedly over 40 years ago, decided against such recommendation (*Nullity of Marriage* (Law Com No. 33, 1970), giving several reasons (at para. 24) in support of this attitude. Although the conceptual divide may no longer mean much to the lawyer, it remains essential to the Christian Church, which attaches particular importance to consent as a prerequisite to marriage. This latter includes consent to sex, so impotence is regarded as vitiating consent.

The Law Commission felt in 1970 that many people, whether they are Christian or not, associate divorce with stigma and would prefer to see illnesses such as mental disorder and impotence treated differently. Those who do not appreciate the existing difference between divorce and nullity and who would not, presumably, oppose assimilation, should not be given greater credence than the 'substantial minority' who would be offended by such change. The Commission's final argument was that the (then) bar on divorce petitions being mounted before the marriage was three years old would be quite inappropriate in nullity cases.

Should these arguments obtain today? The final one is, perhaps, the easiest to dispose of, in that the bar is now one year only and remedies such as judicial separation decrees (which carry virtually the same ancillary redress) are available within that time. Perhaps, also, the all-important conceptual distinction is not as watertight as has been assumed. Wilful refusal to consummate, which accounted for 360 out of 410 decrees in the last year for which such figures were collated (Judicial Statistics (Cm 173, 1986)), is clearly post-marriage behaviour, rather a defect existing at the time of the marriage and should, according to *Bromley's Family Law*, 10th edn, 'be regarded as a reason for divorce' (p. 94). Since 1971, annulment is now permitted for the respondent's mental illness known to the petitioner at the wedding; the reason given for this reform was that the sickness may have worsened during the marriage.

Many would argue that any Anglican objection should be disregarded now that the civil law has parted from religious doctrine; any individual who so chooses is free to seek church approval.

The likelihood today is that nullity proceedings will involve the unpleasantness inherent in medical examination(s) and a full hearing. It is submitted that little would be lost, and much gained, by an affirmative answer to this question so far as voidable marriages are concerned. Cretney for one has consistently urged such reform (*Principles of Family Law*, 8th edn (2008)). Many of the legal consequences of marriage have now been applied even to void 'unions', and virtually all marriages are open to dissolution even if only one spouse wishes it. However, nullity has proved durable; particularly for those who wish to end their marriage yet do not wish to be excluded from their birth families and cultural communities. In *P v R (Forced Marriage: Annulment: Procedure)* [2003] 1 FLR 661 the court heard evidence that a lesser stigma is attached to a woman who obtains a decree of nullity than a woman who obtains a divorce. Proposals to abolish the concept of voidable marriage might therefore face opposition from groups representing women at risk of forced marriage. In fact, many such groups not only support the retention of nullity to protect women forced to marry, but recommend removing the three-year bar contained in s. 13(4). The debate as to whether the concept of a voidable marriage should be abolished has thus acquired a new dimension.

Further reading

Gaffney-Rhys, R. (2010) '*Hudson v Leigh* [2009] The Concept of Non-Marriage'. 22(3) CFLQ 351–63.

Gaffney-Rhys, R. (2010) 'The Legal Status of Forced Marriages: Void, Voidable or Non-Existent?' Int Fam Law 336.

Websites

www.justice.gov.uk/tribunals/gender-recognition-panel

4

Divorce and judicial separation

Introduction

Questions on the current substantive divorce law tend to take the form of problems and the student is usually asked to advise a party to a marriage on whether proceedings would be successful. The introduction of the 'special' procedure meant that decisions of the courts interpreting the technical law were rendered largely 'academic', though still relevant in defended cases (which are very rare indeed). Nevertheless, you will still be expected to be aware of the academic niceties of each of the five 'facts' and to be able to apply them making full and effective use of relevant case law. Even though the district judge does not test or try the evidence filed in the petition, she must be satisfied that the allegations merit a decree as they stand.

Cases that do reach the High Court tend to concern complex issues such as the recognition of foreign divorces and whether the English courts have jurisdiction to dissolve marriages contracted overseas. For example, in *R v M* [2011] EWHC 2132 (Fam) the High Court held that the taliq procedure for divorce was not sufficient to dissolve a marriage that took place in Pakistan even though it would be recognized in the jurisdiction where the marriage was formed. Examination questions are unlikely to focus on jurisdiction or recognition but such issues may form part of a larger question.

The first two questions in this chapter are problem questions and students tackling similar assessments need to remember that the sole ground for divorce is irretrievable breakdown and that the five 'facts' are not grounds. They are, of course, grounds for judicial separation under s. 17 of the Matrimonial Causes Act (MCA) 1973, but given that a mere 227 petitions were lodged in 2011 (a decrease of 24 per cent from 2010), judicial separation will not be considered further in this chapter (Judicial and Court Statistics, 2012). Dates are likely to be extremely relevant in problems questions concerning divorce and always remember to consider the bars and defences contained in the MCA. Students must also look out for riders such as, 'How, if at all, would your answer differ if Wendy were William, wishing to dissolve his civil partnership with Hal?' A key point to note is that **s. 44(5) of the Civil Partnership Act 2004**, which contains the facts that can be used to prove irretrievable breakdown, does not refer to adultery. However, it is assumed that infidelity could constitute 'behaviour' for the purpose of **s. 44(5)(a)**.

As well as questions on the substantive law of divorce, students are likely to face assessments that consider divorce procedure. The third question in this chapter is an essay question which focuses on the role of mediation in divorce proceedings, which is particularly topical at present.

 Question 1

Advise the following spouses:

(a) **Andrew**

He is a successful businessman and six years ago married Barbara, a divorcee. Barbara is a very selfish and lazy woman and as soon as they were married made it clear to Andrew that she was really only interested in him because of his money. Andrew's business is not doing very well at the moment but although he has told her that she must curtail her spending, Barbara spends vast sums on designer clothes and has run up high bills on credit cards. She insists on employing someone to do all the domestic chores, although she does not work herself. For the past few months she has refused all his attempts at sexual intercourse. Andrew is so worried about their financial position that he is taking tranquillizers prescribed by the doctor. Two weeks ago during a row about money, Barbara admitted that she was having an affair with a man 15 years her junior whom she has met at a health club. Andrew does not really mind about the adultery but objects to her attitude towards him and his friends and colleagues.

Andrew seeks advice as to whether he has grounds for divorce.

(b) **Charlotte**

She married David two years ago. They still live in the same house although since April this year they have occupied separate bedrooms and have rarely eaten together.

Charlotte has been having an affair with Edward since Christmas last year and intends to go and live with him as soon as his divorce comes through. David has committed adultery on numerous occasions since their marriage, the last occasion Charlotte remembers being at a New Year's Eve party in the early hours of this year. Neither of them really minded about the other's adultery until recently. David still does not really care and says he has no intention of divorcing Charlotte.

Charlotte wants a divorce.

NB: the parts of this question are equally weighted.

Commentary

This question is an example of a two-part problem question, where you have to advise two spouses in different situations, whether they can establish the ground for divorce and end their respective marriages. The first part of the question focuses on behaviour and the second on adultery; though in each part it may be necessary and advisable to consider other facts. If, as is likely, in your answer to this question you find yourself referring to the adultery 'fact' in both parts, there is no need to produce the same detailed analysis of the fact twice: simply refer the examiner to your response to the other part of the question as and where relevant.

Answer plan

- One ground—'irretrievable breakdown'.
- Demonstrable only by one or more of the five 'facts'.
- Adultery and 'intolerability'—causally connected?
- What constitutes sufficient 'behaviour'?
- 'Living with each other in the same household'.

Examiner's tip

Have the confidence to be selective in what you include in your answer and avoid falling into the trap of writing 'all you know' about the grounds and facts for divorce.

Suggested answer

(a) Andrew

Section 3(1) of the Matrimonial Causes Act (MCA) 1973 provides that a petition for divorce can only be presented after one year from the date of marriage. As Andrew and Barbara have been married for six years, Andrew could commence divorce proceedings immediately, provided that he can establish the ground for divorce.

By **s. 1(1) MCA 1973** the ground for divorce is irretrievable breakdown of marriage. Irretrievable breakdown can only be proved by establishing one of five facts, namely (and in summary) adultery, behaviour, desertion, two years' separation with consent and five years' separation (**s. 1(2) MCA 1973**). Proof of any one of the facts raises a presumption of breakdown (**s. 1(4)**) and although **s. 1(3)** puts a duty of enquiry on the court, the reality is that the 'special procedure' involves no testing of the evidence. The facts which seem to be of relevance to Andrew are behaviour and adultery. In 2009, 16 per cent of divorces were based on adultery, whilst almost 48 per cent were granted due to the respondent's behaviour, making it the most common fact on which to base a divorce (ONS, 2010).

From the information given, the behaviour fact merits detailed discussion here. This fact requires the petitioner to establish that the respondent has behaved in such a way that the petitioner cannot reasonably be expected to live with the respondent (**s. 1(2) (b) MCA 1973**). There are two elements to this fact. First, Andrew must establish that Barbara has behaved in a certain way. Behaviour has been defined in *Katz v Katz* **[1972] 1 WLR 955** as action or conduct by one spouse which affects the other. It may take the form of acts or omissions, it may be a course of conduct but it must have some reference to the marriage. Secondly, Andrew must show that as a result of Barbara's behaviour, he cannot reasonably be expected to live with her. The test is objective, but in assessing whether this is the case, the particular parties, i.e. Andrew and Barbara, will be considered and not 'ordinary reasonable spouses'. Hence, the test could be said to be objective/subjective. In *Ash v Ash* **[1972] Fam 135** the test was enunciated by Bagnall J:

> Can this petitioner with his/her character and personality with his/her faults and other attributes, good and bad, and having regard to his/her behaviour during the marriage, reasonably be expected to live with this respondent.

A similar approach was taken by Dunn J in *Livingstone-Stallard v Livingstone-Stallard* **[1974] 2 All ER 776** and by the Court of Appeal in *Birch v Birch* **[1992] 1 FLR 564**, where it was confirmed that the characters and personalities of the parties are relevant in deciding what conduct they should be expected to bear. This needs to be applied to the facts of the problem. Barbara is selfish and lazy, she has refused sexual intercourse for the past few months and she has admitted to an affair with a man 15 years her junior. In addition, her attitude towards their finances in the circumstances is unreasonable and irresponsible and is adversely affecting Andrew's health. In *Carter-Fea v Carter-Fea* **[1987] Fam Law 130** the husband's financial irresponsibility over a six-year period had affected his family and caused stress to his wife impairing her health. In the wife's words, she 'lived in a world of unpaid bills, bailiffs at the door and second mortgages'. The Court of Appeal said that although running into financial difficulties which upset the other spouse would not as such form the basis of a petition, if one spouse was financially irresponsible and generally unable to manage his affairs, particularly if his attitude had an adverse effect on the other spouse, then this could be classed as behaviour with which the petitioner should not be expected to live. From the information provided and using the authority of *Carter-Fea,* it would seem that Andrew could use Barbara's behaviour as the basis of a petition. Clearly, his health is impaired and he has been prescribed tranquillizers. Applying the objective/subjective test therefore, Andrew will be able to show that as a result of her behaviour, he cannot reasonably be expected to live with Barbara. Andrew should be advised to commence divorce proceedings immediately, relying on the behaviour fact.

In addition, however, as we are told that Barbara has admitted that she is having an affair, Andrew should also be advised on the possibility of using the alternative fact of adultery: that the respondent has committed adultery and the petitioner finds it intolerable to live with the respondent (**s. 1(2)(a) MCA 1973**). This fact will be examined in more detail in part (b) of this answer. For this fact to be established, there has to be adultery. Here Barbara has admitted this, and all that is necessary is for her to respond positively to the question, 'Do you admit the adultery alleged in the petition', and sign the form (**Appendix I, Family Proceedings Rules (FPR) 1991**). In addition, there must be intolerability. It has been decided by the Court of Appeal in *Cleary v Cleary* **[1974] 1 WLR 73** that the two requirements for the fact are independent and that no causal link is required between the adultery and the intolerability. Therefore, the fact that Andrew does not mind about the affair but finds it intolerable to live with Barbara because of her attitude towards him and his friends and colleagues, will not prevent him relying on this fact, provided that the intolerability is genuine. Hence, it would appear that Andrew may successfully petition for divorce on the basis of either adultery or behaviour. Both involve (in the absence of a defence to the petition) a quick divorce by consent. By courtesy of the 'special procedure', the 'adultery' petitioner need, again, merely answer the question, 'Do you find it intolerable to live with the respondent' (**Appendix I, FPR 1991**). The use of adultery may be preferable as the comparative lack of detail required is less potentially exacerbatory than the behaviour fact.

Before proceeding to (b), we should point out that whilst we are not told about Barbara's attitude, we know that David 'has no intention of divorcing Charlotte'. Even David's attitude by no means implies resistance to divorce. Defended petitions are extremely rare, being expensive and discouraged by the courts because of their futility and corrosive effect on family division. Recourse to the 'special procedure' therefore seems likely in each case: so if the district judge is satisfied that the ground for divorce is made out on the face of the petition, then a decree nisi will be pronounced (as part of a batch) in open court, and will be automatically made absolute six weeks thereafter. It should be noted that the *Family Justice Review Final Report* recommends retaining this two-stage process, but changing the name of the decrees, which are outmoded and not understood by many lay people (2011, p. 174).

(b) Charlotte

As Charlotte and David have been married for two years, divorce proceedings could, on establishing the ground, be commenced immediately (**s. 3 MCA 1973**). To obtain a divorce Charlotte must establish the sole ground for divorce: irretrievable breakdown as evidenced by one of the five facts. From the information given, the fact which Charlotte is most likely to want to rely on is adultery: that the respondent has committed adultery and the petitioner finds it intolerable to live with the respondent (**s. 1(2)(a) MCA 1973**).

Adultery is voluntary or consensual sexual intercourse between a married person and a person of the opposite sex, not being the other's spouse. We are told that David has committed adultery on numerous occasions, the last occasion remembered by Charlotte being in the early hours of New Year's Day this year. The onus of proving the fact of adultery and that she finds it intolerable to live with David, rests with Charlotte, the petitioner, the generally accepted standard being on a balance of probabilities. One assumes, however, that David is likely to admit the adultery.

However, in cases involving adultery, the parties must not continue to cohabit for more than six months after the petitioner discovers the respondent's adultery (**s. 2(1) MCA 1973**). If they do, the petitioner cannot rely on that particular act of adultery as evidence of irretrievable breakdown. This is an absolute bar.

Since April this year, Charlotte and David have occupied separate bedrooms and have rarely eaten together. It is possible for a couple to be living apart although in the same house. The test is whether two separate households have been established (**s. 2(6) MCA 1973**). There must be no common domestic life. If Charlotte can establish that she and David have been living apart since April this year, she will be able to rely on the adultery on New Year's Day this year as evidence of irretrievable breakdown. In *Hollens v Hollens* (1971) 115 SJ 327 the unhappy couple were found to be living apart under the same roof when they did not speak, eat or sleep together. Here, the estrangement has not been that extreme and a court might find it closer to *Mouncer v Mouncer* [1972] 1 All ER 289 where the spouses did talk and occasionally eat together. But all may not be lost if David has continued to 'stray'—the six months' grace in **s. 2(1)** continues every time the other spouse discovers a new incident of such infidelity.

In addition to establishing the fact of adultery, the petitioner has also to show that she finds it intolerable to live with the respondent. The test here is subjective. In many cases the intolerability will be because of the adultery, but it has been established by the Court of Appeal that this does not have to be the case. There does not have to be a causal link: *Cleary v Cleary* [1974] 1 WLR 73 and *Carr v Carr* [1974] 1 All ER 1193. In *Cleary* the intolerability was because of the wife's subsequent conduct and attitude after her husband had taken her back, and in *Carr* it was because of the husband's treatment of the children.

In the question we are told that neither David nor Charlotte cared about each other's infidelity until recently and it seems that the reason why Charlotte finds it intolerable to live with David is her desire to be with Edward. The petitioner's intolerability does at least have to be genuine and Charlotte may have difficulty here, particularly as in *Cleary* Lord Denning MR suggested *obiter* that it would not be sufficient that the petitioner simply prefers to live with someone else. As Charlotte clearly wishes to marry and to be with Edward, she may not be able to show genuine intolerability. However, it should be noted that in practice, because of the special procedure, an affirmative answer to the question 'Do you find it intolerable to live with the respondent?' is likely to suffice, and the points raised earlier may thus not become determinative.

If Charlotte is unable to rely on the adultery fact, could she rely on any other? The only fact which would enable her to divorce David immediately is behaviour (**s. 1(2)(b)**). The elements were covered in detail in (a). From the information given, the only behaviour which Charlotte can rely on is David's infidelity. In *Ash v Ash* [1972] Fam

135 it was stated that mutually bad spouses (i.e. spouses who are equally bad in similar respects) can reasonably be expected to live with each other. Here Charlotte has also been having an affair with Edward. Both spouses are 'flirtatious' and it is therefore unlikely—should the truth emerge—that this fact could be successfully used to establish irretrievable breakdown.

The remaining facts involve a qualifying period of separation. Charlotte must be advised that if she is unsuccessful in establishing adultery or behaviour, she cannot commence proceedings immediately. Assuming, as mentioned earlier, that they have been living apart since April this year, then two years thereafter Charlotte will be able to petition on the basis that the parties have lived apart for a continuous period of two years immediately preceding the presentation of the petition and that David consents to the decree being granted (s. 1(2)(d)). Although David says he has no intention of divorcing Charlotte now, it is possible that in two years' time he will be willing to consent. Should he refuse, then Charlotte will have to wait until they have lived apart for five years (s. 1(2)(e)).

Question 2

Robert and Edith were married 30 years ago. They have two grown-up children both married and living away. Robert and Edith have not been happy for several years. They frequently have angry arguments because Edith wants Robert to give up his job as a law lecturer and accept one of the many lucrative offers he has received to go into private practice. Robert refuses to do this and Edith worries that they will have insufficient money to live on after retirement.

Edith and Robert's relationship had deteriorated to such an extent that seven years ago Edith began to refuse to cook, clean or do the washing for Robert. By the start of the following year, they were sleeping in separate rooms and using the bathroom and kitchen at different times on a rota. They communicate by leaving notes for each other. On two occasions the couple have tried to resolve their differences and to live together normally but both attempts failed after just a few weeks. Edith continues to worry about Robert's meagre annual pay increase.

Robert now wants to divorce Edith. Edith is implacably opposed to divorce on religious grounds. She is an active member of the local church and fears divorce would prejudice her position there. She also fears losing the limited pension rights to which she would be entitled as Robert's widow.

Advise Robert.

What would the position be if the parties were Jewish?

Commentary

The focus of your answer to this problem question should be the five-year separation fact and the defence available under **s. 5 of the Matrimonial Causes Act (MCA) 1973**, but other facts should be briefly considered to ensure that full advice is given. Although a petition based on two years' separation with consent appears irrelevant, remember that the passage of time, legal advice and her bargaining position could well lead Edith to change her mind. In 2009, one-quarter of divorces were based on two years' separation which makes it the second most common fact (ONS, 2010). The desertion fact will be relevant, because the petitioner will fear that the respondent will invoke the special defence to a five-year separation petition. However, desertion formed the basis of divorce in less than 1 per cent of cases in 2009 (ONS, 2010). It tends not to be the central issue in a problem question and you should avoid any detailed discussion here, not least because you will not have time.

The final part of the question asks students to consider the position if the parties were Jewish, which is inviting candidates to discuss **s. 10A MCA** inserted by the **Divorce (Religious Marriages) Act 2002**.

Answer plan

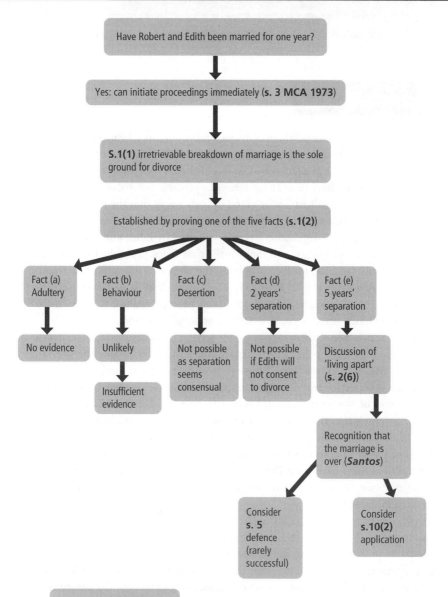

Examiner's tip

The facts of this problem question could lead to a discussion of a number of the five facts, but the emphasis must be on five years' separation.

Suggested answer

Robert wishes to divorce Edith. In order to obtain a divorce, he must establish that their marriage has broken down irretrievably (**s. 1(1) MCA 1973**). To establish irretrievable breakdown, one of the five facts must be established. From the information given, there is no evidence of adultery (**s. 1(2)(a)**). It may be possible for Robert to use the behaviour fact, i.e. that the respondent has behaved in such a way that the petitioner cannot reasonably be expected to live with the respondent (**s. 1(2)(b)**). Robert could point to the fact that their frequent arguments have been caused by Edith and her attitude towards his job and earning capacity, and that for the past seven years she has refused to cook, clean or do any washing for him. Applying the objective/subjective test enunciated by Bagnall J in *Ash v Ash* **[1972] Fam 135**, it is possible that Robert may establish that as a result of her behaviour, he cannot reasonably be expected to live with Edith. But less so today (if at all)—than once, as wives are no longer servants.

Another fact which Robert may consider relying on is desertion, as he may fear that if he chooses to rely on five years' separation, Edith will invoke the special defence under **s. 5 MCA 1973** (see later). However, for this fact to be established he must show that Edith deserted him for a continuous period of two years immediately preceding the presentation of the petition (**s. 1(2)(c)**). This fact involves four elements: the fact of separation, intention to desert, lack of consent by Robert and lack of cause for desertion. There should be no problem in establishing the two-year period of separation (see later) but a state of desertion must immediately precede the presentation of the petition and it would seem likely that Robert and Edith's separation has for some time, if not from the outset, been consensual. Any desertion on Edith's part is terminated by Robert agreeing to the separation.

A petition based on two years' separation with consent (**s.1(2)(d)**) is not, at least as matters stand, practicable as Edith is implacably opposed to divorce and would not give the requisite consent to the decree being granted. It seems, therefore, that Robert should seek to rely on **s. 1(2)(e)**: that the parties to the marriage have lived apart for a continuous period of at least five years immediately preceding the presentation of the petition. The use of this fact enables Robert to divorce Edith against her will and formed the basis of 10 per cent of divorces in 2009 (ONS, 2010). The parties must, however, have lived apart for five years. Robert and Edith still live in the same house. **Section 2(6) MCA 1973** states that a husband and wife are treated as living apart unless living with each other in the same household. Living apart involves both a physical and a mental element. We are told that seven years ago Edith began to refuse to cook, clean or to do the washing but the couple apparently still shared the same bedroom. It is likely therefore that at this stage there was still some 'sharing of domestic life', some matrimonial services being provided. From the following year, the couple slept in separate rooms. Hence, from that time it would seem that Robert and Edith have been living apart and maintaining two separate households.

In *Mouncer v Mouncer* [1972] 1 WLR 321, the wife still did the cooking and cleaning and ate with her husband, but they slept apart. They were still sharing the same household, but were not living apart. In *Fuller v Fuller* [1973] 1 WLR 730, the husband moved in with his wife and her lover after he had suffered a heart attack. He paid for his food and laundry. The couple were held to be living apart: their relationship was that of a landlady and lodger only. Clearly, neither of these cases presents any threat to Robert's petition.

The mental element of living apart involves the recognition throughout the relevant period by at least one of the parties that the marriage is at an end (*Santos v Santos* [1972] Fam 247). This should not present Robert with any problems in practice: under the 'special procedure' he will need merely to state the date he concluded that the marriage was over.

On two occasions, Robert and Edith attempted a reconciliation, on each occasion for just a few weeks. To encourage reconciliation, s. 2(5) MCA 1973 provides that no account is to be taken of a period or periods not exceeding six months of resumed cohabitation, but no such period will count towards the five years. This might conceivably delay Robert's s. 1(2)(d) petition.

Robert and Edith have lived apart for six years and Robert could successfully rely on this fact as evidence of irretrievable breakdown. However, Robert must be advised that s. 5 MCA 1973 provides a special statutory defence available to the respondent to a petition based solely on five years' separation and that, in the circumstances, Edith may raise this defence. The defence, it should be pointed out, is very rarely raised successfully (but it was in *Julian v Julian* [1972] 116 SJ 763 and *Johnson v Johnson* [1981] 12 Fam Law 116, both cases decided very much on their own facts), but where it is, the divorce will not go through.

Section 5 provides that the respondent can oppose the decree nisi on the grounds that (a) the divorce would result in grave financial or other hardship; and (b) in all the circumstances it would be wrong to dissolve the marriage. Both limbs of the defence must be satisfied.

The petition must rely solely on five years' separation and the fact must be established. All the circumstances of the case will be considered, including the conduct of the parties and their interests and the interests of any children or other parties concerned.

Edith must show first that grave hardship will flow from the actual divorce, i.e. from the change in status from being a separated wife to a divorced woman (*Grenfell v Grenfell* [1978] 1 All ER 561). Loss of pension rights has been held to constitute grave financial hardship. Here, Robert has a pension and therefore Edith can make out a case of grave financial hardship. Under old cases Robert might have put forward proposals to offset this loss by, for example a deferred annuity or insurance policy. He would need available capital to do this and, in many cases, the annuity or policy may prove not to be worth much by comparison. In *Le Marchant v Le Marchant* [1977] **1 WLR 559** the loss of an index-linked pension was held to constitute grave financial hardship. The husband made proposals to relieve the hardship including a life insurance policy and his offer was accepted by the court. But today, the problem would probably be soluble by use of the divorce court's enhanced powers with regard to pension 'splitting' and pension 'sharing' under **Part II of the MCA 1973** (as amended).

There will also be no grave financial hardship if the contingency for entitlement is too remote. Grave hardship other than financial is difficult to establish and there is no reported case where it has been. Merely to show that divorce is contrary to religious principles is insufficient (*Rukat v Rukat* [1975] **Fam 63**). There must be some evidence of specific hardship, for example ostracism as alleged but not substantiated by the Hindu wife-respondent in *Banik v Banik (No. 2)* (1973) **117 SJ 874**.

Even if Edith could establish grave financial hardship, she still has to establish that it would be wrong to dissolve the marriage. Here, the conduct of the parties and their respective interests are relevant. There do not seem to be any third parties involved here. It is necessary to weigh the relevant facts and balance the concern to uphold the sanctity of marriage with the desirability of ending empty ties. In *Brickell v Brickell* [1974] **Fam 31** where the wife's conduct had caused the collapse of the family business and she had deserted her husband, the court held that it would not be wrong to dissolve the marriage. As many of Robert and Edith's problems have been caused by Edith's attitude, a similar decision would probably be reached in this case and the divorce would go through.

If the defence is rejected, or indeed if Edith chooses not to raise the defence, she may make an application under **s. 10(2) MCA 1973**. Where a decree is obtained on the basis of two years' separation with consent or five years' separation, the respondent can apply to the court for consideration of her financial position after the divorce. This is not a true defence and such an application merely delays the decree absolute. The court will consider all the circumstances including the age, health, conduct and financial resources and obligations of the parties and what Edith's financial position is likely to be after divorce if Robert should predecease her. The decree will not be made absolute unless the court is satisfied that no financial provision should be made for her or that the provision made is fair and reasonable or the best in the circumstances. In effect, this provision enables the court to make proper financial arrangements prior to the finalizing of the divorce (*Archer v Archer* [1999] **1 FLR 327**). To summarize, the advice to Robert is to petition on the basis of five years' separation, should his wife not change her mind and 'give' him a divorce. If Edith raises the **s. 5** defence, she is most unlikely to succeed.

If Robert and Edith were Jewish, **s. 10A MCA 1973** (as inserted by the **Divorce (Religious Marriages) Act 2002**) would come into play. This section allows either party to apply for the divorce not to be made absolute until a declaration is made by both parties that steps have been taken to dissolve the marriage in accordance with their own religious usages. This provision is designed to ensure that a couple divorced in the eyes of the civil law, also obtain a religious divorce (in this case a *get*) so that they are no longer regarded as married under Jewish law.

Question 3

What role does mediation play in the resolution of disputes during divorce proceedings?

Commentary

Part II of the Family Law Act (FLA) 1996 would have replaced the provisions of the **MCA 1973** discussed earlier in this chapter with a 'no fault' divorce system and mediation was set to play a big part in the practice of divorce. Despite the fact that **Part II** was not implemented, mediation remains part of the divorce process and this essay question requires candidates to review its role. Had the question referred to the use of alternative dispute resolution, students would have had to include reference to other means of reaching a divorce settlement, such as collaborative law. This process involves each party instructing their own lawyer to advise them and all four meet face-to-face in an attempt to reach a settlement. The parties and their lawyers sign a participation agreement, whereby they undertake not to issue court proceedings. If one of the clients wishes to do so, he or she must appoint a different lawyer.

Answer plan

- Meaning of mediation.
- Its introduction to English divorce—**Part II of the FLA 1996**.
- Arguments for and against.
- The role of mediation following the non-implementation of **Part II FLA 1996**.
- The impact of **Practice Direction 3A** and the **Legal Aid, Sentencing and Punishment of Offenders Act 2012**.

Examiner's tip

Demonstrate the currency of your knowledge by referring to **Practice Direction 3A—Pre-Application Protocol for Mediation Information and Assessment** and the **Legal Aid, Sentencing and Punishment of Offenders Act 2012**.

Suggested answer

Mediation is defined as 'a process in which an impartial third person, the mediator, assists couples considering separation or divorce to meet together to deal with the arrangements which need to be made for the future' (*Looking to the Future* (Cm 2799, 1995) para. 5.4). It is a form of Alternative Dispute Resolution which, according to the *Family Justice Review Final Report*, should be rebranded 'Dispute Resolution Services', which suggested that they should be regarded as the 'norm' rather than an 'alternative' (2011, p. 23).

Government thinking on the use of mediation was developed in *Facing the Future, A Discussion Paper on the Grounds for Divorce* (Law Com No. 170, 1988), and *The Ground for Divorce* (Law Com No. 192, 1990). With an eye on the legal aid cost of publicly funded divorce, the official view was that mediation might provide less expensive, as well as better, solutions to divorce problems. But it should also be remembered that mediation and law need not be stark alternatives, given, first, that matrimonial legal work is often geared towards settlement and, secondly, that lawyers may well continue to play a role in mediated disputes. In fact, the Resolution (formerly the Solicitors Family Law Association) Code of Practice 2009 requires members to inform clients of all the options, including mediation, which means that solicitors will actually promote such services.

Mediation in divorce proceedings was due to be institutionalized by the **Family Law Act (FLA) 1996**. If **Part II of the 1996 Act** had come into force, mediation would have been brought to the attention of a spouse contemplating divorce at the earliest possible stage. **Section 8(9)(f)** would have required such information to be disseminated at the information meeting, attendance at which would have been a condition precedent to a divorce application. **Section 12(2)** would have continued this 'early exposure' policy by requiring legal representatives to inform their clients about mediation, to supply them with details of persons qualified to help with mediation and to certify that they have done so. **Section 13** would have enabled the court itself to take a hand by directing that each party attend a meeting at which the facilities for mediation would be explained to them, and to provide an opportunity for them to agree to take advantage of it. The parties would have been required to attend the same meeting unless one or both of them asked for separate sessions, or the court itself thought that such would be more appropriate, for example domestic violence cases. This would not have obliged the spouses to use mediation, as it is generally accepted that compulsion would be a contradiction in terms and counterproductive. The Act's final reference to mediation (**s. 29** repealed by the **Access to Justice Act 1999**) stated that legal aid would be available for mediation in certain circumstances, but it may be unavailable for legal representation, which indicated that initial Government enthusiasm was based more on the supposedly smaller dent mediation would make in the public purse than upon any improvement it may render to the parties' post-divorce arrangements. The pilot studies demonstrated that only 7 per cent of those attending information meetings wanted to use mediation. The pro-mediation arguments: that there is no right answer to a particular dispute; that solutions arrived at by the parties themselves are more likely to stick; that it enables the parties to communicate more effectively, particularly with regard to the emotional issues, are of no avail if mediation is not actually utilized. The other problem was that, according to another pilot study, mediation was not cost-effective.

A further concern regarding the use of mediation in the divorce process is that it disadvantages women (see Ann Bottomley, 'Resolving Family Disputes: A Critical View' in Freeman (ed.) *State, Law and the Family* (1984)). The fear is that it might conceal and continue pre-existing male dominance, thereby putting at risk the recent legal advances made by women in the context of violence and property. A more extensive objection, and possibly a more gender-neutral one, is that it may disadvantage a weak or inarticulate party, although it is claimed that the trained mediator can guard against this happening. Other concerns about the value of mediation include the extent to which it can truly be impartial, that it can be in thrall to society's norms and the extent to which the children themselves should be involved.

Despite the non-implementation of **Part II of the FLA 1996** the use of mediation to resolve family disputes continued to be encouraged. Although **s. 29** was repealed by the **Access to Justice Act 1999,** the essence of it remained in the Legal Services Commission funding code which required a person seeking legal aid for representation first to attend a meeting with a mediator to determine whether mediation would be suitable. This obligation was not limited to divorcing couples, but applied to unmarried couples with disputes relating to children etc. **Part 3 of the Family Procedure Rules 2010 (SI 2010/2955),** which came into force in April 2011, enables the court to adjourn proceedings so that the parties can consider and, where appropriate, utilize alternative dispute resolution services, whilst **Practice Direction 3A—Pre-Application Protocol for Mediation Information and Assessment,** which also came into force in April 2011, extends the duty to consider utilizing mediation services to private paying clients.

The Practice Direction applies where a person is considering applying for an order in 'family proceedings', which covers: private law proceedings relating to children (with some exceptions); proceedings for a financial remedy (with some exceptions) and proceedings to enforce financial orders (**Annex B**). The Practice Direction therefore applies to divorcing couples who wish to utilize the courts to resolve their disputes, but also to cases relating to children that take place outside divorce proceedings. The purpose of the Practice Direction and the accompanying protocol is 'to encourage and facilitate the use of alternative dispute resolution . . . and ensure, as far as possible that all parties have considered mediation as an alternative means of resolving their disputes' (**para. 2.1**). The rationale behind this is that 'there is a general acknowledgement that an adversarial court process is not always best suited to the resolution of family disputes, particularly private law disputes between parents relating to children, with such disputes often best resolved through discussion and agreement' (**para. 3.1**). This suggests that the Government wishes to promote mediation due to the benefits it will bring to the parties and their children, rather than to reduce costs; however, **para. 3.5** proceeds to indicate that 'it is likely to save court time and expense if the parties take steps to resolve their dispute without pursuing court proceedings.'

The court will expect all applicants to have complied with the protocol before commencing relevant family proceedings (**para. 1 of the Pre-Application Protocol**). The protocol requires a person making an application to the court (or their legal representative) to contact a family mediator to arrange for the applicant to attend an information meeting about mediation and other forms of alternative dispute resolution (**para. 2**). **Paragraph 3** indicates that the applicant does not have to attend a meeting if any of the circumstances set out in **Annex C** applies, i.e. the mediator is satisfied that mediation is not suitable because the other party is unwilling to attend; any party has made an allegation of domestic violence which has resulted in a police investigation or civil proceedings; the dispute concerns financial issues and one of the parties is bankrupt; the parties are in agreement; the whereabouts of the other party are unknown; the application is to be made without notice; the application is urgent; there is current social services involvement in respect of a child who would be the subject of the application; a child would be party to the proceedings or the applicant has contacted three mediators within 15 miles of his or her home and none is able to conduct a meeting within 15 days. This extensive list suggests that there will be many cases where the applicant is not obliged to attend an information meeting. The impact of the Practice Direction on the use of mediation during the divorce process therefore remains to be seen.

The most recent changes which will have an impact on the use of mediation in divorce proceedings and other family cases will be introduced as a result of the **Legal Aid, Sentencing and Punishment of Offenders Act 2012**, which received royal assent on 1 May 2012. **Part I** of the Act contains provisions that will reduce the availability of legal aid for representation in the family courts, restricting it to cases involving domestic violence, child abuse or other exceptional circumstances. Divorcing couples (and other family members in dispute) who cannot afford to pay their own legal fees will have to utilize mediation (or another dispute resolution service) as public funding for alternatives to litigation will remain. David Allison, Chair of Resolution, described the measures as 'deeply-flawed' because mediation 'requires both people to be willing to take part. If one parent is denying contact to another or refusing to be reasonable about money they can simply refuse to attend mediation' (Family Law online, 14 February 2011). 'The only option for those then left suffering injustice is to give up, or to represent themselves in court. No easy task at the best of times, let alone at a time of high emotional stress.' The introduction of such measures could therefore lead to injustice and is also likely to lengthen the duration of family cases. According to Resolution members who took part in a recent survey, cases take longer if one or both parties represent themselves. Of those polled, 48 per cent believed that a case would take twice as long if one or both parties represent themselves (Family Law Online, 9 January 2012).

If the recommendations contained in the Family Justice Review 2011 are implemented, the applicant/petitioner will be required to attend a Mediation Information and Assessment Meeting (MIAM) and if the couple have children, they will be required to attend a Separating Parents Information Programme (PIP) (p. 151). If the couple cannot reach an agreement, mediation or another dispute resolution service (e.g. collaborative law) would be utilized in an attempt to resolve the dispute prior to initiating legal proceedings. The Review is thus consistent with previous proposals and reforms in promoting the use of mediation and dispute resolution services.

Further reading

Davies, G., Clisby, S., Cumming, Z. et al (2003) *Monitoring Publicly Funded Family Mediation* (London: Legal Services Commission).

Dingwall, R. (2010) 'Divorce Mediation: Should We Change Our Mind?' 32(2) JSWFL 107–17.

Hunter, R. (2011) 'Doing Violence to Family Law'. 33(4) JSWFL 343–59.

Maclean, M. (2010) 'Family Mediation: Alternative or Additional Dispute Resolution?' 32(2) JSWFL 105–6.

Maclean, M. and Eekelaar, J. (2012) 'Legal Representation in Family Matters and the Reform of Legal Aid: A Research Note on Current Practice'. 24(2) CFLQ 223–33.

Ministry of Justice (2011) *The Family Justice Review Final Report.*

Wright, K. (2011) 'The Evolving Role of the Family Lawyer: The Impact of Collaborative Law on Family Law Practice'. 23(3) CFLQ 370.

Websites

www.divorceaid.co.uk

www.justice.gov.uk/about/moj/independent-reviews/family-justice-review

www.nfm.org.uk

www.resolution.org.uk

5

Domestic violence

Introduction

Part IV of the Family Law Act (FLA) 1996, which came into force on 1 October 1997, provides a single consistent set of remedies for domestic violence, available in all courts having jurisdiction in family matters. The Act does not actually define domestic violence, however, the Home Office has described it as 'any incident of threatening behaviour, violence or abuse (psychological, physical, sexual, financial or emotional) between adults who are or have been intimate partners or family members regardless of gender or sexuality' (*Domestic Violence: A National Report* (2005), para. 10). The Government has since indicated that domestic violence also includes 'honour'-based violence, female genital mutilation and forced marriage (Home Office, *Cross-Government Definition of Domestic Violence* (2011), p. 6).

Although government and public sector bodies should apply the broad definition of domestic violence set out earlier, they do not always do so, as *Yemshaw v Hounslow LBC* **[2011] UKSC 3** demonstrates. The case concerned **s. 177(1) of the Housing Act 1996** which provides that it is not reasonable for a person to continue to occupy accommodation if it is probable that this will lead to domestic violence. A person who leaves a property due to domestic violence is therefore considered unintentionally homeless and the local authority has a duty to house such a person if he or she is in priority need (**s. 175(4)**), for example the person resides with dependent children (**s. 189(1)**). The woman in this particular case left the matrimonial home with her young children because her husband shouted at her in front of the children and she was scared that if she confronted him he might hit her. The local authority housing officers indicated that she was not homeless as a result of domestic violence, because her husband had never hit her, had never threatened to do so and the probability of him doing so was low (para. 17). The Supreme Court held that the housing officers were wrong to restrict the definition of domestic violence to actual violence or the threat of actual violence and emphasized that psychological, financial and emotional abuse can also fall within the definition.

The meaning of domestic violence is currently being reconsidered as a consequence of the Home Office Consultation Paper that was issued in December 2011. The consultation paper asks whether the definition of domestic violence should remain the same, whether it should be extended to include coercive control and whether it should be extend to cover those under the age of 18 (Home Office, *Cross-Government Definition of Domestic Violence* (2011)). It is thus possible that definition of domestic violence will be widened further in the future.

Examination questions are often designed to allow students to demonstrate that they can find their way around the legislation. It may be necessary to identify whether the persons involved fall within the categories covered by **the FLA 1996**. Alternatively, there may be little doubt that the persons are associated, but what may be in issue is whether they are entitled to any orders and, if so, which, and for how long. The three problem questions in this chapter require candidates to tackle both of these issues. However, they do not involve children and, as a consequence, students are not expected to consider the public or private law provisions of the **Children Act 1989** which may be utilized to protect children who witness or are subjected to violence.

Question 1

(a) Amanda began cohabiting with Barnaby when she moved into his house six years ago. After six months of cohabitation they married. Five years ago Amanda was confined to a wheelchair as a result of a riding accident. Barnaby had the house altered to make all areas accessible to Amanda in her wheelchair. New bathrooms and a new kitchen were fitted. Doors were widened and a lift installed. Amanda, who was a journalist before her accident, is now a successful author and has adapted her best-selling novels for television and cinema. Barnaby is editor of the local newspaper. With Amanda's success Barnaby has become more dissatisfied with his life and career. He has been drinking heavily for about six months and on a number of occasions he has lost his temper and hit Amanda, causing severe bruising. On the mornings following these events Barnaby is full of remorse and has promised Amanda he will give up alcohol. After the last incident, two days ago, he moved out of the house and slept on a camp bed in his office.

Advise Amanda. She does not want the police to be involved. She says that although she loves Barnaby, she is frightened of the injuries he may cause her. She wants immediate protection. [20 marks]

(b)   Briefly highlight how your answer would differ if Amanda and Barnaby had never married. [5 marks]

Commentary

This problem question deals with the availability and range of civil remedies to protect family victims of domestic violence under **Part IV of the FLA 1996**. Candidates are required to identify the orders available, identify the relevant sections under which the applications must be made and discuss the principles on which the court will decide whether or not to make an order. Part (b) of the answer should not repeat advice that is common to part (a). One vital fact has been changed: candidates are therefore urged to deal with that change as 'briefly' as possible. It is always useful to note the marks allocated to each part of a subdivided question.

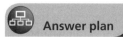 **Answer plan**

Occupation orders—Part IV, Family Law Act 1996

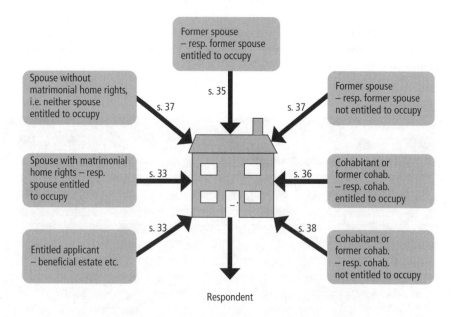

- Identify relevant area of law—domestic violence—**Part IV FLA 1996**.

- Associated persons.

- Orders available—non-molestation and occupation orders.

- The meaning of molestation. Factors courts take into account when deciding to grant order.

- Occupation order—matrimonial home rights, **s. 30**. Application under **s. 33**. Factors courts take into account. Balance of harm test.

- Power of arrest, **s. 47**.

- Cohabitants. Occupation order, **s. 36**. Balance of harm test—court's discretion not duty. Duration of order.

Examiner's tip

The question does not state that Amanda wishes to end the marriage, therefore a detailed survey of the ground for divorce (**Matrimonial Causes Act (MCA) 1973**) would not be expected here.

Suggested answer

(a) As Amanda wants 'immediate protection', but does not want the police to be involved, she can be advised that **Part IV of the Family Law Act (FLA) 1996** empowers courts which have jurisdiction in family matters to make two types of order, one which can provide protection (a non-molestation order) and another which deals with occupation of the family home (an occupation order). The case could be brought before the court in as little as two clear days and in emergency situations the court may, where it considers that it is just and convenient to do so, make an occupation order or a non-molestation order without notice (**s. 45(1)**). This would mean that Barnaby would have no notice of Amanda's application and no opportunity to reply, at this stage, with his version of events. If the court were to make an order without notice it must give Barnaby an opportunity to make representations relating to the order as soon as just and convenient at a full hearing (**s. 45(3)**). In the present circumstances, with Barnaby out of the house, it may be thought unnecessary to apply for an order without notice.

At this stage Amanda's first priority is her own protection and occupation of the home. The court may make a non-molestation order where an application has been made by a person associated with the respondent, whether or not other family proceedings have been instituted (**s. 42(2)(a)**); or, of its own motion in any family proceedings (**s. 42(2) (b)**). Amanda and Barnaby are married to each other and therefore come within the definition of associated persons (**s. 62(3)(a)**). Although molestation is not defined in the Act, the lack of a statutory definition has not given rise to difficulty in the past. Molestation has been described as 'pestering' in *Vaughan v Vaughan* [1973] 3 All ER 449; and in *Horner v Horner* [1982] 2 All ER 495 included 'any conduct which could be regarded as such a degree of harassment as to call for the intervention of the court' (see *C v C (Non-Molestation Order: Jurisdiction)* [1998] 2 WLR 599). In deciding whether to grant Amanda's application for a non-molestation order and, if so, in what manner, the court must have regard to all the circumstances including the need to secure her health, safety and well-being (**s. 42(5)**). Barnaby's violence, resulting in severe bruising to Amanda, would—surely—seem to be sufficient to justify a non-molestation order.

It would appear that Amanda is neither a legal nor a beneficial owner of the property. However, by virtue of **s. 30**, Amanda has matrimonial home rights which give a spouse the right, if in occupation, not to be evicted or excluded from the house (which is, or has been, or was intended to be, the associated couple's home), by the other spouse, except with the leave of the court given under **s. 33**. (If not in occupation, she has the right, with the leave of the court, to enter and occupy the house.) Matrimonial home rights are a charge on the house (**s. 31(2)**). To bind third parties, where the land is unregistered, the charge must be protected by the registration of a Class F land charge against the name of the property owner in the register of land charges (**Land Charges Act 1972**), or, in the case of registered land, by the entry of a notice in the Charges Register under the **Land Registration Act 1925** (**s. 31(10) of the 1996 Act**). Occupation orders are available under five different sections of the Act (**ss. 33, 35, 36, 37, 38**). Amanda is 'a person entitled', due to her matrimonial home rights, and, therefore, would make her application under **s. 33**. An order may enforce Amanda's entitlement to remain in occupation as against Barnaby (**s. 33(3)(a)**); prohibit, suspend or restrict Barnaby's right to occupy the house (**s. 33(3)(d)**); or exclude him from a defined area in which the dwelling-house is included (**s. 33(3)(g)**). In deciding whether to exercise its powers under **s. 33(3)** and, if so, in what manner, the court is to have regard to all the circumstances including the housing needs and housing resources of each of the parties and any relevant children; the financial resources of the parties; the likely effect of any order, or of any decision by the court not to exercise its powers to make regulatory orders, on the health, safety or well-being of the parties and any relevant child; and the conduct of the parties in relation to each other and otherwise (**s. 33(6)**). As Amanda is an entitled person the court has a duty to make an order if it appears that she is likely to suffer significant harm attributable to Barnaby's conduct, if an order is not made, which is as great or greater than the harm likely to be suffered by Barnaby (**s. 33(7)**). Conduct is attributable to the respondent even if it is unintentional. The important issue is the effect on the applicant not the respondent's intention (*G v G (Occupation Order: Conduct)*[1999] 1 FLR 392). Harm, in relation to Amanda, who is at least 18, means ill-treatment or impairment of health (**s. 63(1)**). Significant harm is likely to be interpreted, as in the **Children Act 1989** proceedings, as 'considerable, noteworthy or important' (*Humberside CC v B* [1993] 1 FLR 257 at 263, *per* Booth J). Amanda's need for a specially adapted home is more difficult to satisfy than Barnaby's housing needs. Although Amanda may be more affluent, Barnaby would appear to have an adequate income. The violence inflicted on Amanda is likely to be a decisive factor in the court's deliberations. On the balance of harm test, an order should be made in favour of Amanda. In contrast, in *B v B* [1999] 1 FLR 715, despite the respondent's violence, the harm to the husband and his child was likely to be greater if an order were made than the harm likely to be suffered by the applicant wife and the couple's child if an order were not made. If the balance is tipped in the applicant's favour under **s. 33** then the court has a duty to make the order. However, if the scales do not tip in the applicant's favour, the court still has a discretion to make the order after considering **s. 33(6)** (*Chalmers v Johns* [1999] 1 FLR 392). The court should consider **s. 33(7)** and then if the test for significant harm is not satisfied it should move on to **s. 33(6)** (*G v G (Occupation Order: Conduct)*[2000] 2 FLR 36 confirming *Chalmers* (mentioned earlier)). The order may be made for a specified period, until the occurrence of a specified event or until further order (**s. 33(10) of the 1996 Act**). The court may impose on Amanda obligations as to repair and maintenance, discharge of rent, mortgage payments or any other outgoings affecting the home (**s. 40(1)(a)**). She could be ordered to pay rent to Barnaby (**s. 40(1)(b)**). Either party may be granted possession or use of the furniture or other contents of the house (**s. 40(1)(c)**). There is, however, no power to commit a defaulter to prison (***Nwogbe v Nwogbe*** [2000] 2 FLR 744). In deciding how to exercise these powers the court is to have regard to all the circumstances of the case including the financial needs and financial resources of the parties (**s. 40(2)(a)**). A payment of rent by Amanda to Barnaby should allow him to find more comfortable accommodation.

The court would attach a power of arrest to the occupation order, as Barnaby has used or threatened violence against Amanda, unless the court was satisfied that in all the circumstances of the case Amanda would be adequately protected without such a power of arrest (**s. 47(2)**). Although **the FLA 1996** gives the court the power to accept undertakings, where it has power to make an occupation order, there is no power to attach a power of arrest to an undertaking. The court cannot accept an undertaking in any case where a power of arrest would be attached to the order. Were the court to accept Barnaby's undertaking, he would not be required to admit that the allegations are true and the court would make no finding of fact regarding his conduct. If the couple hope for a reconciliation this may be sufficient to force Barnaby to take stock of the situation. However, Amanda's protection must take precedence over Barnaby's feelings.

The **Domestic Violence, Crime and Victims Act (DVCVA) 2004** amended **s. 42** to make breach of a non-molestation order a criminal offence. A person guilty of the offence would be liable on conviction on indictment, to imprisonment for a maximum sentence of five years, or a fine, or both; or on summary conviction, to 12 months' imprisonment or a fine, or both. The police are able to arrest for breach of a non-molestation order, without the need for the attachment of a power of arrest to the order, or for the applicant to apply to the civil court for an arrest warrant. The respondent would only be guilty of a criminal offence if he were aware of the existence of the non-molestation order (**s. 42A**).

When the court is considering whether to make an occupation order under the **FLA 1996, s. 42** (as amended by **the DVCVA 2004**) places a duty on the court to consider making a non-molestation order. Breach of an occupation order was not made a criminal offence, as past conduct of violence or molestation is not a requirement for the grant of an occupation order. Hence, a power of arrest can still be attached to an occupation order. If Amanda did not wish to pursue criminal proceedings for breach, she could follow the civil route. If that were to happen, and Barnaby were to be punished for contempt in the civil court, he could be convicted of breach of a non-molestation order. This would not prevent a prosecution for other offences, for example assault or grievous bodily harm.

The choice of civil or criminal proceedings would be Amanda's. She may have been reluctant to involve the police initially, but may take a different view on breach.

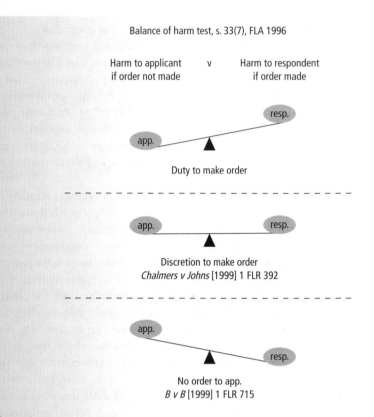

Balance of harm test, s. 33(7), FLA 1996

Harm to applicant   v   Harm to respondent
if order not made   if order made

resp.

app.

Duty to make order

app.   resp.

Discretion to make order
Chalmers v Johns [1999] 1 FLR 392

app.

resp.

No order to app.
B v B [1999] 1 FLR 715

Figure 1

(b) Cohabitants are defined as a man and woman who, although not married to each other, are living together as husband and wife (**s. 62(1)(a)**); and former cohabitants is to be read accordingly (**s. 62(1)(b)**). However, under the **DVCVA 2004** the definition of cohabitants is amended to include, 'two persons who, although not married to each other, are living together as husband and wife or as if they were civil partners' (**s. 62(1)(a) FLA 1996**); and 'former cohabitants is to be read accordingly' (**s. 62(1) (b)**). As cohabitants, or former cohabitants, Amanda and Barnaby would come within the definition of associated persons (**s. 62(3)(b)**) and, as such, Amanda may apply for a non-molestation order (**s. 42(2)(a)**) (with the same outcome as in part (**a**) of this answer).

Amanda, a cohabitant, would not be entitled to matrimonial home rights. Her occupation order application would be as a cohabitant with no existing right to occupy (**s. 36**). In addition to circumstances comparable to those contained in **s. 33(6)**, the court considered the nature of the parties' relationship; the length of time they lived together as cohabitants; any children of both parties or for whom both parties have or have had parental responsibility; the time elapsed since they lived together; and any pending proceedings relating to ownership of the house, or financial relief for a child under the

Children Act 1989 (s. 36(6) FLA 1996). Before the enactment of the **DVCVA 2004** the court had to have regard to the fact that the couple had not given each other the commitment involved in marriage (**s. 41**). As a result of the definition of cohabitants being amended to include same-sex couples (who do not have the capacity to marry), **s. 41 FLA 1996** was repealed and **s. 36(6)** was amended to provide that, when considering the nature of the parties' relationship, the court must take into account, in particular, the level of commitment involved in that relationship (**s. 36(6)(e)**).

The court has a discretion (not a duty as it does with entitled persons, spouses and former spouses) to make an occupation order, if the balance of harm test tips in a cohabitant applicant's favour (**s. 36(8)**). For Amanda (a non-entitled cohabitant) the order must not exceed six months, but may be extended on one occasion for a further specified period not exceeding six months (**s. 36(10)**). However, non-molestation orders can be made for a specified period or until further order. That may not provide much consolation for Amanda if there is no reconciliation and she is compelled to seek alternative accommodation.

Question 2

(a)   Charles and Damian, 19-year-old twin brothers, are nephews of Edward, who is a 70-year-old widower. The twins leave home to attend the university in the town where Edward lives. During term time they live (rent-free) with Edward in his large house on the edge of town. As he likes to take an early morning run, Edward aims to be asleep by 11 pm. He has told Charles and Damian that they can come and go as they please, play music whenever they want, and as loudly as they want, provided it does not keep him awake. Charles keeps his door closed and does not disturb his uncle. However, Damian insists on leaving his door open. On a number of occasions Edward has gone along to Damian's room to complain about the noise, only to be met by verbal abuse and threats of violence. Charles went to his uncle's aid each time and was punched and kicked by Damian. Damian received some minor bruising from Charles in the last scuffle. Edward is very upset by these incidents and has become nervous and withdrawn. Damian's parents say they cannot cope with him. They confess to Edward that Damian has been a bully for years.

As a result of Damian's behaviour Charles is sleeping on the floor of the room of a fellow student who lives nearby. Edward has gone to a local bed and breakfast guest house. Damian remains in Edward's home. The family does not wish to involve the police.

Damian seeks your advice. He tells you that he likes 'having the house to myself'. He has heard that as a 'victim of domestic violence' he can go to court to get orders that will protect him and exclude Edward and Charles. [20 marks]

(b)   How would your answer differ if Charles were not Damian's twin brother, but his homosexual partner? [5 marks]

Commentary

This question is here to illustrate that at some time you will be asked to advise the unpleasant, the devious and the morally reprehensible as well as the deserving and/or downtrodden. Everyone is entitled to ask for legal advice: it is not your function to pass judgment. Remember that sometimes you have to give 'bad news'; the person who has asked for your advice may have to be told that he does not stand a chance of being granted an order. You have to explain why that is so. This question is inviting you to discuss the remedies available to relatives and same-sex couples under **Part IV of the FLA 1996** as amended by the **DVCVA 2004**.

Answer plan

- Identify relevant area of law—domestic violence—**Part IV FLA 1996**.
- Associated persons—relatives—**s. 62 and s. 63**.
- Orders available—non-molestation and occupation orders.
- Molestation—meaning. Factors courts take into account when deciding whether to grant order.
- Apply relevant cases and statutes to facts. Occupation order—who may apply? Appropriate section? Factors considered by court. Balance of harm test.
- Power of arrest, **s. 47** for occupation orders.
- Same-sex couples. Cohabitants, **s. 62(1)(a)**? Associated persons, **s. 62(3)(c)** living in same household.

Examiner's tip

In order to advise Damien properly you must not only explain the likelihood of him being granted an order, but must also warn him that other persons are likely to apply, and succeed, in their applications for orders against him.

Suggested answer

(a) As 'relatives' Damian and Edward come into the category of 'associated persons' who may apply for orders under **Part IV of the Family Law Act (FLA) 1996 (s. 62(3) (d))**. 'Relatives' are defined in **s. 63(1)** to include uncle and nephew. Damian and Charles are also relatives and therefore associated persons for the purpose of the Act (*Chechi v Bashier* [1999] 2 FLR 489). The court may make a non-molestation order where an application has been made by a person associated with the respondent, whether or not other family proceedings have been instituted (**s. 42(2)(a)**); or, of its own motion in any family proceedings (**s. 42(2)(b)**). A non-molestation order extends beyond restraining violence to forbidding the respondent from pestering (*Vaughan v Vaughan* [1973] 3 All ER 449) or harassing (*Horner v Horner* [1982] 2 All ER 495) the applicant. A non-molestation order application by Damian against Edward would be doomed to failure as there appears to be no evidence of anything which could be described as molestation by Edward directed against Damian; a similar application against Charles would also fail (*C v C (Non-Molestation: Jurisdiction)* [1998] 2 WLR 599). Even though Damian received some minor bruising in the last scuffle with his twin, the court, in deciding whether to exercise its powers, must have regard to all the circumstances including the need to secure the health, safety and well-being of the applicant (**s. 42(5)(a)**). When set in the context of all the incidents, it would be seen by the court that it is not Damian who needs a non-molestation order but Charles and Edward; it is their health, safety and well-being that needs to be secured. Charles was punched and kicked by Damian and Edward was met by verbal abuse and threats of violence and has become nervous and withdrawn. The court can go ahead and make the non-molestation orders against Damian of its own motion even though no such applications have been made by Charles and Edward (**s. 42(2)(b)**). In *Davis v Johnson* [1979] AC 264, at 334, Viscount Dilhorne said, 'violence is a form of molestation, but molestation may take place without the threat or use of violence and still be serious and inimical to mental or physical health.'

Although Damian and Edward are associated persons, Damian would not be entitled to apply under **Part IV FLA 1996** for an occupation order excluding Edward from the dwelling-house which is or has been their home. Damian has no estate or interest in the dwelling-house so could not make an application under **s. 33**. Nor does he fit into any of the other four categories of applicant, i.e. spouse (**ss. 33, 37**), former spouse (**ss. 33, 35**), cohabitant (**ss. 33, 36, 38**) or former cohabitant (**ss. 33, 36, 38**). By the same reasoning Damian could not apply for an occupation order against Charles. Furthermore, having strongly suggested to Damian that his own applications have little chance of success, you must warn him that he may face applications from the others. Edward (an entitled applicant by virtue of a beneficial estate) may apply for an occupation order requiring Damian to leave the dwelling-house which has been his and Damian's (the associated person's) home (**s. 33(3)(f)**). In deciding whether to exercise its powers under **s. 33(3)** and, if so, in what manner, the court is to have regard to all the circumstances, including the housing needs and housing resources of each of the parties; the financial resources of the parties; the likely effect of any order, or of any decision by the court not to exercise its powers to make regulatory orders, on the health, safety or well-being of the parties; and the conduct of the parties in relation to each other and otherwise (**s. 33(6)**). As Edward is an entitled person the court has a duty to make an order if it appears that he is likely to suffer significant harm attributable to Damian's conduct, if an order is not made, which is as great or greater than the harm likely to be suffered by Damian (**s. 33(7)**). Harm, in relation to Edward, who is at least 18, means ill-treatment or impairment of health (**s. 63(1)**). Significant harm is likely to be interpreted, as in the **Children Act 1989** proceedings, as 'considerable, noteworthy or important' (*Humberside CC v B* [1993] 1 FLR 257 at 263, *per* Booth J). It is highly likely that

Damian, threatened with exclusion on account of his behaviour, would be able to establish a degree of hardship in terms of the difficulty in finding similarly comfortable, congenial and convenient accommodation. However, he is unlikely to suffer significant harm, whereas Edward who is being subjected to abuse and threats of violence may very easily suffer harm if Damian remains in the house, as it seems likely that the incidents would be repeated. The Law Commission (*Domestic Violence and Occupation of the Family Home* (Law Com No. 207, 1992), para. 4.34) thought that the law would treat violence or other forms of abuse as deserving immediate relief. If it were thought to be appropriate, the occupation order could also include a term excluding Damian from a defined area in which the dwelling-house is included (**s. 33(3)(g)**). An order under **s. 33** may, in so far as it has a continuing effect, be made for a specified period, until the occurrence of a specified event or until further order (**s. 33(10)**). There is a presumption that the court will attach a power of arrest to the occupation order and the breach of a non-molestation order is now an arrestable offence. Damian has used violence against Charles and threatened violence against Edward, so unless the court was satisfied that in all the circumstances of the case Edward and Charles would be adequately protected without such a power of arrest in relation to the occupation order, a power of arrest would be attached (**s. 47(2)**). Where a court decides not to attach a power of arrest to an order it may accept an undertaking, for example by the respondent not to molest the applicant (**s. 46(1)**). The undertaking is enforceable as if it were an order of the court.

The **Domestic Violence, Crime and Victims Act (DVCVA) 2004** made breach of a non-molestation order a criminal offence with a maximum penalty of five years' imprisonment. The police are, therefore, able to arrest for breach of a non-molestation order, without the need for the attachment of a power of arrest or for the applicant to apply to the civil court for an arrest warrant. The respondent would only be guilty of a criminal offence if he were aware of the existence of the non-molestation order. If Charles or Edward did not wish to pursue criminal proceedings, they could follow the civil route. If that were to happen, and Damian were to be punished for contempt in the civil court, he could not be convicted of breach of a non-molestation order. This would not prevent a prosecution for other offences, for example assault or grievous bodily harm.

(b) Prior to the amendments introduced by the **DVCVA 2004**, homosexual partners were not classed as cohabitants or former cohabitants but could be associated persons if they lived or had lived in the same household, otherwise than merely by reason of one of them being the other's employee, tenant, lodger or boarder (**s. 62(c)**). A person living with another in a homosexual relationship has always been able to apply for a non-molestation order, despite the fact that they did not originally fall within the definition of cohabitants. **The DVCVA 2004** amended the definition of cohabitants to include two persons who are neither married to each other nor civil partners of each other but are living together as husband and wife or as if they were civil partners. This allows either Charles or Damian to apply for an occupation order under **s. 38** (neither cohabitant nor former cohabitant entitled to occupy, i.e. they have no beneficial estate, interest or contract or statutory right to remain). Taking into account the balance of harm test in **s. 38(5)** and Damian's conduct (**s. 36 (4)(d)**), it is unlikely that Damian would be successful in his application. However, Charles would have a much greater chance of a positive outcome.

Also, Charles would be able to apply for a non-molestation order as a cohabitant, rather than being part of the same household as Damian. Otherwise, all the advice given earlier in part (a) would remain the same.

? Question 3

Three years ago a group of friends (Fiona, George and Ian) who had been medical students at the same hospital, bought and became joint owners of a large house with the intention of living there together.

(a) Fiona and George were engaged at the time of the purchase and intended to marry after a five-year engagement (the lengthy engagement was Fiona's idea). Fiona has never lived in the intended matrimonial home. George moved in at the time of the purchase and suggested that Fiona should join him. Fiona thinks that George has consistently failed to show sufficient respect for her. A year ago, on George's suggestion that they should bring forward the date of the wedding, Fiona terminated the engagement. George has bombarded Fiona with flowers and begged her to reinstate the engagement. Fiona has decided that George is an unsuitable partner.

Advise Fiona. She wishes to remove George from the house and live there herself as it is nearer to the hospital than her present accommodation. Fiona wants George to refrain from sending pleading letters and flowers.

(b) Harriet and Ian had been living together for two years before they moved into the house three years ago. Although Harriet made a contribution to the purchase price Ian told her that there was a limit to the number of names that could appear on the deeds to the property. Harriet worked as a nurse until she gave birth two years ago. The baby died a few days after he was born. Harriet has suffered two miscarriages since then. Ian has been very unsympathetic and said to Harriet that it is just as well that he had not bothered to marry her. Eight months ago he left to live with June. That relationship has now ended. During the last month he has called on Harriet every day. He told her to get out of his house. He has told her that she 'looks a mess' and has 'let herself go'. He has threatened to display, on the railings outside the house, photographs of Harriet in the nude, so that, he says, everyone can compare her present appearance with that of four years ago. Yesterday he bundled her out of the house and threw her clothes after her.

Harriet has no family and her close friends live near to the house. She is at a women's refuge. However, the close proximity of so many young children and babies is making her very tearful.

Advise Harriet.

The parts of this question are equally weighted.

Commentary

This is a demanding question which requires a detailed answer. It is the type of question which may be set for coursework or as a 'pre-seen' exam question or in an open book exam.

Part (a) concentrates on an engaged couple and the conditions they must fulfil to be eligible to make an application for remedies under **Part IV FLA 1996**. There also appears to be some doubt about whether George's behaviour is sufficient to warrant any orders under the Act.

Part (b) raises little doubt about behaviour and worthiness. However, what is required is a discussion about the choice of the appropriate section under which to make an application.

Answer plan

- Identify relevant area of law—domestic violence—**Part IV FLA 1996**.
- Associated persons. Engaged couples. Evidence of engagement.
- Orders available. Non-molestation and occupation orders.
- Molestation—meaning. Factors courts take into account when deciding whether to make an order.
- Power of arrest, **s. 47**—undertakings, **s. 46**.
- Apply relevant cases and statutes to facts. Occupation order—entitled applicant, **s. 33**. Factors. Balance of harm test.
- Cohabitants. Occupation order, **s. 36**. Factors. Balance of harm test. Contrast with entitled applicant.

Examiner's tip

Avoid rushing into this question—it is a lengthy, two-part case study that requires careful reading prior to commencing the answer.

Suggested answer

(a) A wide group of 'associated persons' may apply for non-molestation orders and a narrower group may apply for occupation orders under **Part IV of the Family Law Act (FLA) 1996**. Fiona and George agreed to marry one another, therefore they are associated persons, even though the engagement is over (**s. 62(3)(e)**). As Fiona ended the engagement only a year ago, her application will be within the three-year limit (**s. 42(4)**). The court can neither make a non-molestation order under **s. 42** nor an occupation order under **s. 33** (entitled applicants) unless there is evidence in writing (**s. 44(1)**) of the agreement; however, **s. 44(1)** does not apply if the court is satisfied that the agreement to marry was evidenced by the gift of an engagement ring in contemplation of marriage (**s. 44(2)(a)**), or a ceremony entered into by the couple in the presence of one or more witnesses (**s. 44(2)(b)**).

If Fiona could not prove the existence of an engagement, or she was outside the three-year limit, she may nonetheless be able to apply for a non-molestation order due to the amendments made by **the Domestic Violence, Crime and Victims Act (DVCVA) 2004.** **Section 62(3)(ea)** includes in the definition of associated persons, those who have or have had an intimate personal relationship with each other, which is or was of a significant duration. This will cover a long-standing relationship which may, or may not, be a sexual relationship. However, it must be an intimate and personal relationship. This will not include long-term platonic friends or 'one-night stands'.

In deciding whether to exercise its powers to grant a non-molestation order and, if so, in what manner, the court must have regard to all the circumstances including the need to secure the health, safety and well-being of Fiona (**s. 42(5)(a)**). 'Molestation may take place without the threat or use of violence and still be serious and inimical to mental or physical health' (*Davis v Johnson* [1979] **AC 264**). A non-molestation order has been held to extend beyond restraining violence to forbidding the respondent from pestering (*Vaughan v Vaughan* [1973] **3 All ER 449**) or harassing (*Horner v Horner* [1982] **2 All ER 495**) the applicant, and includes the forcing by the other party of his society on the unwilling suffering party for the purpose of seeking to resume affectionate relations (*F v F* [1989] **2 FLR 451**). The court would consider the number and frequency of the letters and bouquets along with their effect on Fiona. It may be thought appropriate in the circumstances for George to give an undertaking not to molest Fiona (**s. 46(1)**). George, in giving an undertaking to the court, would not have to admit the truth of Fiona's allegations and the court would make no finding of fact regarding his conduct. A breach of the undertaking would be contempt of court (**s. 46(4)**).

Fiona's application for an occupation order would be under **s. 33** as an entitled person. Fiona is one of the legal owners of the property. She is entitled to occupy the dwelling-house by virtue of a beneficial estate or interest giving her the right to remain in occupation (**s. 33(1)(a)(i)**). Although the dwelling-house has never been Fiona's home (**s. 33(1)(b)(i)**), the couple intended it to be their home (**s. 33(1)(b)(ii)**). As with the non-molestation order, the occupation order application must be within three years of the termination of the engagement (**s. 33(2)**). She may claim to be an associated person because of their 'intimate personal relationship' (**s. 62(3)(ea)**) and as an entitled person she would be able to apply under **s. 33(1)(b)(ii)**. Fiona would wish the order to contain a term requiring George to leave the house (**s. 33(3)(f)**). In deciding whether to grant such an order and (if so) in what manner, the court is to have regard to all the circumstances including the housing needs and housing resources of Fiona and George; their financial resources; the likely effect of any order, or of any decision by the court not to make an order, on the health, safety and well-being of Fiona and George; and the conduct of the parties in relation to each other (**s. 33(6)**). As Fiona is an entitled person, the court has a duty to make an order if it appears that she is likely to suffer significant harm attributable to George's conduct, if an order is not made, which is as great or greater than the harm likely to be suffered by George (**s. 33(7)**). Harm, in relation to Fiona, who is at least 18, means ill-treatment or impairment of health (**s. 63(1)**). Significant harm is likely to be interpreted, as in the **Children Act 1989** proceedings, as 'considerable, noteworthy or important' (*Humberside CC v B* **[1993] 1 FLR 257** at 263, *per* Booth J). It is difficult to conclude on the facts given that, without an order, Fiona would suffer significant harm due to George's conduct. As in *Wiseman v Simpson* **[1988] 1 All ER 245** it appears that Fiona has 'simply ceased to be in love' with George (if she ever were). However, in *Scott v Scott* **[1992] 1 FLR 529** the Court of Appeal upheld an order prohibiting the husband from exercising his right to occupy the matrimonial home where there was no violence, because the husband, who would not accept the marriage was over, had repeatedly tried to persuade his wife to effect a reconciliation and had also broken an earlier undertaking.

Were an occupation order to be made in Fiona's favour either party could be granted possession or use of the furniture or other contents (**s. 40(1)(c)–(e)**). Obligations as to repair, maintenance and the discharge of outgoings in respect of the house could be imposed by the court (**s. 40(1)(a)**). Additionally, Fiona could be ordered to pay rent to George (**s. 40(1)(b)**) (the guidelines to be followed by the court when exercising its discretion to make such orders are contained in **s. 40(2)**). (Note: there is no power of enforcement in **s. 40**: *Nwogbe v Nwogbe* **[2000] 2 FLR 744**.)

The advice to Fiona is that she and George need to decide what to do with their property, for example sell it, or one buy the other out (of course, any such arrangement would need both the consent and formal participation of Ian). **Part IV** orders should be unnecessary here.

(b) Harriet and Ian are former cohabitants, a man and woman who, although not married to each other, were living together as husband and wife (**s. 62(1)(b)**) and therefore they are associated persons (**s. 62(3)(b)**). Harriet could apply for an occupation order giving her the right to enter and occupy and requiring Ian to leave the dwelling-house which has been their home. The application may be either as a former cohabitant with no existing right to occupy (**s. 36**), or as an entitled person, by virtue of a beneficial estate or interest, under **s. 33**. Although Harriet is not a legal owner of the property, she should be able to establish a beneficial interest by way of a resulting trust as she made a financial contribution to the purchase price of the property (*Sekhon v Alissa* **[1989] 2 FLR 94**) or a constructive trust. As a **s. 36** applicant, Harriet is only entitled to an order for a specified period not exceeding six months and to one extension for a further specified period not exceeding six months. However, a **s. 33** order may be granted for an unlimited period. Also, under **s. 36**, the order must contain a provision giving Harriet the right to enter and occupy the dwelling-house for the period specified and requiring Ian to permit the exercise of that right (**s. 36(4)**). This provision is necessary, as an applicant under **s. 36** is, by definition, non-entitled.

In deciding whether to make an order, if she is 'entitled', the court would look to s. 33(6) (see part (a)) but if she is not entitled, s. 36(6) would be applied, which requires the court, additionally, to consider the nature of the parties' relationship, the length of time they lived together as husband and wife and the length of time that has elapsed since they lived together.

When, on the balance of harm test, the scales tip in favour of an entitled applicant (s. 33(7)) the court is under a duty to grant an order. However, for a s. 36 applicant, the court has a discretion to grant an order (s. 36(7)). Considering the heart-rending circumstances, coupled with Ian's dastardly behaviour, it is almost certain that the court would grant an occupation order whether it be as a result of a duty (s. 33) or merely a discretion (s. 36).

The dilemma, then, is under which section should Harriet make her application? If she makes the wrong choice, will it jeopardize her chance of an order? If an application is made under one section and the court considers that it has no power to make an order under that section, but that it has power to make an order under another section, then the court may make an order under that other section (s. 39(3)). Were Harriet to be granted an order under s. 36, could Ian claim that there has been a finding of fact that an order had been granted to Harriet as a cohabitant with no rights in the property. That danger appears to have been defused by s. 39(4) which states that the fact that a person has applied for an occupation order under ss. 35 to 38, or that an occupation order has been made, does not affect the right of any person to claim a legal or equitable interest in any property in any subsequent proceedings (including **Part IV**). This allows the more urgent **Part IV** applications to proceed without the need to get bogged down in a property dispute at this stage.

Molestation covers a wide range of behaviour (see part (a)). In *Johnson v Walton* [1990] 1 FLR 350, sending photographs of the partially nude applicant to a national newspaper with the intention of causing her distress was held to constitute molestation. On the basis of this decision, threatening to pin nude photographs of Harriet to the railings outside the house could also amount to harassment. A non-molestation order may include terms which prohibit threats, harassment or pestering. Harriet seems eminently deserving of an order which will secure her health, safety and well-being (s. 42(5)(a)).

Further reading

Burton, M. (2009) 'Civil Law Remedies for Domestic Violence: Why are Applications for Non-Molestation Orders Declining?' 31(2) JSWFL 109–20.

Donovan, C. and Hester, M. (2011) 'Seeking Help from the Enemy: Help-Seeking Strategies of Those in Same-Sex Relationship Who Have Experienced Domestic Abuse'. 23(1) CFLQ 26.

Edwards, S.S.M. (2011) 'Domestic Violence: Not a Term of Art but a State of Consciousness'. Fam Law 1244.

Herring, J. (2011) 'The Meaning of Domestic Violence: *Yemshaw v London Borough of Hounslow* [2011] UKSC 3'. 33(3) JSWFL 297–304.

Knight, C.J.S. (2012) 'Doing (Linguistic) Violence to Prevent (Domestic) Violence? *Yemshaw v Hounslow LBC* in the Supreme Court'. 24(1) CFLQ 95.

Websites

www.domesticviolence.co.uk

www.womensaid.org.uk

6 Children: general principles, concepts, status and wardship

Introduction

Family law is increasingly child-centred. For example, **s. 25 of the Matrimonial Causes Act 1973** (as amended by the **Matrimonial and Family Proceedings Act 1984**) provides that the welfare of minor children is the first consideration when the court is assessing financial relief for spouses. If a court is determining questions regarding the upbringing of a child or the administration of a child's property under the **Children Act (CA) 1989**, the child's welfare shall be the court's 'paramount' consideration (**s. 1(1)**). The same principle applies to adoption under the **Adoption and Children Act 2002 (s. 1(2))**. At an international level, the **United Nations Convention on the Rights of the Child (UNCRC) 1989** reflects the view that children and family relationships should have special protection and that their rights as individuals should be guaranteed with regard to such matters as nationality and freedom of expression.

All students need to have a sound knowledge of the general principles of welfare and 'non-intervention' and the concept of parental responsibility as they permeate child law. This chapter contains a hotchpotch of questions on, as the title suggests, general principles and concepts of child law, the status of children (recognizing the rise of the recorded non-marital birth rate in recent years) and wardship, whose role was significantly affected by the **CA 1989**. Such topics lend themselves to essay-type questions and three of the questions take this form, but there is one problem question too.

 Question 1

Analyse the rights and responsibilities of a father who has never been married to the mother of his child.

Commentary

This question requires candidates to analyse the legal position of a father who has never been married to the mother of his child. If the question had referred to a father who *is* not married to the mother of his child, a discussion of the rights and responsibilities of a father post-divorce would also be needed. Students should explain the position under the original **CA 1989**, the changes that were introduced by the **Adoption and Children Act 2002** and the potential impact of the Registration of Births (Parents Not Married and Not Acting Together) Regulations 2010. As the question asks students to discuss rights and *responsibilities*, a brief explanation of liability for child support should be included, which is discussed in more detail in **Chapter 14**.

 Answer plan

- Numbers.
- Sorts of 'unmarried fathers'.
- Meaning of parental responsibility.
- **CA 1989, s. 4**—'agreements' and 'orders'.
- **Adoption and Children Act 2002**—joint registration.
- **CA 1989, s. 8** orders.
- Child support—**Child Support Act 1991** as amended.

 Examiner's tip

Although it is tempting to refer to the 'unmarried father', this is inaccurate, as the father of a child may be married to someone other than the child's mother.

 Suggested answer

Statistics show that the number of children born out of wedlock is increasing. In 2010, 47 per cent of births in the UK were non-marital, but only 5.9 per cent of births outside marriage were registered by the mother alone (ONS, 2010). Eighty-four per cent of babies are born to parents who are married, civil partners or cohabiting (ONS, 2010), which would seem to indicate that a significant number of children are born into stable extra-marital relationships with two actively involved parents. At the other end of the spectrum, a man may father a child as the result of a one-night stand, or even by rape; this father is not likely to play any part in the child's life.

Historically, there was no legal procedure to enable an actively involved father, living with the mother, to acquire legal recognition of this fact, and there was no way in which he could legally share parental responsibility with the mother. The Law Commission decided in its *Report on Illegitimacy* (Law Com No. 118, 1982), not to abolish illegitimacy altogether, as to do so would not only mean that all children would be the same, but that all parents would be the same and have equal parental rights and duties in relation to their children. It was felt that to give all fathers equal rights fails to distinguish between the many different types and situations and could lead to harassment, blackmail and disruption of new family units.

The starting point is, therefore, that a father who is not married to the child's mother has no automatic 'parental responsibility' (PR): the mother of a non-marital child has sole PR (**s. 2(2), Children Act (CA) 1989**). PR is defined by **s. 3 CA 1989** as 'all the rights, duties, powers, responsibilities and authority which by law a parent of a child has in relation to the child and his property.' A father who is not married to the mother can, however, acquire PR, but he has to take positive steps to do so.

So what are the options available to him? Under the original provisions of the **CA 1989** a father who was not married to the mother could only acquire PR if he entered into a parental responsibility agreement with the mother, if he obtained a parental responsibility order from the court or if he was granted a residence order by the court. However, the **Adoption and Children Act 2002** inserted s. 4(1)(a) into the **CA 1989** to enable a father who was not married to the mother to acquire parental responsibility by jointly registering the birth. This provision came into effect on 1 December 2003 and since then thousands of men have acquired PR by registering their child's birth. As explained earlier, only 5.9 per cent of births outside marriage were registered by the mother alone in 2010, which means that the majority of fathers acquired PR for their children. Presumably those who oppose fathers who are not married to the mother having automatic status, would not object to these fathers obtaining PR, as such men are presumably acting as social parents.

If a father does not jointly register the birth or if the child in question was born before 1 December 2003, he could suggest a parental responsibility agreement, whereby the father and mother can, by agreement, provide for the father to have parental responsibility (**s. 4(1)(b)**). The agreement is only effective if in the form prescribed by regulations and filed in the Principal Registry of the Family Division. The court's role here is administrative only, i.e. there is no investigation of the child's welfare. However, the agreement can be terminated by court order and at this point the welfare principle does apply (**s. 1(1)**). In the early years it seemed that many agreements were forged and that, after witnessing by a court official or JP was introduced in 1994, numbers fell. Between 1994 and 2004 only a few thousand agreements were registered each year and since then numbers have dropped significantly as many unmarried fathers acquire PR by joint registration of birth.

If the relationship with the mother has broken down then a parental responsibility agreement is unlikely to be a realistic option and the father who is not married to the mother would need to apply to the court for a parental responsibility order (PRO) for the child (**s. 4(1)(a) CA 1989**). This is assuming that he did not acquire parental responsibility by jointly registering the birth of the child in question. On an application by the father for a PRO, the welfare of the child is the paramount consideration (**s. 1 CA 1989**). The 'non-intervention principle' (**s. 1(5)**) also applies and the court will only make an order if it is in the child's best interests to do so. The **1989 Act** is silent as to the factors which the court should consider, but there is judicial guidance. In *Re H (Illegitimate Children: Father: Parental Rights) (No. 2)* **[1991] 1 FLR 214** Balcombe LJ indicated that relevant factors could include: how the PRO is likely to benefit the child, the relationship the father has with the child, the reasons for the application, his level of commitment to and involvement with the child, and whether making the order is likely to destabilize the child's new family unit. But in *Re H (Parental Responsibility)* **[1998] 1 FLR 855**, the Court of Appeal held that the Balcombe list is neither exhaustive nor determinative and that the welfare principle is the overriding criterion.

In 2011, approximately 5,224 parental responsibility orders were granted, 40 orders of 'no order' were made and 45 applications were actually refused (Judicial and Court Statistics, 2012, Table 2.4). Injuring both the child concerned and another child by a former partner *(Re H (Parental Responsibility)* **[1998] 1 FLR 855**), possession of pederastic material *(Re P (Parental Responsibility)* **[1998] 2 FLR 96**) and being brain-damaged in a road accident *(M v M (Parental Responsibility)* **[1999] 2 FLR 737**), have all led to refusals. In contrast, a finding of violence against the father did not preclude a PRO in *Re J-S (Contact: Parental Responsibility)* **[2003] 1 FLR 399 (CA)** as the father had shown commitment, attachment and reasons.

Applications for a PRO are 'family proceedings' and the court may make any **s. 8 CA 1989** order (e.g. a contact order) instead of a PRO if it considers that the best way of promoting the child's welfare. A father who has not been married to the child's mother may also apply as of right *(M v C and Calderdale MBC* **[1992] Fam Law 571**) for a **s. 8** order. Hence he may apply for a residence order. If successful, the court must make a PRO to confer on him the powers and responsibilities of a parent (**s. 12(1)**) otherwise his parental responsibility would be limited (e.g. no right to appoint a guardian) and would end if the residence order ended.

A father who has not been married to the mother is likely to apply for a **s. 8** contact order with a PRO (although it is possible to apply for contact on its own). Probert points out that there is now a 'widespread assumption among the judiciary that it is generally in the interests of the child to maintain contact with both parents and that in practice the courts will order contact unless there are good reasons not to do so' (*Cretney and Probert's Family Law* (2009), p. 285). But the assumption that contact is in the child's interests is far weaker if there is no relationship between the father and child. In the absence of 'good reasons', an application for contact by a committed father who has a relationship with his child is likely to be successful.

If a father obtains parental responsibility then it means that he acquires the status of a parent for adoption proceedings and his consent must be obtained or dispensed with. He also acquires the right to appoint a guardian for the child (**s. 5(3) CA 1989**), the right to consent to the child's marriage (**s. 3 Marriage Act 1949** as amended) and the right to object to the provision of and removal from local authority accommodation (**s. 20 CA 1989**). Furthermore, acquiring PR has important implications for **Hague Convention** (abduction) proceedings. However, the ability to make decisions regarding a child on a daily basis will vary from case to case. A father who acquires PR because he has been granted a residence order will in practice be in a position to make more decisions than a man who is estranged from his child's mother and obtained a PRO from the court.

It should be noted that the court can withdraw PR from a father on the application of anyone with parental responsibility, or the child with leave of the court. Such an order was made in *Re P (Terminating Parental Responsibility)* [1995] **1 FLR 1048** on the basis that the father had been imprisoned for assaulting the nine-week-old daughter in question.

As explained earlier, a father who has never been married to the mother of his child has the right to apply for a **s. 8** order, i.e. a residence order, a contact order, a specific issue order or a prohibited steps order, and this is the case whether or not he has acquired parental responsibility. His status is therefore recognized and he has the ability to request orders that would enable him to participate in his child's life. Of course, an order will only be granted if it is in the child's interests (**s. 1(1) CA 1989**), which emphasizes that the provisions exist to benefit the child. In addition, a father without parental responsibility is required to maintain his child financially, in the same way as a father with parental responsibility. **Section 1(1) of the Child Support Act 1991** (as amended) provides that each parent of a qualifying child is responsible for maintaining him and **s. 54** defines a parent as a person who is in the eyes of the law the mother or father of a child. No reference is made to parental responsibility. It thus remains the case that many men are legally obliged to support their children financially under the **Child Support Act 1991** but do not have parental responsibility in relation to them, which many claim is unfair. Again, this state of affairs demonstrates the child-centred nature of the law in England and Wales.

This answer has demonstrated that a father who has never been married to his child's mother has potentially significant status as he can acquire parental responsibility in relation to his children. The amendment introduced by the **Adoption and Children Act 2002** has improved the position of the unmarried father and has meant that most children born outside wedlock have two parents with PR. But if the parents' relationship has broken down before the child is born, the father is likely to have to initiate court proceedings to acquire PR even if he is a committed and responsible father, as joint registration and PR agreements require the mother's cooperation. If/when the Registration of Births (Parents Not Married and Not Acting Together) Regulations 2010 come into force, the position of such a father who does not have a good relationship with the child's mother will improve, as the regulations are designed to ensure that wherever possible the names of both parents are registered. A mother who is not married to the child's father and attends the register office alone will be required to provide details about the father so that he can be contacted and registered on the birth certificate. Although the mother will be able to refuse in exceptional cases (e.g. if she fears for her safety), many more unmarried fathers will register the birth of their child and will thus acquire PR for them.

Question 2

Last year, Rose (a single woman) had a brief affair with Fred, a wealthy married man 20 years older than her. After Rose had ended the relationship, she discovered that she was pregnant. Fred offered to leave his wife and to marry Rose but Rose did not want anything more to do with him. The baby, John, was born six months ago. Fred and his wife never had any children and he is delighted that he now has a son. He continually asks to see John and says that he wants to be actively involved in the child's upbringing. Rose is now living with Simon who is willing and able to support both of them. They plan to marry and wish to bring John up as their own child without interference from Fred.

Last week Fred told Rose that John would be at a real disadvantage if they (Fred and Rose) did not get married and make him legitimate. During the heated argument which followed, and in an attempt to make Fred leave them alone, Rose told Fred that he might not be John's father anyway.

Rose has no intention of claiming anything from Fred. She has, however, discovered that Fred's father has just died leaving his estate to be divided equally between all his grand-children, and wonders whether John would have a claim.

Advise Rose.

Commentary

This question asks you to advise the mother of a child born outside marriage, who is being (she will argue) pestered by the child's father. With any problem involving children you can expect to have to weave into your answer the pervasive principles and concepts, i.e. parental responsibility, welfare and non-intervention. You can begin by reassuring a mother in such circumstances on the issue of prima facie parental responsibility and then go on to deal with the specific areas of concern. The main one is obviously what the father's rights are and what action he could take in relation to the child, both of which are dependent on proof of paternity. Indeed, the relationship will also have to be proved before any claim can be made on the grandfather's estate. You will therefore need to discuss how paternity can be proved.

You are told that 'Rose has no intention of claiming anything from Fred', indicating that you are not expected to consider child support (see **Chapter 14**). In reality, of course, despite what Rose says, the issue of child support would be discussed, to ensure that Rose is properly advised. You should also consider the issue of inheritance as Rose has specifically mentioned the fact that Fred's father has recently died leaving his estate to his grandchildren.

Answer plan

- Legal position of a father not married to the mother.
- Proof of paternity.
- **CA 1989, s. 8** orders.
- Distinctions between 'legitimate' and 'illegitimate' children.
- Succession rights.

Examiner's tip

Fred has suggested that John will be disadvantaged if his parents do not marry—ensure that you address this point by explaining the status of children born outside marriage.

Suggested answer

As Rose and Fred are not and have never been married, parental responsibility is currently vested in Rose alone (**s. 2 Children Act (CA) 1989**). Fred wants to be recognized as John's father and may take legal action in order to achieve this. When considering any application, the paramount objective will be the welfare of John (**s. 1(1)**) and any order made must be in his best interests. The 'non-intervention' principle (**s. 1(5)**) will also apply, so the court will only make an order if it thinks that to do so is better for the child than making no order at all.

Before Fred can acquire any legal status in relation to John, the relationship has to be established and paternity will have to be proved, particularly as Rose has told Fred that he might not be John's father. The **Family Law Reform Act 1969, s. 20(1)**, empowers a court to require the use of genetic tests in any civil proceedings involving an issue of paternity. DNA testing, which can be carried out on bloods, bodily fluids and tissue, would determine beyond any reasonable doubt whether Fred is John's father. To ensure integrity, such court-ordered tests can only be administered by an accredited body (**s. 20(1A) Family Law Reform Act (FLRA) 1969**). It should be noted that if Rose opposes his application for blood or DNA tests, Fred may be stopped in his tracks at this point, like the natural father (if such he was) in *Re F (A Minor: Paternity Tests)* **[1993] Fam Law 163**. The court may decide, as it did in that case, that there is no realistic prospect of Fred succeeding in his application for parental responsibility or contact, as it would not be for John's benefit, and that consequently to establish who John's natural father is would make no real difference. An order for blood tests might disturb the stability of the family unit and should therefore be refused. However, Rose should be advised that the court generally prefers the truth to come out. In *Re H (Paternity: Blood Test)* **[1996]**

2 FLR 65 Ward LJ said that 'every child has the right to know the truth unless his welfare clearly justifies the cover up', citing **art. 7 of the United Nations Convention on the Rights of the Child (UNCRC) 1989** which refers to the 'right to know' one's parents. Following this, a test was ordered in *Re H and A (Children)* [2002] EWCA Civ 383, despite the husband's statement that he would leave the wife and children were it to show that he had not fathered them. Rose should be advised that it is not advantageous to refuse to supply her and John's samples, as that would allow the court to presume Fred's paternity under **s. 23(1) FLRA 1969**. In addition, it is in Rose's interests for paternity to be established if a claim is to be made on Fred's father's estate, or should child support become an issue.

Assuming that paternity is proved, what options are available to Fred? Two options can be quickly dismissed as unrealistic: a **s. 4** parental responsibility agreement (as Rose will obviously not agree to Fred acquiring equal parental responsibility) and a **s. 8** residence order (as, on the facts, the welfare of the child would dictate that John should remain with Rose). Fred could, however, apply for a **s. 4** parental responsibility order (PRO) and/or a **s. 8** contact order. The effect of the PRO would be to equate Fred's legal position, at least for the duration of the order, with that of a married father. The court, applying the welfare principle (**s. 1 CA 1989**), must be satisfied that it is appropriate so to do. The court will look at how the PRO is likely to benefit John; what relationship Fred has with John and why he is applying for parental responsibility; how committed he is and whether the PRO would be likely to destabilize John's family unit *(Re H (Illegitimate Children: Father: Parental Rights) (No. 2)* [1991] 1 FLR 214). Fred would obviously be applying for a PRO because he genuinely wants to be actively involved with the child's upbringing and Rose should be advised that he could well succeed. In *Re C (Minors) (Parental Rights)* [1992] 2 All ER 86, it was held that a PRO may be granted even though there may be a problem enforcing the rights which arise as this can be resolved by a **s. 8** order. Even acrimony between the parties *(Re P (A Minor) (Parental Responsibility Order)* [1994] 1 FLR 578), or violence *(Re J-S (Contact: Parental Responsibility)* [2003] 1 FLR 399 (CA)), need not be fatal.

In any event, Fred as father could apply for a contact order (**s. 8 CA 1989**). Although there is now a 'widespread assumption among the judiciary that it is generally in the interests of the child to maintain contact with both parents' this assumption 'is weaker if there were no existing relationship between the child and the parent' (*Cretney and Probert's Family Law* (2009), p. 285). It is arguable whether John's welfare would be served by having contact with Fred whose only real claim here is that he is the natural father. There is no meaningful father/son relationship here, and Rose does not want to be reminded of their brief affair, particularly now that she intends to marry Simon. In *Re O (Contact: Imposition of Conditions)* [1995] 2 FLR 124, the mother was required to supply the father with updates on the boy's progress. Such indirect contact may be the answer in this case. Furthermore, in *Re H (A Minor) (Parental Responsibility)* [1993] 1 FLR 484, the Court of Appeal held that although the mother's new relationship might preclude a contact order, a PRO would not be ruled out. Another possibility, also with reference to reluctant resident parents, might be 'supervised' contact as in

F v F (Contempt: Committal) [1998] 2 FLR 237 where the mother was ordered to hand over the children to the person in charge of a contact centre.

If an order for contact is made, Rose must be advised that she may be required to pay a fine or face imprisonment for contempt if she persistently defies a court order (see *Re S (Contact Dispute: Committal)* [2004] EWCA Civ 1790). Furthermore, the **Children and Adoption Act 2006** introduced new powers to enforce contact (contained in ss. **11A–11P CA 1989**). **Section 11I of the CA 1989** (as amended) provides that when a contact order is made after 8 December 2008 the court must attach a warning notice which indicates the consequences of non-compliance. In relation to contact orders made prior to 8 December 2008, a warning notice can be attached if a question arises before the court in relation to that order or a specific application to attach a warning is made. The existence of the warning notice means that the court can make a variety of orders to enforce contact. For example, a resident parent who fails to comply with a contact order can be required to compensate the other (**s. 11O**) or he or she can be ordered to carry out unpaid work (**s. 11J**).

Two further issues need to be discussed. First, is it true that John will be disadvantaged if Fred and Rose do not marry? The general principle, now embodied in the **FLRA 1987**, is that there should be equality for all children at law, regardless of whether they are born in wedlock or not. **Section 1 of the 1987 Act** introduced a rule of construction that references to relationship are to be construed without regard to whether or not the mother and father were married to each other at any particular time. Discrimination cannot be justified and is inconsistent with UK international obligations under the **European Convention on Human Rights (1950)** and the **European Convention on the Legal Status of Children Born out of Wedlock (1981)**. The position of the child born to unmarried parents in relation to maintenance and inheritance was largely assimilated with that of the child born to a married couple by the **1987 Act**. Furthermore **s. 9 of the Nationality, Immigration and Asylum Act 2002** now enables British citizenship to be bestowed by a proven parental link (although this is not an issue in John's case). John could not, however, inherit his father's title if he has one (*Re Moynihan* [2000] 1 FLR 113).

The last issue needing to be discussed is that Fred's father has died leaving his estate to be divided equally between all his grandchildren. One assumes from this that there is a will in which case, by **s. 19 FLRA 1987**, all words such as 'children', or as here 'grandchildren', are to be construed as including illegitimate children unless a contrary intention appears. In the absence of such a contrary intention, John will in fact have a claim on Fred's father's estate, provided of course that the relationship can be proved.

 Question 3

Discuss the extent to which the role of wardship has diminished since the Children Act 1989.

Commentary

Most family law courses cover wardship, which is one expression of the inherent jurisdiction of the High Court. It is a long-established, extremely flexible jurisdiction which was much used prior to the activation of the **CA 1989**.

In 1991, 4,961 originating summonses were issued, 2,752 by local authorities and 2,209 by others (Judicial Statistics, 1991). By 1993, there were only 269 wardship applications (White, Carr and Lowe, *The Children Act in Practice*, 2nd edn (1995)). The *Judicial Statistics Annual Reports* ceased to give statistics about wardship in 1992.

This question is asking you to consider the role of wardship in the light of the **CA 1989**. In order to assess whether its role has diminished you will need to explain its role prior to the **1989 Act** in both public and private law cases, which may not have been covered in lectures. As a result, this type of essay question is likely to be set as an assignment to enable you to demonstrate your research skills.

 Answer plan

	Private law	Public law
Pre-Children Act 1989	Wardship was used to resolve novel cases between individuals or cases where freezing required	– Child in care could be made a ward – Wardship could provide a route into care – Wardship could not be used to review local authority decisions
Post-Children Act 1989	– Open door policy and range of orders means wardship is used less often – Still used when freezing required, e.g. abduction	– Cannot be used by individuals in immigration cases – Wardship and care are incompatible – Wardship can be an alternative to care

 Examiner's tip

Ensure that you not only define wardship and explain its features, but also consider the continuing significance of it—refer to recent cases such as **KY v DD [2011] EWHC 1277 (Fam)** and **Wardship: T v S (Wardship) [2011] EWHC 1608 (Fam)**.

Suggested answer

Wardship is just one use of the High Court's inherent jurisdiction over children and provides what many see as an essential residual protection for children. Anyone with a sufficient and proper interest in a child may, without leave, seek to make the child a ward of court. The child becomes a ward immediately on the issuing of the originating summons (**s. 41(2) Supreme Court Act 1981**) and no ground needs to be established to invoke the jurisdiction.

A child can be made a ward of the court provided that he or she is physically present in the jurisdiction (*H v D* [2007] EWHC 802) or is habitually resident in the jurisdiction but currently overseas (*Lewisham London Borough Council v D* [2008] 2 FLR 1449). In *Re B, RB v FB and MA (Forced Marriage: Wardship: Jurisdiction)* [2008] EWHC 1436 (Fam) the High Court made a 15-year-old British national a ward of the court even though she had never so much as visited the UK; however, this is unusual.

The advantages of wardship stem from the fact that cases are heard in the High Court (which is suited to hearing long and complex cases, with one continuous hearing by an experienced judge), under a largely non-statutory jurisdiction in which there are the widest possible powers to protect a child, and which can easily adapt to changing conditions. The unique feature of wardship, however, is that legal control over the child vests in the court, which takes over ultimate responsibility for the child and 'no important step in the child's life can be taken without the court's consent' (*per* Cross J in *Re S (Infants)* [1967] 1 All ER 202) without committing contempt of court. The prior sanction of the court is therefore required if, for example, a ward wishes to marry or to leave the jurisdiction. When the court is determining such issues the welfare of the child is considered 'first, last and all the time' (*per* Dunn J in *Re D (A Minor) (Justices' Decision: Review)* [1977] 3 All ER 481). The need to apply to the court for permission to take any important step in relation to the child obviously places a considerable burden on judicial resources and is seen by some as a disadvantage of the jurisdiction, others being delay and cost.

So what role did wardship play before the **Children Act (CA) 1989**? First, it was used in private law disputes by individuals, for example parents, relatives and friends, in situations where immediate freezing of the position was required. Examples included preventing child abduction, preventing irrevocable surgery such as abortion (*Re G-U (A Minor) (Wardship)* [1984] FLR 811) or solving novel cases where the court's expertise and wide powers were advantageous (*Re F (In Utero)* [1988] 2 All ER 193). Wardship also had a role in public law cases as until the **1989 Act**, a child in care could be made a ward. However, in *A v Liverpool City Council* [1981] 2 FLR 222, where a mother wished in effect to challenge the access arrangements to her child, the House of Lords decided that there is no general reviewing power in the court over local authority decisions and wardship cannot be used to this end. The same principle applied wherever other statutory powers were exercisable, for example wardship could not be used to resist the deportation of a child. In contrast, local authorities were encouraged to use wardship as providing another route into care, if the ground for an order under the **Children and Young Persons Act 1969** could not be established. Similarly, where a court refused an order and the authority had no right of appeal, wardship would be used (*Re C (A Minor) (Justices' Decision: Review)* [1981] 2 FLR 62). It could also be used to supplement local authority powers in relation to children in care, for example to solve medical problems, to prevent publicity, to obtain injunctions.

The activation of the **CA 1989** reduced the need to invoke wardship for several reasons. First, the **CA 1989** introduced an 'open door' policy of access to the courts including easier access to the High Court. Prior to the Act, many individuals were only able to access the courts through wardship, however the **1989 Act** enables a wide range of persons to apply for a **s. 8** order. Secondly, hearsay evidence is admissible in all 'family proceedings' (which includes wardship) and the whole range of **s. 8** orders can be made. The courts can thus make the order that is in the best interest of the child, rather than the order that has been applied for. In addition, the introduction of prohibited steps orders and specific issue orders (**s. 8**) provides flexibility that was previously only obtainable in wardship cases.

Private law cases are probably the least affected by the **1989 Act** as wardship remains as an alternative to the statutory orders, even if it would be possible to achieve the same result under the statutory scheme. However, in the rare event that a private individual resorts to wardship, it may be declined by the court. Wardship is expensive and the prohibited steps and specific issue orders (**s. 8**) often enable the same result to be achieved. But in extreme cases, where parents are continually applying for prohibited steps and specific issue orders, a judge might make the child a ward of the court and treat the parents as forfeiting their parental responsibility, as evidenced in *Wardship: T v S (Wardship)* [2011] EWHC 1608 (Fam). Furthermore, wardship retains unique features which make it attractive, for example no leave is required; there is immediate access as of right to the High Court and immediate freezing of the *status quo*. Consequently, it continues to be of particular use in child abduction cases (see *KY v DD* [2011] EWHC 1277 (Fam) for a recent example) and others where continuing judicial control is considered desirable (*Re T (A Minor) (Child: Representation)* [1993] 4 All ER 518). In *B v D (Abduction: Wardship)* [2008] EWHC 1246 (Fam) wardship was used to secure the return of children from Portugal despite the fact that the **Hague Convention on the Civil Aspects of International Child Abduction (1983)** could have been utilized. Wardship has also been used to protect British children at risk of being forced into marriage. In *Re SK (Abduction: Forcible Removal by Parents)* [1999] 2 FLR 542 and *Re B, RB v FB and MA* [2008] (see earlier) young British girls physically situated overseas were made wards of the court and consequently permitted to travel to the UK where the risk of forced marriage was not present. However, the use of wardship to protect those at risk of being forced to marry is likely to diminish following the **Forced Marriage (Civil Protection) Act 2007** (see **Chapter 2**).

In public law cases, the Act is silent on the use of wardship by individuals against a local authority and it is assumed that the judicial restrictions imposed by *A v Liverpool City Council* [1981] 2 FLR 222 are preserved. The provisions of the **CA 1989**, particularly the presumption of reasonable contact (**s. 34**) and the rights of appeal contained in the Act, mean that it is often unnecessary for individuals to resort to wardship in public cases. In addition, it remains the case that wardship cannot be utilized if other statutory powers are exercisable. Consequently, in *R (Anton) v Secretary of State for the Home Department; Re Anton* [2004] EWHC 2730/2731 (**Admin/Fam**) it was held that the inherent jurisdiction cannot be used to grant an injunction restraining the removal from the jurisdiction of a child subject to immigration control. Similarly, *S v S* [2008] **EWHC 2288** (**Fam**) concerned a child whose mother was attempting to resist deportation as a failed asylum seeker. The application to make the child a ward of the court was rejected on the basis that wardship cannot impinge upon the Secretary of State's powers in relation to immigration.

It is in the context of use of wardship by a local authority that the **Act** has had the greatest impact. Previously the main function of wardship here was to underpin the statutory scheme and to remedy any deficiencies. As the **CA 1989** modernized the system and remedied many of the defects, the need for local authority use of wardship was eliminated. But the Act went further by expressly indicating that wardship and care are incompatible (**s. 100**). The effect is that a local authority is precluded from acquiring rights over children which it cannot get under the statute, which in turn aims to provide improved machinery for protecting children. **Section 31** now provides the sole ground for compulsory action and a local authority cannot ever use wardship to take a child into care, to keep a child in local authority accommodation or to acquire any aspect of parental responsibility (**s. 100(2)**). However, in exceptional cases wardship can be utilized as an alternative to care proceedings, where the latter would not be in the child's best interests. In *Re M and J (Wardship: Supervision and Residence Orders)* [2003] 2 FLR 541, the local authority applied for care orders in respect of two children. It was held that, in the exceptional circumstances of the case, it was appropriate to take the exceptional course of continuing wardship and also making both supervision and residence orders. Under the wardship jurisdiction, the various adults involved would be allowed to return to court and ask a third party to assist with decision-making about the children. In another case *(Re W and X (Wardship: Relatives Rejected as Foster Carers)* [2004] 1 FLR 415) a care order would not have achieved what the local authority wanted for children who were with maternal grandparents as an emergency placement. Even though there were some serious concerns about aspects of the grandparents' parenting skills, the local authority considered that the children should remain with the grandparents on the basis that the authority and the grandparents shared parental responsibility. However, the grandparents were then rejected as foster carers. The problem then was that under the **Fostering Services Regulations 2002** (**SI 2002/57**), the local authority could not place children in their care with a person not approved as a foster carer. However, the best interests of the children required that they remain in the care of the grandparents. Yet, outstanding concerns meant that the placement should be subject to long-term external scrutiny. Here, it was decided that the wardship jurisdiction could justifiably be used to fill this significant lacuna. Wardship, together with a supervision order and a raft of orders under the **CA 1989, s. 8**, provided the best available solution for the needs of these children.

If a local authority wishes to resolve a specific question about a child being looked after, then it may now with leave invoke the inherent jurisdiction of the High Court (**s. 100**), a jurisdiction quite separate from wardship and use of which does not place the child under the ultimate responsibility of the court. Leave under **s. 100(3)** will be granted if the court is satisfied that, first, the result sought cannot be achieved under any statutory jurisdiction and, secondly, that there is reasonable cause to believe that if the jurisdiction is not exercised the child is likely to suffer significant harm. In relation to a child in care, the first condition should cause no problems, as none of the **s. 8** orders is available to the local authority (**s. 9(1) and (2)**) and use of the inherent jurisdiction is now the only option. If leave is granted, the authority will be able to seek High Court assistance on difficult or sensitive issues (a sort of specific issues jurisdiction for children in care) (see *Re W (A Minor) (Medical Treatment: Court's Jurisdiction)* [1992] 4 All ER 627, *Re O (A Minor) (Medical Treatment)* [1993] 2 FLR 149 and *Re M (Care: Leave to Interview Child)* [1995] 1 FLR 825). However, the court will not assume overall control as with wardship. It should also be noted that private individuals can make an application to the High Court under its inherent jurisdiction to resolve specific issues that require immediate attention (e.g. emergency medical treatment) if the continual control that wardship provides is not required (*Re M (Medical Treatment: Consent)* [1999] 2 FLR 1097).

As a means of resolving all kinds of disputes over children wardship cannot really be matched, even by the statutory framework of the **1989 Act**. Wardship still has a role to play, but one has to agree that the restrictions imposed on its use, and the greater flexibility in other family proceedings mean that the role has indeed been greatly reduced.

 Question 4

One of the principal aims of the **Children Act 1989** was to ensure that more attention was paid to the child's voice. Consider the extent to which this aim has been achieved.

 Commentary

A general question on such a significant piece of legislation as the **CA 1989** will quite commonly be included on an exam paper. You may be asked to assess the Act from any one of a number of different viewpoints, for example the child, the parents, the local authority or the court. Here it is in terms of the child's voice. This requires a sound knowledge and appreciation of the statute's provisions and its underlying philosophy, so that you can scan the Act and pick out provisions which appear to give more attention to the child's voice and, therefore, lend support to the title statement. You could quite legitimately, by way of introduction, refer briefly to the previous position, including common law and the *Gillick* decision, as the phrase 'more attention' begs the question how much was paid before, but emphasis must be on the **Children Act** provisions and their subsequent development. You will need to consider the general principles and then to review both the private and public law provisions from the perspective required by the title.

Answer plan

- ***Gillick*-**competence.
- The welfare principle.
- **S. 1(3)(a)**—child's 'wishes and feelings'.
- **S. 8** applications by children.
- Public law and children's guardians.

 Examiner's tip

Bring your discussion up to date by referring to the recommendations contained in the *Family Justice Review Final Report* (2011).

 Suggested answer

Prior to the implementation of the **Children Act (CA) 1989**, mature children were sometimes able to express their views in both public and private law cases, but often only lip-service was paid to them. However, the law did recognize that it was usually futile for a parent to try to force his views on a mature child; the child's level of intellectual or emotional development was not relevant in deciding the extent of parental authority. In *Gillick v West Norfolk and Wisbech Area Health Authority* [1986] 1 FLR 224, the House of Lords held that parents' rights to take decisions 'yield to the child's right to make his own decisions when he reaches a sufficient understanding and intelligence to be capable of making up his own mind on the matter requiring decision' (*per* Lord Scarman). Whether a child is *Gillick*-competent depends on his emotional and intellectual maturity. The decision means that the mature minor can decide whether to do or not to do something provided that he understands fully the complexity of the issues involved. This includes the right to consent to medical treatment, though Lord Donaldson has said that a parent can still give valid consent even if a mature minor refuses treatment (***Re R (A Minor) (Wardship: Medical Treatment)* [1991] 4 All ER 177**), and the court can override the mature minor's refusal or consent in the interests of the child's welfare (***Re S (A Minor) (Consent to Medical Treatment)* [1994] 2 FLR 1065**).

A number of provisions in the **CA 1989** now give statutory recognition to the claims of children to have an independent say on issues affecting them, and a greater degree of involvement in decision-making. **Section 1** provides that when a court determines any question with respect to the upbringing of a child or the administration of a child's property, the child's welfare is to be the court's paramount consideration. This could be described as the main message of the Act and ensures that any decision taken in either a public or private law case, where the child's upbringing is central, is the one which best promotes the child's welfare. **Section 1(3)** contains a checklist of factors to which the court must normally have regard when considering whether to make an order. No weight is ascribed to any particular factor but the list focuses on the needs of the child and his views. The first factor on the list (**s. 1(3)(a)**) is the 'ascertainable wishes and feelings of the child' (considered in the light of his age and understanding). This obviously gives the child a voice, though being first on the list does not give the child's wishes priority over other items (*Re J (A Minor)* [1992] 2 FCR 785). To ascertain the child's wishes the court will normally rely on the investigations made by a CAFCASS officer or children's guardian.

Clearly the age of the child is likely to be crucial in determining how much weight should be given to his wishes. In *Re H (A Child)* [2011] EWCA Civ 762 the Court of Appeal overturned a residence order in the mother's favour because the 11-year-old girl wanted to live with her father, whilst in *Re R (A Child)* [2009] EWCA Civ 445 the Court of Appeal overturned a residence order granted to the 9-year-old child's father on the basis that insufficient weight had been placed on the child's wish to return to his mother. In *Re R (Residence: Shared Case: Children's Views)* [2005] EWCA Civ 42, 7- and 9-year-old siblings were given the right to participate in private law proceedings and to have weight given to their views. It is, thus, clear that the views of quite young children may be taken into account. Other factors considered by the court when assessing the weight to be attached to the child's views include the dangers of coaching, the relative importance of the issue, the factual basis of his or her views and the danger to the child of being asked to choose between parents. *Re S (Contact: Children's Views)* [2002] EWHC 540 may serve as a warning to parents who do not listen to their children. A father who sought contact with his three children aged 16, 14 and 12 was found to have hectored them, failing to learn that his attitude was counter-productive. It was held that there was no point in making an order with regard to the eldest who was opposed to it; the middle boy was required merely to make himself available for contact by common agreement; and the youngest, who had maintained contact, was allowed some choice about the form it should take in future. The court doubted the quality of contact achievable only by court order.

The other two general principles in **s. 1 of the CA 1989**, i.e. non-intervention (**s. 1(5)**) and the disapproval of delay (**s. 1(2)**), can also be viewed in terms of listening to a child's voice. The non-intervention principle ensures that no order is made unless it is shown to be the best for the child and tends to prioritize adults' views. The court may fail to consider the child's wishes (to listen to his voice) if, for example, on divorce, parents agree and no order is made. On the other hand, the 'delay is harmful' principle recognizes that a child's sense of time is more acute than that of an adult.

The **CA 1989** allows a child to apply, with leave, for one of the **s. 8** orders, i.e. residence, contact, prohibited steps, specific issues, and can instruct a solicitor to act on his behalf. Children may therefore apply with leave for orders allowing them to live with whom they want (*Re T (A Minor) (Child Representation)* [1994] **Fam 49**) and to have contact *(Re F (Contact: Child in Care)* [1995] 1 FLR 510) with those people they want to see. Leave will be granted if the court is satisfied that the child has sufficient understanding to make the application (**s. 10(8)**). The judge must be convinced that the child can understand the consequences of his action. Although children can seek leave to apply for a specific issue order or a prohibited steps order if they do not agree with their parents, Sir Stephen Brown P has said that children cannot start proceedings just because they do not get their own way at home. Consequently, in *Re C (A Minor) (Leave to Seek Section 8 Order)* [1994] 1 FLR 26 FD a 15-year-old girl was denied leave to apply for a **s. 8** order to enable her to go on holiday with her friend's family. But the Act does give children the right to be heard and the court will assess their best interests. There is thus some compliance with **Art. 12 of the United Nations Convention on the Rights of the Child 1989** which requires the child to be provided with the opportunity to be heard in judicial proceedings affecting him, but the child's voiced opinion may not prove determinative.

In addition to these issues, there are other examples of situations where a child has access to the court. The child is a party in all public law cases and will usually be separately represented. By **s. 41** the court must appoint a children's guardian for a child unless it is not necessary to safeguard his interests. Children's guardians are now appointed at an earlier stage and their role includes investigating the case, explaining matters to the child and advising the court on the child's best interests and *wishes*. It should be noted that the **Adoption and Children Act 2002** added **s. 8** proceedings to the list of 'specified proceedings' which involve the appointment of a children's guardian and solicitor (**s. 41(6) CA 1989**). In reality, the appointment of a guardian is reserved for complex private law cases. For example, in *Re C (A Child)* [2011] EWCA Civ 261 the Court of Appeal held that a 12-year-old child should be joined as a party with a solicitor and guardian to ensure that someone put forward the child's views independently of both parents.

A number of other public law provisions embody the *Gillick* principle that a mature minor has the right to decide. Under **s. 34**, a child in care can apply for contact to be refused where the presumption of contact operates and may question decisions relating to contact in court. He may also apply for a residence order to discharge the care order and make an application to discharge an emergency protection order made under **s. 44**. Where a child assessment order (**s. 43**), an emergency protection order (**s. 44**) or an interim care or supervision order (**s. 38**) is made with a direction relating to examination or assessment, the mature minor has the right to refuse to submit to the assessment. The orders do not authorize medical or psychiatric examination or other assessment which a child of sufficient age and understanding refuses to undergo. Here, unlike other provisions of the Act, it seems that it is not just a case of ascertaining and giving consideration to the child's wishes but that if the child is capable of making an informed decision then his wishes are conclusive. The right to refuse under these provisions has been held at first instance to be limited to the stage of assessment, and not to actual treatment, when the court could override the child's decision (*per* Thorpe J in *Re J (A Minor)* [1992] 2 FCR 785).

A final example of attention being paid to the child's voice is **s. 22** of the Act which requires a local authority to ascertain the wishes and feelings of a child being looked after and to give due consideration to them, depending on his age and understanding, before taking a decision which affects him. Local authorities must give the child information and explanations so that he can make an informed choice. The child must know his rights and what is available and feel that what he says is not being ignored. Each local authority has to establish a procedure for considering complaints and representations which must be publicized and should be 'user friendly' (**s. 26**). A child has the right to complain under this provision and must be told of the panel's findings and what changes should result.

The **CA 1989**, as seen from the provisions examined earlier, certainly pays more than lip-service to the child's wishes. The child is to be treated as an individual with a right to be consulted, kept fully informed and treated with respect commensurate with his age and understanding. If the recommendations contained in the *Family Justice Review Final Report* (2011) are enacted, the interests of children will be at the heart of the operation of the Family Justice Service. Children will 'be given age appropriate information which explains what is happening when they are included in disputes' and should 'as early as possible in a case be supported to be able to make their views known and older children should be offered a menu of options, to lay out the ways in which they could—if they wish—do this' (p. 45). It is therefore likely that greater attention will be paid to the child's voice in the future.

Further reading

Baroness Hale of Richmond (2012) 'Can You Hear Me Your Honour?' Fam Law 30.

Cave, E. (2011) 'Maximisation of Minors' Capacity'. 23(3) CFLQ 431.

Fortin, J. (2009) *Children's Rights and the Developing Law* (London: Butterworths).

Gilmore, S. and Herring, J. (2011) 'Children's Refusal of Medical Treatment: Could *Re W* be Distinguished?' Fam Law 715.

Gilmore, S. and Herring, J. (2011) '"No" is the Hardest Word: Consent and Children's Autonomy'. 23(1) CFLQ 3.

Guidelines in Relation to Children Giving Evidence in Family Proceedings. Working Party of the Family Justice Council (2011).

Websites

www.cafcass.gov.uk

www.crae.org.uk

www.childrenscommissioner.gov.uk

www.direct.gov.uk/en/parents/parentsrights/dg_4002954

www.rights4me.org

7

Assisted reproduction

Introduction

Assisted reproduction is a fascinating area of family law which raises moral, ethical and legal dilemmas and is of practical interest due to the increasing numbers of people who are involved. The Human Fertilisation and Embryology Authority's annual figures from licensed clinics demonstrate that in 2009 over 13,000 babies were born as a result of assisted reproduction (www.hfea.gov.uk). In the vast majority of cases the couple seeking treatment provide the genetic materials. In 2009, only 585 babies were born using sperm or egg donors. It is these cases (some of which also involve surrogacy) which give rise to legal issues as the law has to decide to whom parentage should be attributed. The **Human Fertilisation and Embryology Act (HFEA) 1990** was enacted to define the legal parents of a child born as a result of artificial methods of conception and to legislate on other issues connected with assisted reproduction, such as the storage of embryos. The **1990 Act** was amended by the **Human Fertilisation and Embryology (Deceased Fathers) Act 2003**, to allow a man to be registered as the father of a child conceived after his death (if written consent was provided). More recently, the **HFEA 2008** made changes to the law in the light of medical and social developments. Students should be aware of these changes and recent case law such as *A and A v P, P and B* **[2011] EWHC 1738 (Fam)** where the High Court declared that it was not necessary for both applicants to be alive when a parental order is made provided that they were when the application was submitted.

This chapter contains two problem questions both of which focus on parenthood. The first considers surrogacy, whilst the second concerns the more common scenario whereby a couple experiencing fertility problems have *in vitro* fertilization (IVF) treatment.

Question 1

Mary, who is two months pregnant, is married to Harry; they have four children. As Sarah, Mary's sister, is able to conceive a child but unable to carry a child to full term, Mary agreed to a full surrogacy arrangement. The *in vitro* fertilization treatment was carried out at a licensed clinic using Sarah's egg and her husband's (Frank) sperm. Harry disapproves of the arrangement. Mary has received results of tests which show that the child will be born disabled. Frank did not reveal, but was aware at the time of the donation, that there was a history of such a disability in his family. Harry wants Mary to give birth and then hand the child over to Sarah and Frank. Sarah wants Mary to have an abortion but she refuses. Frank wants Mary to give birth but he does not wish to raise or acknowledge the child as his own.

(a) Advise Mary as the legal parenthood of her child. [17 marks]

(b) What would the position be if Sarah and Frank wanted the child but Mary changed her mind? [8 marks]

Commentary

This case study requires students to explain who is the legal mother and father of Mary's unborn child. As Mary received treatment in a licensed clinic, the provisions of the **HFEA 2008** will apply. However, it should be noted that a surrogacy situation can easily arise without medical assistance and in such cases the common law rules relating to parentage are applicable. This is also the case if assisted reproduction treatment is not obtained at a clinic licensed by the Human Fertilisation and Embryology Authority. The second part of the question asks candidates to explain the position if Sarah and Frank wanted the child and Mary changed her mind.

Answer plan

- Relevant area of law—assisted reproduction, **HFEA 2008**.

- Define surrogacy—full/partial. **Surrogacy Arrangements Act 1985**. Arrangements not enforceable.

- Define legal mother/father. Apply to facts.

- Parental order, **s. 54 HFEA 2008**. Adoption. Apply to facts.

- **Congenital Disabilities (Civil Liability) Act 1976** as amended by **HFEA 1990**.

- Can Mary change her mind? Compare *Re P (Surrogacy: Residence)* [2008] **Fam Law 18** and *Re TT (Surrogacy)* [2011] **EWHC 33 (Fam)**.

Examiner's tip

Given the possibility that none of the adults want to take responsibility for the child, your answer should mention local authority intervention.

Suggested answer

The **Human Fertilisation and Embryology Act (HFEA) 2008** regulates treatment services which assist women to carry children. The Act provides definitions of the legal mother and legal father of a child who has been born as a result of artificial methods of conception.

As the clinic was licensed by the Human Fertilisation and Embryology Authority, Mary will have received counselling before going ahead with the treatment. Mary is pregnant and involved in a full surrogacy arrangement. A surrogate mother is a woman who carries a child as a result of an arrangement made before she began to carry the child and with a view to the child being handed over to, and the parental responsibility being met (so far as practicable) by, another person or persons (**Surrogacy Arrangements Act 1985, s. 1(2)** as amended by the **Children Act (CA) 1989, Sch. 13, para. 56**). The 'arrangement' must have been made before she began to carry the child *and* with a view to the child being handed over to, and parental responsibility being exercised by, another person or persons (**s. 1(1) and (2)**).

Section 33(1) of the HFEA 2008 provides that the woman who is carrying or has carried a child as a result of the placing in her of an embryo or sperm and eggs, and no other woman, is to be treated as the mother of the child. So, in law, Mary is the mother of the child. The father of the resulting child is defined in **s. 35(1) HFEA 2008** as being a husband whose wife receives donated sperm, or an embryo created from donated sperm, unless it is shown that he did not consent. Harry would not therefore be considered the child's legal father and his lack of consent and desire that Mary hand the child over would rebut the common law presumption that a child born to a wife is that of her husband.

The donor whose sperm is used to establish a pregnancy, to which a married woman's husband has not consented, is not to be treated as the father of the child (**s. 41(1) HFEA 2008**). However, in *Re B (Parentage)* [1996] 2 FLR 15, the sperm donor was not anonymous and there was evidence of a joint enterprise in the artificial insemination, which took place at a licensed clinic. The genetic father was held to be the legal father of the child. He had played an essential role in aiding the woman to achieve what they had both been trying for, namely a pregnancy. If the court were to follow *Re B* then Frank would be the legal as well as the genetic father. However, Frank cannot be forced to comply with the surrogacy agreement. The common law position adopted in *A v C* (1978) [1985] FLR 445, that no surrogacy arrangement is enforceable by or against any of the persons making it, was put on a statutory footing in **s. 1(A) of the Surrogacy**

Arrangements Act 1985. Harry and Mary cannot therefore force Sarah and Frank to take the child. It seems unlikely that Sarah and Frank will apply for a parental order (see later).

The **CA 1989** does not state when parental responsibility begins, but a child in the Act is taken to refer to a live child, so although Sarah has stated that she wants Mary to have an abortion, no one other than the woman who is carrying the child, the mother, has the right to be consulted in respect of termination of pregnancy (*Paton v British Pregnancy Advisory Service Trustees* [1978] 2 All ER 987 (approved by the European Court of Human Rights, *Paton v UK* [1981] EHRR 408)).

Mary may not be able to enforce the surrogacy agreement against Frank but he may find that the child born as a result of that agreement may be able to sue him where the child is born disabled. The **Congenital Disabilities (Civil Liability) Act 1976, s. 1(A)** as amended by the **HFEA 1990**, states that such a child may sue if the child has been born disabled following the placing in the woman of an embryo, or sperm and eggs, or following her artificial insemination and, inter alia, the disability results from an act or omission in the course of selection of the embryo or the gametes used to bring about the embryo. The clinic, as defendant, would not be answerable to the child if, at the time the embryo was placed in Mary, Frank knew of the particular risk of the child being born disabled. If Frank had failed to reveal the genetic disease, and the condition could not be revealed by testing, then the clinic would not be at fault. The child would have to sue Frank. In cases where the donor is not known, the child may apply to the court for an order requiring the authority to provide identifying information so that the child may sue under the **1976 Act**.

If none of the adults take responsibility when the child is born, the local authority will need to intervene. If the child is abandoned at the hospital, the local authority would owe the child, who would be a child in need, not only a general duty to safeguard and protect his or her interests, but a duty to accommodate the child (**CA 1989, s. 20**). Care proceedings may be considered with a view to adoption.

If Sarah and Frank want the child

If Sarah and Frank want the child, they could apply for a parental order under **s. 54 HFEA 2008**. The court may make the order subject to certain preconditions, amongst them being the situation which applies here, that the gametes of the man and/or woman who constitute the commissioning couple were used to bring about the creation of the embryo (following the **2008 Act** it is no longer necessary for the couple to be married). Sarah and Frank must apply for an order within six months of the child's birth and the child's home must be with them. Mary (and Harry) must agree unconditionally to the making of the order and the court must be satisfied that no money or benefit other than expenses has been given or received in connection with the order. As applications for a parental order rank as family proceedings under the **CA 1989**, it is possible that, in addition, or as an alternative, the court could make **s. 8** orders, for example it could make a contact order for Mary to visit, or decide that Mary remain the legal parent and grant a residence order in favour of Sarah and Frank.

If Mary wants to keep the child, Sarah and Frank cannot force her to hand the child over because, as explained earlier, **s. 1A of the Surrogacy Arrangements Act 1985** provides that surrogacy agreements are unenforceable. In addition, the court would not make a parental order as Mary's consent is required. However, Sarah and Frank could apply for a residence order under **s. 8 CA 1989** and in *Re P (Surrogacy: Residence)* **[2008] Fam Law 18** the commissioning couple were granted residence when the surrogate mother refused to hand the child over. In this case the surrogate mother had told the intended father that she had miscarried and there was evidence that she had done the same to several other men. When the father discovered that a child had been born, he and his wife applied for residence. Their application was successful because the mother's psychological state was such that she would not be able to parent in the long term. In contrast, the commissioning couple in *CW v NT and another* [2011] EWHC 33 were not granted residence of a child born as a result of a surrogacy arrangement. This was because the surrogate mother did not set out to deceive the couple: she genuinely changed her mind after the child was born. In addition, the child had formed an attachment to the surrogate mother and the mother was more likely to promote contact with the father than vice versa. Residence was therefore granted to the mother with contact to the father. The same decision was reached by the court in *Re TT (Surrogacy)* **[2011] EWHC 33 (Fam)**. Case law thus suggests that a court would not grant residence to Sarah and Frank if Mary changed her mind.

Question 2

Chris and Jane have been living together for ten years. In 2010 they decided to start a family and two years later they sought advice from a fertility specialist at a licensed clinic because Jane had not become pregnant. They were advised to try *in vitro* fertilization (IVF) using Jane's eggs and donated sperm. Chris and Jane attended all appointments together and although the first cycle of IVF was unsuccessful, the second cycle was successful and Jane gave birth to Ben. Chris never bonded with Ben and as a result Chris and Jane's relationship deteriorated. Chris has just left Jane and has told her that he doesn't want anything to do with Ben as he isn't his father anyway.

(a) Jane seeks your advice as to whether Chris is considered in law to be Ben's father.

(b) What would the position be if Chris left Jane before the second embryo was implanted?

(c) What would the position be if Jane was supposed to be implanted with an embryo created using her eggs and Chris's sperm but there was a mix-up at the clinic and Jane's egg was mixed with David's sperm (David and his wife were also having treatment at the clinic)?

(d) What would the position be if Jane and Chris were a lesbian couple?

The parts to this question are equally weighted.

Commentary

This question is an example of a problem where students are asked to provide advice in relation to several alternative scenarios. Candidates are required to consider whether Chris is Ben's legal parent; on the basis that he cohabits with and sought treatment with Jane; if he left Jane before the successful implantation; if there was a mix-up at the clinic and if Chris is female. As treatment was received at a licensed clinic, the provisions of the **HFEA 2008** will need to be examined, including the changes made by the **2008 Act** in relation to the legal position of male cohabitants and lesbian partners, which came into effect in 2009.

 Answer plan

Scenario	Relevant law
Is Chris Ben's father?	**HFEA 2008** **– s. 41**: the donor is not the father **– ss. 36 and 37**: agreed fatherhood conditions would be satisfied
What if Chris left before the treatment?	**HFEA 2008** **– s. 41**: the donor is not the father **– ss. 36 and 37**: agreed fatherhood conditions probably not satisfied
What if there was a mix-up?	**HFEA 2008** does not apply: common law applies (**Leeds Teaching Hospital NHS Trust v A [2003]**)
What if Chris is female?	**HFEA 2008, ss. 42 and 43**

 Examiner's tip

Focus on the question, which is all about identifying the legal parents—it is not necessary to discuss the consequence of parenthood (e.g. liability for child support and the right to apply for **s. 8** orders) in any detail.

Suggested answer

Jane and Chris received IVF treatment at a licensed clinic and, as a consequence, the provisions of the **Human Fertilisation and Embryology Act (HFEA) 2008** must be considered. The first point to note is that the sperm donor is not treated as the child's legal father (**s. 41(1) HFEA 2008**). This does not mean that children born as a result of donor insemination will always be fatherless as the Act enables the mother's husband or partner to be treated as the child's legal father. As Jane and Chris are not married, **s. 36 HFEA 2008** is relevant. This provision enables a woman's male partner to be treated as the child's legal father if the requirements set out in **s. 37** (the agreed fatherhood conditions) are satisfied. Under **s. 37** the man in question must give the person responsible at the licensed clinic a notice stating that he consents to being treated as the father of any child resulting from treatment provided to his partner. In addition, the woman in question must give notice that she consents to her partner being treated as her child's father. In both cases the notice must be in writing and signed by the parties. This amends the position under the **1990 Act, s. 28(3)** of which provided that a male partner would be treated as the child's father if the woman was implanted/inseminated in the course of treatment services provided for her and the man together. The question indicates that Chris and Jane sought treatment in 2010 and as a result **ss. 36 and 37 HFEA 2008** apply rather than **s. 28(3) of the 1990 Act**. Given that Chris attended all appointments with Jane, it is assumed that both parties gave the required written notices to the clinic as the clinic would not have provided treatment without them. It is also assumed that Chris did not withdraw the notice (**s. 37(1)(c)**) as it appears that he only changed his mind after Ben was born. Chris would therefore be treated as Ben's legal father and, although he cannot be forced to have any contact with Ben, he would be considered Ben's father for the purpose of child support, inheritance etc.

If Chris left Jane before the second embryo was implanted

If Chris left Jane before the second embryo was implanted, the position could be quite different. **Section 37 HFEA 2008** (the agreed fatherhood conditions) provides that a woman's partner will be treated as the father of a child if both parties have given written notice of consent (**s. 37(1)(a)** and **(b)**) and neither party has given the person responsible notice of withdrawal of consent (**s. 37(1)(c)**). A notice of withdrawal of consent must be made in writing under **s. 37(2)**. The **2008 Act** thus provides explicit requirements that must be complied with if a person changes his or her mind in this sort of situation. In contrast, the **1990 Act** did not contain express provisions relating to withdrawal of consent. The courts therefore had to decide whether a couple could be classed as receiving treatment together if they separated before the successful implantation. In *Re R (A Child) (IVF: Paternity of Child)* [2005] UKHL 33 the man consented to his partner's treatment but after the first unsuccessful cycle of IVF the couple separated. The woman proceeded with treatment and had a second cycle which was successful. At first instance the court held that the former partner was the legal father as he had consented to treatment which envisaged two cycles of IVF from the outset. However, the Court of Appeal and the House of Lords held that consent must be present at the time of the successful conception or implantation and that if a couple separated prior to this, they were not having treatment together. **Section 28(3)** would not therefore apply. **Section 37 HFEA 2008** makes it clear that Chris would have to have withdrawn his consent in writing to avoid being treated as Ben's legal father. Based on *Re R* (see earlier), consent can be withdrawn in between treatment cycles. If Chris has done so, he will not be considered Ben's legal father.

If Jane was implanted with an embryo created using David's sperm

If Jane was supposed to be implanted with an embryo created using her eggs and Chris's sperm, but the embryo was accidentally created using David's sperm, the situation is quite complex. Chris has not consented to this and as a consequence cannot be treated as the father of the child under **ss. 36 and 37** (see earlier). **Section 41(1)** of the **Act** provides that where the sperm of a man who had given consent to its use for the purpose of treatment services was used for such a purpose, he is not to be treated as father of the child. In other words, a sperm donor is not considered the legal father of any children born as a result of insemination using his sperm or the implantation of an embryo created using his sperm. If the embryo implanted into Jane had been created using donated sperm, the donor would not therefore be treated as Ben's father. However, this provision would not apply to David, who is receiving treatment with his wife, as David would not have consented to his sperm being used to inseminate other women or to create embryos for the use of other couples. A similar issue arose in the case of *Leeds Teaching Hospital NHS Trust v A* [2003] EWHC 259 where two couples, one black and one white, were receiving IVF treatment at the same clinic at the same time. When Mrs A gave birth to mixed-race twins it was evident that her eggs had been mixed with Mr B's sperm. The court held that Mr A could not be considered the father of his wife's children as he had only consented to his sperm being mixed with his wife's eggs. Furthermore, Mr B could not claim the exemption contained in **s. 28(6)(a) of the 1990 Act** (**s. 41(1) of the 2008 Act**) as he had not consented to his sperm being used to treat others. As none of the provisions of the **HFEA 2008** were applicable, the common law rule, which provides that the genetic father is the legal father, was applied. Mr B was thus considered the legal father of Mrs A's twins. Following *Leeds Teaching Hospital NHS Trust v A* [2003], David would be treated as Ben's legal father. He would be liable for child support and could apply for orders under **s. 8 CA 1989**, for example, contact. Chris, on the other hand, has no rights or responsibilities in relation to Ben.

If Chris is female

If Chris is female, her status is governed by **ss. 42–5 HFEA 2008**. Under the **1990 Act** a woman could not be treated as the legal parent of a child born to her female partner and this remained the case even after the **Civil Partnership Act 2004**. A lesbian couple could, however, be granted a joint residence order to reflect the social role that the mother's partner played (*Re M (Sperm Donor Father)* [2003] **Fam 94** and *Re A (Joint Residence: Parental Responsibility)* [2008] **EWCA Civ 867**). In 2006, the Department of Health concluded that reform was required 'to better recognize the wider range of people who seek and receive assisted reproduction' (*Review of the Human Fertilisation and Embryology Act* (2006), para. 2.67). This led to the adoption of the **HFEA 2008**, which enables the mother's female partner to be treated as a legal parent. If Chris and Jane are civil partners, **s. 42** provides that Chris will be classed as Ben's other parent unless it is shown that she did not consent to the treatment. A civil partner is therefore treated in the same way as the husband of a woman who receives treatment under **s. 35**. Similarly, if Chris and Jane are not civil partners, **ss. 43–4** put them in the same position as an unmarried heterosexual couple. Chris would therefore be treated as Ben's other parent if the 'agreed female parenthood conditions' set out in **s. 44** are satisfied, i.e. both women give written notice indicating that they wish Chris to become a legal parent. As with heterosexual couples, it is essential that the notice given by either party has not been withdrawn prior to implantation/insemination.

Further reading

Blain, S. and Worwood, A. (2011) 'Alternative Families and Changing Perceptions of Parenthood'. Fam Law 289.

Johnson, S. (2012) 'How Many Parents Does a Child Need?' Fam Law 313.

Welstead, M. (2011) 'This Child is My Child; This Child is Your Child, This Child was Made for You and Me—Surrogacy in England and Wales' in B. Atkin (ed.) *International Survey of Family Law* (Bristol: Jordan, for the International Society of Family Law), p. 165.

Websites

www.ukdonorlink.org.uk

www.hfea.gov.uk

www.surrogacy.org.uk

8 Adoption

Introduction

Adoption is one of the more segregable family law topics and, as a consequence, it will not be covered on all family law courses. If it is examined, some of its components are virtually guaranteed a place, such as dispensing with parental consent and relative/non-relative adoption. Students should be aware of the role of adoption agencies and local authorities, the minimum and maximum ages of the parties and how long the child must have been placed with the applicants before the court hearing, all of which are governed by the **Adoption and Children Act (ACA) 2002,** which reformed adoption law and came into force in December 2005. We are likely to see further changes to this area of law as the Government has recently issued two discussion papers (*Placing Children in Sibling Groups for Adoption: A Call for Views* and *Contact Arrangements for Children: A Call for Views* (Department of Education, 2012)). In addition, the Children and Families Bill (expected 2013) is proposed to contain provisions to reform the adoption process.

Despite the comparative conceptual isolation of adoption it is, of course, an example of 'family proceedings' for the purposes of the **Children Act (CA) 1989** and therefore any **s. 8** order may be made in lieu, residence or contact, for example. In addition, candidates should be prepared to discuss the possibility of the court making a special guardianship order under **s. 14A CA 1989** as such an order is viewed as a viable alternative to the adoption of older children who wish to remain in contact with their birth family.

So far as inter-country adoption is concerned, the **Children and Adoption Act 2006** provides a statutory framework for the restriction of adoption from countries where there are public policy concerns, for example child trafficking. As this topic is often omitted from family law modules, it will not be considered in this chapter.

Question 1

Five years ago Mary, an unmarried medical student, gave birth to Nick following her affair with Tim (who has since died). During her pregnancy Mary had arranged for Hal and Wendy, a married couple, to give the child a home 'for the time being'. They are now both aged 50: Hal is a labourer and Wendy a shop assistant; they have no children of their own.

Since making this arrangement, Mary has qualified as a doctor. During her student days she saw Nick regularly, often offering Hal and Wendy money (for the boy's keep) which they occasionally accepted. Nick understands, as well as his age permits, that Mary is his natural mother, but looks upon Hal and Wendy as his 'mummy and daddy'.

Mary, now aged 24 and recently married to Cecil, a solicitor aged 29, has now told Hal and Wendy that she and Cecil want to bring Nick up as their child. Hal and Wendy want to keep Nick and have applied to adopt him themselves.

Will the law do right by Nick?

 Commentary

This problem question on adoption requires candidates to address the issue of dispensing with parental consent, the legality of the placement, the role of the local authority and, crucially, the range of orders available. Note that although adoption can be omitted from the course or from your revision without causing much damage to other topics, it cannot itself be dealt with in isolation. This question thus requires knowledge of the **CA 1989** as well as the **Adoption and Children Act (ACA) 2002**.

 Answer plan

Key issue/principle	Relevant legislation
The welfare principle	**S. 1(2) ACA 2002**
	S. 1(1) CA 1989
	Art. 21 UNCRC 1989
The welfare checklist	**S. 1(4)(a) ACA**
	S. 1(3) CA
Local authority investigation	**S. 44 ACA**
Age and status	**Ss. 50(1), 47(9) ACA**
Probationary period	**S. 42 ACA**

Key issue/principle	Relevant legislation
Parental consent	S. 52(1)(b) ACA
Alternatives to adoption: residence and contact, special guardianship	S. 8 CA
	S. 14A CA

 Examiner's tip

This question does not instruct you to 'Advise Hal and Wendy' or 'Advise Mary and Cecil' but asks you whether 'the law will do right by Nick'. Your answer should therefore be child-centred.

 Suggested answer

This situation will be dealt with either by the **Adoption and Children Act (ACA) 2002** or the **Children Act (CA) 1989**, and in each case the governing principle, **s. 1(2) and s. 1(1)** respectively, is the paramountcy of the child's welfare—'throughout his life' in the former case. So the law will at least be *trying* to 'do right' by Nick. This is consistent with **Art. 21 of the UN Convention on the Rights of the Child 1989** which provides that 'States Parties that recognize and/or permit the system of adoption shall ensure that the best interests of the child shall be the paramount consideration. . . .'

Section 1(3)(a) of the 1989 Act and **s. 1(4)(a) of the 2002 Act** both indicate that the court shall have regard to the ascertainable wishes of the child concerned (considered in the light of his age and understanding). Five-year-old Nick understands 'as well as his age permits' that Mary is his mother, but sees Hal and Wendy as his 'mummy and daddy'. It seems that the combination of his extreme youth and the ambivalence of his perceptions renders it difficult to weigh the latter in any appropriate manner.

So far as Nick's immediate future is concerned, it seems that Hal and Wendy could take advantage of **ss. 36(1)(a) and 40(2)(a) of the 2002 Act** whereby a child may not, pending the hearing, be removed from adoption applicants with whom he has had his home (other than by leave of the court). Better for Nick that only one separation occur, if separation there must be. During this period his welfare will be monitored by the local authority (which must be notified of the application) under **s. 44** and which will also undertake the investigatory and reporting functions normally undertaken, in 'stranger' adoptions, by the agency responsible for 'placing' the child. These include a health history of the birth parents, an investigation into the applicants' circumstances and a counselling service. Nick will be medically examined. Because Mary is opposing the adoption, an officer of the Children and Family Court Advisory and Support Service (CAFCASS) will be appointed whose overall duty will be to safeguard Nick's interests.

If it is right for Nick to be adopted, there will be no difficulty with the basic legal requirements. Hal and Wendy are both over 21 and are a couple (**s. 50(1)**) and Nick is under 19 years old (s. 47(9)). Additionally, there is the suggestion of 'prohibited' payments under s. 95 but, it is unlikely that the money Hal and Wendy 'occasionally' accepted from Mary would be held to be so tainted. Their application would comply with s. 42 in that Nick has lived with them for at least three of the last five years. By the same token, they are also eligible for a residence order (see later) and a 'special guardianship' order under s.14A CA 1989. The latter would allow them to exercise PR to the exclusion of Mary, and qualify them for financial support.

Crucial to Nick's future is the designation of adoption proceedings as 'family proceedings' under s. 8(4)(d) CA 1989. The upshot is that the court, either on its own motion or upon application, can make s. 8 orders, one or more of which, as we will see, may well be right for Nick. Similarly, the court has the duty, under s. 46(6) of the 2002 Act, to consider whether 'there should be arrangements for allowing any person contact with the child' before making an adoption order.

The welfare principle (s. 1(2) ACA 2002) is elaborated by s. 1(4) which lists the specific factors to which the court or adoption agency must have regard when making decisions. Section 1(4)(c) refers to 'the likely effect on the child (throughout his life) of having ceased to be a member of the original family' whilst s. 1(4)(f) refers to the relationship 'which the child has with relatives'. If an adoption order was made in favour of Hal and Wendy, it would sever for all time Nick's legal link with his 24-year-old natural mother, replacing her with a couple who will be in their 60s whilst he is still a schoolboy. In *Re K (A Minor) (Wardship: Adoption)* [1991] 1 FLR 57, a key factor was that the applicant 'mother' would be 57 when the child was ten, and that the natural mother genuinely wanted her child back. In addition, Mary and Cecil may well provide Nick with siblings, unlike, surely, Hal and Wendy. In *Re L (A Minor) (Care Proceedings: Wardship) (No. 2)*[1991] 1 FLR 29, Willis J stated that every child had a right, where possible, to be brought up by 'its' own family and that there must be 'strong, cogent and positive reasons' for denying that right. Other things being equal, it is in the interests of the child to be brought up by his parent: *Re W (A Minor) (Residence Order)* [1993] 2 FLR 625.

If Hal and Wendy proceed with their application, it will clearly be without Mary's consent and, as a consequence, the court would have to consider whether Mary's consent can be dispensed with under s. 52(1)(b) of the 2002 Act. Under the previous law (the Adoption Act 1976) the welfare principle did not apply to the issue of dispensing with consent and the court could dispense with consent if the parent was withholding it unreasonably (*Re P (An Infant) (Adoption: Parental Agreement)* [1977] Fam 25). However, s. 52(1)(b) of the 2002 Act provides that consent can be dispensed with if the welfare of the child so requires. In this case Mary's consent would not be dispensed with. It is therefore likely that Hal and Wendy's application for adoption would be refused. It is also unlikely that Hal and Wendy would be granted a special guardianship order under s.14A CA 1989, which is viewed as an alternative to adoption, as the court might not wish to restrict Mary's parental responsibility.

In the short term it *might* be that the law would best serve Nick's interests by taking advantage (in the absence of appropriate private ordering) of the court's ability to make s. 8 CA 1989 orders in the adoption proceedings. Surely Nick must live with one couple and see another, his filial link to Mary intact? But with which couple should he make his home? We know little of Cecil, Nick's 'stepfather', other than his apparent respectability. Now that **s. 8** orders are being considered, **s. 1(5) of the 1989 Act** applies, so the court must be sure that 'making an order would be better for the child than making no order at all'. Perhaps Hal, Wendy, Mary and Cecil can come together for Nick's continued well-being, with the former couple becoming invaluable 'social grandparents', Nick seeing them and staying with them as often as possible, to the pleasure and advantage of all concerned. Perhaps the parties can arrive at that stage consensually and instead of, not after, abortive adoption proceedings. If not, residence orders under **s. 8(1)** in favour of Mary (who already has 'parental responsibility' as mother under **s. 2(2)(a) CA 1989**) and Cecil (who would thereby obtain PR for the duration) with Hal and Wendy able to apply for contact, also under **s. 8(1)**. Finally, we must note that Mary and Cecil are eligible to adopt under **s. 50(2)** as a couple where one of the couple is the mother of the adoptee. But under **s. 42(3)** such step-parent adoption applications cannot be made until the child has lived with the applicant(s) for at least six months and the local authority has made the investigations required under **s. 44** (see earlier). If they make an application, **s.46(6) of the ACA 2002** requires the court to consider whether any arrangements for contact should be made before making an adoption order. However, it is highly unusual to impose contact on the adopters (*Re R (Adoption: Contact)* [2005] **EWCA Civ 1128**). Consequently, in *Re T (Adoption: Contact)* [2010] EWCA Civ 1527 the maternal grandmother's application for contact was refused because the adoptive parents were not in favour of it. Adoption by Mary and Cecil might not therefore serve Nick's interests if they opposed contact with Hal and Wendy and, as explained, an order under the **CA 1989** might be preferable.

 Question 2

The Adoption and Children Act 2002 ensured that the 'welfare principle' applies to adoption, extended the categories of those eligible to adopt, introduced placement orders and encouraged the adoption of children in local authority care.

Analyse the significance of these changes.

 Commentary

As ever, a description of the relevant material is not what is asked for. Rather, students are required to analyse the significance of the changes made by the **Adoption and Children Act (ACA) 2002** that are identified in the question. To do this, you should refer to the official documents which led up to the Act and explore the implications of reform from a human rights perspective. In addition, your answer should consider whether the **ACA 2002** has increased the number of adoptions from care and whether more recent initiatives will achieve this goal.

Answer plan

- **Adoption Act 1976.**
- **CA 1989.**
- Welfare principle/statutory checklist.
- 'Couples' as adopters.
- Placement orders.
- Increasing numbers adopted from care.
- Recent developments.

Examiner's tip

Demonstrate the currency of your knowledge by referring to the provisions to be included in the Children and Families Bill.

Suggested answer

The **Adoption and Children Act (ACA) 2002** repealed and replaced the **Adoption Act 1976. Section 6 of the 1976 Act** had provided that the child's welfare was the first consideration of the court, however **s. 1 ACA 2002** states that 'whenever a court or an adoption agency is coming to a decision relating to the adoption of a child the paramount consideration of the court or adoption agency must be the child's welfare, throughout his life.' **Section 1(1)** is an 'overarching' provision, just like the welfare principle contained in **s. 1(1) of the Children Act (CA) 1989.** The ACA thus aligns adoption law with the relevant provisions of the **CA 1989,** but unlike the **CA** it applies 'throughout his life' and not merely 'throughout his childhood'. Furthermore, whilst **s. 1 ACA** imports much of the 'checklist' found in **s. 1(3) of the 1989 Act** (the child's wishes, needs, characteristics, any likely harm) it also refers to the wishes and feelings of the any of the child's relatives or 'of any such person' and their ability to serve him or her.

But none of this was earth-shattering: the upgrading of the child's welfare from 'first' to 'paramount' in the **2002 Act,** has cut little ice since it came into force. What *is* important is that the paramountcy principle was extended to the dispensing of parental consent, with specific reference to both the placement order, which is required if the parents have not consented to the child being placed for adoption, and the final adoption order. Under **s. 16(2)(b) of the Adoption Act 1976** the necessary consent of a parent with parental responsibility could be overridden if it was unreasonable for the parent to withhold it (*Re P (An Infant) (Adoption: Parental Agreement)* **[1977] Fam 25**). This arguably contravened one of the most fundamental of societal principles: that the claims of the birth family, or at least the birth mother, have priority in the absence of proven unsuitability. Indeed, in recommending the extension of the welfare principle to adoption, the *Review of Adoption Law: Report to Ministers of an Interdepartmental Working Group* (Dept of Health and Welsh Office, 1992), indicated that the ability 'to override completely a parent's wishes' is 'unacceptable in relation to an order which irrevocably terminates a parent's legal relationship with a child' (para. 7.1). **Section 52 ACA 2002** now provides that consent cannot be dispensed with unless the welfare of the child *requires* it. In *Re P (Placement Orders: Parental Consent)*[2008] EWCA Civ 535 Wall J explained that this means that the adoption of a child must be imperative rather than optional or reasonable (paras 124–5). Applying the welfare principle to the dispensing of parental consent was an important development as it ensured that adoption law complied with **Art. 21 of the UN Convention on the Rights of the Child 1989** which requires state parties to guarantee that the best interest of the child is the paramount consideration.

The official documents that preceded the **2002 Act** did not propose to change the minimum eligibility requirements (which had remained constant since the **Adoption of Children Act 1926**). So, for example, adoption would have remained restricted to married couples or (generally) unmarried individuals. The reason advanced in para. 4.37 of *Adoption: The Future* (Cm 2288, 1993) was that: 'marriage remains the most common permanent relationship in which the upbringing of children is undertaken' and at the time it was the only relationship 'registrable under legislation' and was the only one which required 'a court to bring it to an end'. Eventually, the legislature accepted a backbench amendment **(s. 144(4))** which provided that adoption by a 'couple' included: (a) a married couple or (b) two people (whether of different sexes or the same sex) living as partners in an enduring family relationship. Two years later, the **Civil Partnership Act 2004** further amended the definition of a couple to include civil partners. Allowing unmarried couples to adopt was significant for several reasons. First, the courts had previously granted joint residence orders to unmarried couples when they were satisfied that such orders were in the child's best interests. They usually made joint residence orders if the arrangement had been working for some time and the couple's relationship was enduring (which is what the Act requires). The **ACA 2002** thus allowed such arrangements to be formalized by way of adoption. Secondly, the Joint Select Committee on Human Rights suggested that restricting adoption to married couples contravened the UK's human rights obligations and, finally, permitting unmarried couples to adopt would expand the pool of potential adopters. The latter could serve to fulfil one of the key aims of the legislation, namely to increase adoption from care (see *Adoption—The Prime Minister's Review* (Performance and Innovation Unit, July 2000) and the White Paper *Adoption: A New Approach* (Cm 5017, December 2000)). According to para. 2.5 of the White Paper, the proportion of looked-after children adopted in 1999–2000 varied by council between 0.5 per cent and 10.5 per cent, and para. 4.16 recorded the Government's belief that an increase of up to 50 per cent was viable. The supposed shortfall was due to: social workers receiving little training in making decisions for permanence for children; would-be adopters believing that the system is drawn-out and arbitrary; insufficient support, both post-placement and post-adoption; the lack of a nationwide system and court delays. The following measures were introduced to ensure that more 'looked-after' children would be adopted: 'National Standards for Adoption' which standardized the expectations of all concerned, the encouragement of applications by outlawing blanket exclusions other than for certain criminal convictions, a countrywide Adoption Register for England and Wales to suggest matches between children waiting to be adopted and approved prospective adopters; and a requirement that councils pay the court fees when its 'looked-after' children are adopted. In addition, **s. 22 ACA 2002** provides that a local authority *must* apply for a placement order over its accommodated children, if a care order is in place or if it thinks that the care order criteria apply, and that the child should be adopted. A placement order is defined as 'an order made by the court authorizing an adoption agency to place a child for adoption with any prospective adopters who may be chosen by the agency' (**s. 21(1)**). They were introduced by the **2002 Act** 'to bring the decision making process about adoption forward to a point before the child and prospective adopters are personally committed to each other' (Hughes LJ in *Re T (Placement Order)* [2008] **EWCA Civ 248, para. 16**). This formal change reflected the earlier reality, whereby the court granted an adoption order following an administrative decision that adoption was in the child's interests. The requirement contained in **s. 22** should have produced an increase in the number of adoptions from care, but statistics demonstrate that this has not been the case. In the year ending 31 March 2008, 3,200 children in care were adopted in England and Wales which was a decrease from previous years' figures. Data for the year ending 31 March 2011 shows a slight increase, as 3,050 children were adopted from care in England (BAAF, 2012) with a further 252 children adopted from care in Wales (www.assemblywales.org). However, the number of looked-after children is 65,520 in England (www.education.gov.uk) and 5,419 in Wales (www.assembly-wales.org) and although some of these will be looked after under a voluntary arrangement, the Government's target of a 50 per cent increase has evidently not been met. This may be partly due to the changes made to the **CA 1989** by the **Children and Young Persons Act 2008** which require a local authority to make arrangements for the child to live with a parent, or a person with parental responsibility or a person in whose favour a residence order had been made prior to the care order, unless to do so would be inconsistent with the child's welfare or was not reasonably practicable (**s. 22C(3) and (4)**). If it is not possible, the authority should attempt to accommodate the child with other relatives or friends (**ss. 22C(6)(a) and 7(a)**). The latter need to be approved as local authority foster parents. In the year ending 31 March 2008, 8 per cent of children in care lived with a parent and 11 per cent were placed with a relative or friend. As Probert explains, both of these figures are likely to rise in the future (*Cretney and Probert's Family Law*, 7th edn (2009), pp. 338–9). It should also be noted that special guardianship orders, which are defined as 'a half-way house between a residence order and an adoption order' are growing in number (Ward LJ in *Re L (Special Guardianship: Surname)* [2007] **EWCA Civ 196, para. 3.1**). Such orders were introduced by the **ACA**

2002 (inserting **ss. 14A–F** into the **CA 1989**) and confer parental responsibility on the guardian. They differ from adoption orders as they are not permanent, do not confer parental status on the guardian and do not extinguish the parental responsibility of the birth parent(s). However, the special guardian can actually exercise parental responsibility to the exclusion of all others, including the birth parents. This can be useful if the child in question is older, has contact with his or her birth family and does not wish to be legally separated from them (*Adoption—A New Approach* (2000), para. 5.8). The increase in special guardianship orders and placements with relatives and friends may go some way to explaining why the number of adoptions has not grown. The proposed Children and Families Bill (which is expected in 2013) will also contain provisions which may lead to an increase in the number of children adopted from care. It is suggested that infants subject to a care order should be placed with foster carers who wish to adopt them and have already been approved for this purpose. In addition, if an adoption is not arranged by the local authority within three months, the child should be placed on the national adoption register (www.education.gov.uk). It is therefore possible that we will witness an increase in adoptions from care in the future.

Further reading

Department of Education (2011) *The Adoption and Children Act 2002. Adoption Statutory Guidance* (first revised February 2011).

Department of Education (2012) *Proposals for Placing Children with Their Potential Adopters Earlier.*

Department of Education (2012) *Placing Children in Sibling Groups for Adoption: A Call for Views.*

Department of Education (2012) *Contact Arrangements for Children: A Call for Views.*

Department of Health (2000) *Adoption—A New Approach* (Cm 5017).

Hughes, K. and Sloan, B. (2011) 'Post-Adoption Photographs: Welfare, Rights and Judicial Reasoning'. 23(3) CFLQ 393.

Katz, S. and Katz, D.R. (2012) *Adoption Law in a Nutshell* (St Paul, MN: Thomson West).

McFarlane, A. and Reardon, M. (2010) *Child Care and Adoption Law: A Practical Guide* (Bristol: Family Law).

Websites

www.baaf.org.uk

www.adoption.org.uk

9

Children: private ordering

Introduction

Decisions about what should happen to children after the separation or divorce of their parents, for example where they should live and how much contact they should have with each parent, affect large numbers of families each year. In 2011, the number of children involved in private law applications was 109,656 (Judicial and Court Statistics, 2012). The vast majority of them were under **s. 8 of the Children Act (CA) 1989**, which allows the court to make residence, contact prohibited steps and specific issue orders.

  This area of family law tends to be popular with students and there is likely to be a question on the paper. To answer it properly you will need to know not just the **s. 8** orders, but also the context in which they operate. The general principles and concepts of the **1989 Act** as they relate to private law proceedings will be particularly relevant, i.e. the welfare principle and the statutory checklist, the 'non-intervention' principle and continuing parental responsibility. Specific issues which may arise include: change of child's name, leaving the jurisdiction and problems with contact. Private orders for children may, of course, also come up in questions on other areas such as finance and property or the ground for divorce.

 Question 1

While the law can sever the legal bond between husband and wife, the law in family disputes should do nothing that appears to weaken the bond between parent and child. That bond is vital. (Lord Mackay, Lord Chancellor when the Children Act 1989 was passed.)

Assess the extent to which the **Children Act 1989** accepts and advances this view.

Commentary

It should be quite clear from the title quotation that the point Lord Mackay was making is that when a husband and wife end their relationship by divorce (sever the legal bond), their relationship with their children should survive intact. He claimed that the relationship between parent and child is 'vital' and that the law should not do anything that could be seen as weakening the bond. The question asks you to assess the extent to which the **CA 1989** accepts and advances the view expressed by Lord Mackay. You will need a sound knowledge of the private law provisions of the Act and its underlying philosophy and an appreciation of the approach now taken to private ordering. You should include examples of provisions which have an effect on the parent/child bond referred to by Lord Mackay and assess each one in terms of the title quotation.

Answer plan

- The position prior to the **CA 1989**.
- Continuing 'PR' post-divorce.
- The 'non-intervention' principle and **s. 41 Matrimonial Causes Act (MCA) 1973**.
- **S. 8**, residence and contact orders.
- The **Children and Adoption Act 2006**.
- Recent developments.

Examiner's tip

To gain extra marks, make reference to the recommendations contained in the *Family Justice Review Final Report* (2011) and the Government's proposals to introduce a legislative statement regarding the importance of children maintaining an ongoing relationship with both parents.

Suggested answer

The view being expressed by Lord Mackay is that when a couple divorce, it is their spousal relationship which ends, not their relationship with their children, and that the law, when dealing with children after divorce, should be seen to support this continuing parent/child relationship. No law can make someone be an active involved parent, but it can at least encourage those who would like to continue in that role to do so. Prior to the **Children Act (CA) 1989**, there was very little to encourage joint responsibility or to preserve a real relationship between a child and the non-custodial parent. Two orders which did go some way towards achieving this were joint custody orders and access orders. But joint custody orders were often symbolic and when one parent had 'sole custody' and the other 'access', the latter would often feel redundant or inferior and would sometimes stop playing any useful part in the child's life as a result.

Generally, it is true to say that the **CA 1989** does accept that on separation and divorce both parents should continue in their role as parents and a number of its provisions support this view. First, married parents both have parental responsibility for their children (**s. 2 CA 1989**) and this is totally unaffected by separation or divorce. Court intervention is not seen as lessening a parent's duty to continue to play a full role. If a **s. 8** order is made, parental responsibility is limited only to the extent that the order settles a particular issue (e.g. where the child should live) between the parties. For many items, parental responsibility runs with the child; either parent can exercise it when the child is with him, each can act independently in meeting his responsibility and there is no consultation requirement in the Act (**s. 2(7)**). In the past the courts have indicated that the non-resident parent should be consulted in relation to key issues, such as sending a child to boarding school (*Re G (Parental Responsibility: Education)* [1994] 2 **FLR 964**) or medical treatment (*Re C (Welfare of Child: Immunisation)* [2003] 2 FLR **1095 (CA)**). However, the Department for Children, Schools and Families has emphasized that each parent can act alone and that there is no consultation requirement in the Act (DCSF, *The Children Act 1989 Guidance and Regulations Vol. 1: Court Orders* (2008), para. 2.31). One statutory limitation is that neither must act incompatibly with any order made (**s. 2(8)**). In the absence of an order, if one parent objects to what the other is doing, then application must be made to the court (see *M v H (Education Welfare)* [2008] EWHC 324 (Fam)). Thus, perhaps more than any other provision of the Act, this concept of continuing parental responsibility goes some way to ensuring that no matter what happens to the marital relationship, the parent/child relationship continues.

One of the most innovative principles in the **1989 Act** is the non-intervention or no order principle (**s. 1(5)**). It is relevant in all family proceedings but in practice the most important situation in which it operates is on divorce. The principle reflects the basic philosophy of the **1989 Act** that responsibility for children rests with their parents and state intervention is only justified when it is best for the child. The 'presumption' that no order will be made unless it is required in the best interests of the child, in this context, discourages parents from expecting a court order in every case. Wherever possible, parents should be left to make their own arrangements for their children. An order will always have to be justified on the basis of the child's welfare and will be desirable where there is a dispute, vital where there is the possibility of abduction and practical where housing is a problem and the local authority requires an order for the purpose of determining housing needs. But an order is unlikely to be made, just because a parent will feel more secure.

Section 41 of the Matrimonial Causes Act 1973 (as amended by **Sch. 12, CA 1989**) is in line with the non-intervention principle. There is no requirement of judicial approval of private agreements regarding children on divorce; the court's duty is the more modest one of considering what order, if any, to make. Scrutiny of the arrangements made for children is a paper exercise; there is only a hearing when the form seems to indicate something is amiss, and the discretion to direct that the decree is not to be made absolute until further order, is exercised in exceptional circumstances only. Again, the procedure leaves the parental responsibility to the parents wherever possible and does not interfere unnecessarily.

The private orders available under **s. 8** also help to advance the view that the bond between parent and child is vital, and recognize the potential psychological impact on a parent of 'labelling'. The two principal orders, i.e. residence and contact, reflect the issues most likely to need resolving, namely: where the child should live and how much the child should see of both parents. The court is no longer concerned with wholesale reallocation of rights; each parent retains parental responsibility and does not lose parental status. In *Re G (A Child)* **[2008] EWCA Civ 1468** Ward LJ emphasized that the parent with residence does not have more power than the other (para. 18). The 'winner takes all' situation, which led many absent parents to feel redundant under the old system, is thus avoided. The *Family Justice Review Final Report* (2011) recommends abolishing residence and contact orders and replacing them with a 'child arrangements order' which would further emphasize the importance of both parents maintaining relationships with their children.

If a residence order is made, the two automatic conditions contained in the order relating to change of the child's surname and removal of the child from the UK (both only being possible with the consent of every person who has parental responsibility for the child or leave of the court) emphasize the importance of a continuing link with the non-residential parent (**s. 13 CA 1989**). The 'residential' parent is not prevented from removing the child from the UK for less than one month. A parent of a child under 16 may be committing an offence if he takes or sends the child out of the UK without the appropriate consent (**s. 1 Child Abduction Act 1984**). In addition, **s. 11(4)** makes shared residence possible and in *D v D (Shared Residence Order)* **[2001] 1 FLR 495** the Court of Appeal held that, contrary to earlier case law, it is not necessary to show that exceptional circumstances exist before a shared residence order may be granted. What should be demonstrated is that the order is in the interests of the child, in accordance with **s. 1 CA 1989**. The court should exercise its discretion based on the facts and, in opposed cases, the welfare checklist (**s. 1(3) CA 1989**). However, Gilmore points out that although shared residence orders are no longer unusual, they are not normally practicable ('Shared Residence: A Summary of the Courts' Guidance' [2010] Fam Law 285). They will normally be granted if such an order actually reflects the reality of where the children live (*Re H (Children)*[2009] EWCA Civ 902). This does not mean that the children should be spending an equal amount of time with both parents as both *D v D* and *Re F (Shared Residence Order)* **[2003] 2 FLR 397** demonstrate. Indeed, in *Re W (Shared Residence Order)* **[2009] EWCA Civ 370** the Court of Appeal upheld a shared residence order where the child would spend approximately 25 per cent of his time with the father. In addition, considerable distance between the parents' homes does not preclude the possibility that the child's year would be divided between the two homes in such a way as to validate the making of a shared residence order (see *Re F* earlier).

The most common type of order made under **s. 8** is an order for contact (108,552 orders were made in private law proceedings in 2011 (Judicial and Court Statistics, 2012, Table 2.4)). Probert points out that there is now a 'widespread assumption among the judiciary that it is generally in the interests of the child to maintain contact with both parents and that in practice the courts will order contact unless there are good reasons not to do so' (*Cretney and Probert's Family Law* (2009), p. 285). This attitude is reflected in the amendments made to the **CA 1989** by the **Children and Adoption Act 2006** which are designed to promote contact. **Section 11A of the CA 1989** allows the court to make a contact activity direction when an application for contact is made and a contact activity condition (**s. 11C**) when the final order is made. Contact activities can take the form of programmes or counselling aimed at persuading the resident parent of the benefits of contact. CAFCASS officers may be asked to provide information in support of the court's efforts to find solutions to contact difficulties. The courts also have powers to enforce contact orders (in addition to their existing powers to fine or imprison parents who obstruct contact). For example, an unpaid work requirement can be imposed on the recalcitrant parent under **s. 11J CA 1989** (inserted by the **Children and Adoption Act 2006**). Furthermore, residence can be transferred from the parent obstructing contact to the other, as a last resort (*Re A (Residence Order)* [2009] EWCA Civ 1141). This actually occurred in *TE v SH and S* [2010] EWCA 192 (Fam). These developments designed to promote contact reinforce Lord Mackay's statement regarding the importance of maintaining the bond between parent and child.

Many parents (perhaps the majority) after divorce need information and short-term help to organize their shared responsibilities, and mediation is consequently a feature of many of these cases. It aims to civilize the consequences of marriage breakdown, to diffuse a potentially acrimonious situation and to help pave the way for good working relationships, particularly with the children, after divorce. The use of mediation will increase as a result of recent reforms (see **Chapter 4**) and if the recommendations contained in the *Family Justice Review Final Report* are implemented, parents will also be required to attend a Separating Parents Information Programme (PIP) which may help parents to resolve any issues they have and ensure that the parent/child relationship is maintained (2011, p. 151). The *Final Report* also suggests that mothers and fathers should form a parenting agreement but the weight to be accorded to it is currently unclear.

At present, the court may of its own motion make a family assistance order (**s. 16 CA 1989**) to help a family resolve the conflicts flowing from breakdown and to smooth the transition period. This short-term order (12 months since the **Children and Adoption Act 2006**) has to be voluntary and the child's welfare is paramount. The Act has widened the scope of family assistance orders by removing the requirement that such orders may only be made in exceptional circumstances, specifically focusing on advice and assistance on contact where needed, and more power in reporting back to court on whatever matters relating to **s. 8** the court requires. The Code of Practice of Resolution (formerly known as the Solicitors' Family Law Association (SFLA)) advocates that solicitors should explain to their clients how the attitude of parents towards each other in negotiations involving children may affect their relationship with the children.

In conclusion, the **CA 1989** (as amended) reflects the view that ex-spouses remain parents and ought to retain a commitment to their children. One can never legislate for human nature; no legal provision can make an unwilling parent be an active and involved parent and there will always be situations where it is not in the child's best interests to preserve the bond. The Act clearly recognizes, however, the importance of the parent/child relationship and through a number of its provisions seeks to encourage its preservation where practicable, thus advancing the view expressed by Lord Mackay. The present Government wishes to take this a stage further by introducing an express 'legislative statement of the importance of children having an ongoing relationship with both parents after family separation, where that is safe, and in the child's best interests' (*Government Response to the Family Justice Review* (2012), p. 18). The Government has consequently established a working group to develop proposals for legislative change. It thus appears that the sentiment expressed by Lord Mackay may be explicitly included in legislation.

 Question 2

Ruth is a 15-year-old girl whose parents are in the throes of a very acrimonious divorce. Ruth's father has moved away, and was happy for Ruth to stay with her mother, so that she could remain at the same school. Ruth does not get on with Bill, the man with whom her mother is now living. He constantly finds fault with Ruth and makes it very plain that he would prefer it if she were not around. Ruth's mother always takes his side. Ruth is a very intelligent and sensitive girl and the stressful situation at home has started adversely to affect her school work. Last week when her mother told her that she was going to marry Bill, Ruth left home and moved in with her aunt and uncle, who are happy for her to stay with them indefinitely. Ruth's mother is not happy with the situation and is insisting that Ruth returns home immediately. Yesterday she turned up at Ruth's school and tried to bundle Ruth into the back of her car to take her home. Ruth wants to stay where she is.

Discuss.

 Commentary

The facts contained in this question raise several legal issues which require the identification and discussion of specific statutory provisions. The answer should include the child's right to apply for orders, the types of order available, the welfare principle, the relevance of the child's wishes and feelings and the possible appointment of a guardian to represent Ruth. Candidates should also discuss Ruth's ability to make her own decisions and wardship.

Answer plan

Advice for Ruth	Advice for Ruth's mother
Ruth can apply for **s. 8** orders with leave (**s. 10(8) CA 1989**)	Ruth's mother has an automatic right to apply for **s. 8** orders
Leave may be granted if Ruth has sufficient understanding and a chance of success	Ruth's mother must be advised that Ruth will be *Gillick*-competent
Ruth can instruct her own solicitor and a guardian may be appointed (**s. 41 CA 1989**)	Ruth's mother may apply for Ruth to be made a ward of the court: **s. 41 Supreme Court Act 1981**
Ruth may apply for a residence order to live with her uncle and aunt or a PSO to prevent her removal	Ruth's welfare is first consideration Wardship is unlikely
The welfare principle (**s. 1(1) CA 1979**) and the welfare checklist apply (**s. 1(3) CA 1989**)	Adoption is the only way to sever the tie between Ruth and her mother but this is unlikely

 Examiner's tip

As you are asked to 'discuss', rather than advise a particular party, you can take the opportunity to assess the situation from the mother's point of view, as well as Ruth's.

 Suggested answer

This question concerns a dispute between a mother and her teenage daughter over where the daughter should live. The issue is whether the mother can insist that her child returns home to live with her and whether the daughter can take any steps to ensure that she can stay where she is.

One of the principal aims of the **Children Act (CA) 1989** was to give the child a voice, and one way in which it seeks to achieve this is by empowering the child to make application to the court. Similarly, **Art. 12 of the UN Convention on the Rights of the Child 1989** gives the child the right to express an opinion, and to have it taken into account in judicial proceedings. Under **s. 8 CA 1989**, Ruth can apply for a range of orders; residence, contact, prohibited steps and specific issue. She cannot apply as of right, however; leave is required under **s. 10(8)** which *may* be granted if the court is satisfied that the child has sufficient understanding to make the proposed application. The level of understanding required is high: Ruth will have to convince the judge that she is able to understand the consequences of her actions (***Re S (A Minor) (Independent Representation)***

[1993] Fam 263). Age is obviously relevant, though no minimum age is specified in the Act. As Ruth is 15 years old, the court is likely to listen very carefully to what she has to say. In *Re P (A Minor) (Education: Child's Wishes)* [1992] 1 FCR 145 where the child involved was 14, the court emphasized the importance of listening and paying respect to the views of older children who are mature enough to make up their own minds as to what they think is best for them. Hence, leave may well be granted. In *Re H (Residence Order: Child's Application for Leave)* [2000] 1 FLR 780, it was held that the court may also consider the likely success of the proposed application, and that the child's welfare is an important, but not paramount, consideration. The courts have made it clear that their doors are open to genuine cases of last resort, where there has been a severe breakdown in a child's relationship with his parents, and not, for example, in cases where a child is peeved because he or she is not getting his own way at home *(Re C (A Minor) (Leave to Seek Section 8 Order)* [1994] 1 FLR 26). We are told that Ruth is an intelligent and sensitive girl whose school work is being adversely affected by the stressful situation at home. As she is 15 years old she is obviously at an important stage of her education. It is not a case of her not getting her own way at home, there is obviously a breakdown. It is therefore likely that leave would be granted. Applications should be made in the High Court or transferred there if made in the lower courts. Ruth will be able to instruct her own solicitor, if the court gives leave or the solicitor agrees to act (**s. 41**). She must have sufficient understanding to instruct and be able to give rational, coherent and consistent instructions (*Re H (A Minor)*[1991] 2 FCR 330). It should also be noted that **r. 9(5) of the Family Proceedings Rules 1991** permits the court to appoint a guardian to represent the child in family proceedings. Following amendments made by **s. 122 of the Adoption and Children Act 2002**, a guardian can be appointed to represent a child during **s. 8** proceedings (**s. 41 CA 1989**). However, such representation should only be required in cases of 'significant difficulty'. For example, in *Re C (A Child)* [2011] EWCA Civ 261 the Court of Appeal held that the 12-year-old child should be joined as a party with a solicitor and guardian to ensure that someone put forward the child's views independently of both parents.

As Ruth wants to be allowed to live with her aunt and uncle and to prevent her mother taking her away from their home, she should apply for a residence order which is an order settling the arrangements to be made as to the person with whom a child is to live, and a prohibited steps order which is an order that no step which could be taken by a parent in meeting his parental responsibility for a child and which is of a kind specified in the order, is to be taken by any person without the consent of the court. The residence order would allow her to stay where she wants, at least for the time being. The court may decide to make an interim residence order pending final determination of the matter, but in any event residence orders are subject to review. The effect of the order would be to vest parental responsibility in Ruth's aunt and uncle, though Ruth's parents would, of course, retain parental responsibility. The prohibited steps order would be used to prevent Ruth's mother taking her away from her aunt and uncle's home; this will be the issue specified in the order which has to be referred to the court. Both the orders will cease when Ruth reaches 16.

When the court is considering the applications, Ruth's welfare will be the paramount consideration (**s. 1 CA 1989**) and the court's task is to assess her best interests. In an opposed **s. 8** order application (as this is likely to be) the welfare checklist applies (**s. 1(3)**) and Ruth's wishes and feelings will be taken into account, commensurate with her age and understanding. It seems likely that the court would make the orders applied for as they represent the best solution for Ruth.

As we are asked to 'discuss' the scenario rather than to advise Ruth, we should also consider the mother's position. Perhaps understandably she is trying to enforce her right, as she sees it, to 'custody' of her daughter. Even before the implementation of the **CA 1989** it was recognized that a wise parent would not try to force his views on a mature child and since the House of Lords decision in *Gillick v West Norfolk and Wisbech Area Health Authority* [1986] 1 FLR 224, the child's level of intellectual or emotional development has been relevant in deciding the extent of parental authority. Ruth is *Gillick*-competent and would be regarded as sufficiently mature to decide for herself what she wants to do. There is no doubt that she will fully understand all the issues involved here.

The mother could turn to the inherent jurisdiction of the High Court and ask for Ruth to be made a ward of court under **s. 41 Supreme Court Act 1981** (as happened in *Re AD (A Minor)* [1993] Fam Law 405). Legal control over Ruth would then vest in the court which takes over ultimate responsibility for her welfare. All important decisions about her upbringing must subsequently be referred to the court including, of course, where and with whom she should live. In wardship, Ruth's welfare will be considered 'first, last and all the time' (*per* Dunn J in *Re D (A Minor) (Justices' Decision: Review)* [1977] Fam 158). The High Court may well ask that a children's guardian be appointed for Ruth and give directions that he or she should investigate the case. Ruth will be able to retain her own solicitor and the two separate applications, both being 'family proceedings', would be heard together in the High Court. In *Re CT (A Minor) (Wardship: Representation)* [1993] 2 FLR 278, the Court of Appeal indicated that giving a child ward status is exceptional under the modern law but in *Wardship: T v S (Wardship)* [2011] EWHC 1608 (Fam) the child was made a ward of the court because the parents could not resolve issues themselves: they were therefore taken to have forfeited their parental responsibility. However, Ruth's mother will not be encouraged to use wardship: it is therefore more likely that the application will proceed as one for **s. 8** orders. Indeed, Ruth's mother can automatically apply for a residence order if she wants Ruth to live with her. Finally, Ruth's mother can be reassured that the only way in which her relationship with her daughter can be totally severed is by adoption, which is highly unlikely in the circumstances. Assuming that Ruth successfully obtains a prohibited steps order and a residence order, it is likely that some continued contact with her mother will be maintained and encouraged.

Question 3

Caroline and Robin were divorced two years ago after an eight-year marriage. The divorce was largely due to Robin's involvement with a somewhat extreme religious sect whose beliefs he tried to impose on all the family. Robin is a strict disciplinarian and expects very high standards of his family. The two children, Debbie, now aged 7, and Linda, now 4, stayed with Caroline after the divorce but see their father regularly.

For the past six months, Philippa, an engineer, has been living with Caroline and they are involved in a lesbian relationship. Robin has only just discovered the nature of Caroline and Philippa's friendship and is horrified. He says that Caroline is not fit to bring up children and that his daughters are not staying in that immoral environment. He intends to apply for a residence order and to ensure that Caroline sees the girls as little as possible. He lives alone but says that his sect friends will look after the girls when he is at work.

Caroline only works part time to enable her to look after the girls, who are both at school.

Advise Caroline.

Commentary

Solicitors should encourage the attitude that a family dispute is not a contest with a winner and a loser, but a search for fair solutions (see Resolution Code of Practice). In cases such as this one, this may take some doing. The facts indicate the likelihood of a fully contested application for residence: fortunately in practice such cases are rare. They may generate a great deal of bitterness, as each parent perceives the other's unfitness as the main issue. An opposed **s. 8** application does, however, provide you with the opportunity to discuss the welfare principle (**s. 1**) and use the statutory checklist in **s. 1(3) CA 1989**. Your answer should also consider the non-intervention principle (**s. 1(5)**) which is relevant in such cases.

Answer plan

- Both have PR.
- **S. 8**—residence and contact.
- The welfare principle—**s. 1**.
- Statutory checklist, **s. 1(3)**.
- The homosexual parent.
- The 'religious' parent.

Examiner's tip

Ensure that you utilize the information given in the question to identify which factors on the checklist are relevant and make use of relevant case law.

Suggested answer

One assumes that Caroline wants the two girls, Debbie and Linda, to continue to live with her and that she is concerned that Robin will be allowed to take them away from her. Obviously, on such facts there is likely to be a full-blown dispute over the children. Mediation is perhaps unlikely to be successful and the court will order a welfare report to be prepared (**s. 7 CA 1989**).

As married parents, Caroline and Robin both have parental responsibility for Debbie and Linda (**s. 2 CA 1989**) and this has not been affected by their divorce. They may both exercise their responsibility independently of each other when the girls are with them. Any **s. 8** order will only affect parental responsibility in so far as it deals with a concrete issue concerning the girls' upbringing, and neither parent must act incompatibly with such an order. Robin says that he intends to apply for a residence order but Caroline will oppose any such application. In private family disputes such as this one, it is not automatic that an order will be made. The court will be influenced by the non-intervention principle (**s. 1(5) CA 1989**) and will only make an order if satisfied that there is a demonstrable need for one. Robin and Caroline will have to justify an order being made, but where there is a dispute, as here, an order is probably going to be desirable. **Section 11(4) CA 1989** permits a residence order in favour of more than one person, but this also brings problems of stability for the child. In *Re W (Shared Residence Order)* [2009] 2 FLR 436 the Court of Appeal indicated that although the inability of parents to work in harmony is not a reason to decline an order, it is not a reason to make an order either. Furthermore, shared residence orders are usually made to reflect existing arrangements. In this case the children do not spend a substantial amount of time with their father. A shared residence order is therefore unlikely.

In deciding with whom Debbie and Linda should live, their welfare will be the court's paramount consideration (**s. 1 CA 1989**). As the **s. 8** application for a residence order is opposed, the checklist in **s. 1(3) CA 1989** is applicable to assist the court with the balancing exercise necessary to assess the children's welfare. It is not necessary for the court to consider every guideline in every case, merely the relevant ones (*B v B (Minor: Residence Order: Reasons)* [1997] 2 FLR 602). Applying the checklist to the given facts, as appropriate, first on the list (though this does not give them priority over other factors (*Re J (A Minor)* [1992] Fam Law 229)) are the ascertainable wishes and feelings of the children, considered in the light of their age and understanding. Children can be influenced by all sorts of things when expressing a view and the court will not be constricted by a child's wishes particularly if they appear to be at odds with the child's welfare; at the end of the day it is the court's decision. The court will listen to and pay respect to the views of older children (see *Re S (Contact: Children's Views)* [2002] 1 FLR 1156, which concerned children of 16, 14 and 12) but the views of younger children have also been considered in contact and residence disputes. For example, in *Re R (A Child)* [2009] EWCA Civ 445 the Court of Appeal overturned a residence order made in favour of the 9-year-old child's father on the basis that insufficient weight had been placed on the child's wish to return to his mother. Here, the girls here are only 7 and 4, and the court is most unlikely to hear them directly, relying instead on the children and family reporter's interview. In *Re A (Specific Issue Order: Parental Dispute)* [2001] 1 FLR 121, the court was influenced by the psychological evidence that it is harmful to require children to choose between parents.

The girls' physical, emotional and educational needs must also be considered. Initially it was felt that young children should be with their mother (*M v M* [1982] 4 FLR 603) but there is, in fact, no legal presumption of maternal preference. In the Scottish case of *Brixey v Lynas* [1996] 2 FLR 499 the House of Lords referred to 'the workings of nature . . . where a very young child has been with its mother since birth and there is no criticism of her ability to care for the child only the strongest competing advantages are likely to prevail.' If the mother is unable to care for the children, the courts will grant residence to the father even if the child is very young (*Re D (A Child) (Residence: Ability to Parent)* [2001] 2 FCR 751 (CA)). In this case there are no concerns regarding Caroline's ability to look after the children. Certainly, there should be no question of separating the two girls *(C v C (Custody of Children)* [1988] 2 FLR 291; siblings should be brought up together in same household), particularly in view of the age proximity. A further factor in Caroline's favour is the fact that since she and Robin divorced two years ago the girls have lived with her. In practice, preservation of the status quo tends to be the most important factor (s. 1(3)(c)). Continuity of care is important and the court will be reluctant to disturb the girls' settled environment, unless there is good reason for doing so (*Re B (Residence Order: Status Quo)* [1998] 1 FLR 368).

In considering any harm suffered or likely to be suffered by Debbie and Linda (s. 1(3)(e)) the court will look at their parents' lifestyle and behaviour, such behaviour being relevant if it reflects on the individual as a parent. In this particular case, two aspects of parental behaviour require discussion. First, we are told that Robin is involved with an extreme religious sect and that the marriage broke down because of his attempts to impose his beliefs on the rest of the family. He is also described as being a strict disciplinarian with very high standards, factors which will not necessarily work against him (*May v May* [1986] 1 FLR 325). His religion is, however, a different matter. Usually a parent's religious beliefs will not be of particular relevance in such cases but, if the parent's beliefs are extreme and result in social isolation, psychological damage or physical suffering for the children, then they will be relevant. In *Re B and G (Minors) (Custody)* [1985] FLR 493 the father was a member of the Church of Scientology which set out to indoctrinate children making them 'unquestioning captives and tools of the cult, withdrawn from ordinary thought, living and relationship with others.' As a consequence, custody (as it then was) was granted to the mother. Furthermore, in *Hoffman v Austria* (1993) **17 EHRR 293 (ECtHR)**, it was held permissible to deny 'custody' to a parent because of the *effect* of any religious practices on the child. If the court found that there was a risk of any sort of harm to Debbie and Linda as a result of their father's involvement with what is described as an extreme sect, Robin would not be given a residence order. Robin's determination to limit contact between Caroline and the children will also damage his case. In *Re C (Residence Order)* [2007] **EWCA Civ 866** the court ordered the transfer of residence from the mother to the father as the former obstructed contact.

Secondly, we are told that Caroline is involved in a lesbian relationship with Philippa, which according to Robin means that she is not fit to bring up the girls. The fact that Caroline is a lesbian does not in itself render her unfit to care for Debbie and Linda as Robin contends. In fact, the European Court of Human Rights has held that homosexuality cannot justify denying a parent custody of (or access to) a child (*Da Silva Mouta v Portugal* 1999 (Application No. 33290/96)). The change in attitude towards lesbian parents is reflected in the **Human Fertilisation and Embryology Act 2008**, which allows a mother's female partner to be treated as the legal parent of a child born through assisted reproduction (see **Chapter 7**). Caroline's lesbian relationship should not therefore operate against her.

Caroline only works part time and is able to look after the girls herself when they are not at school. Robin, on the other hand, intends to leave the girls with other members of the sect whilst he is at work. Child-care arrangements are another relevant factor and the court may well be reluctant to see Debbie and Linda being looked after by sect members at times when they could be with their own loving mother.

On balance, taking all relevant factors into account, it would seem likely that the court will decide that Debbie and Linda's welfare demands that they stay with Caroline, and make an unconditional residence order in Caroline's favour. A joint residence order (s. 11(4)) would appear unlikely and impracticable in the circumstances. Robin would, however, undoubtedly be allowed regular and frequent contact with his daughters and there is nothing to suggest that Caroline will obstruct this.

? Question 4

Matthew and Liz divorced amicably 18 months ago. They have two sons, Tom, now 8, and Jack, now 10, and Matthew has always been happy for them to stay with Liz. No orders were made in relation to the boys on the divorce.

Matthew tries to see the boys two or three times a week and they frequently spend weekends with him. These arrangements worked well until recently, but Matthew is now experiencing a number of problems.

A few months ago Liz met Bruce, a New Zealander living in the UK, and there is now talk of marriage. On a number of occasions in the last few weeks, Matthew's arrangements to see Tom and Jack have been cancelled at the last minute, as the boys were going out with

Bruce. Last week when Matthew actually got to see the boys, Tom was talking excitedly about a possible trip to New Zealand with Bruce. Matthew feels that Bruce is trying to replace him as the boys' father. Liz refuses to discuss this, or indeed anything to do with Tom and Jack, with Matthew.

The boys are happy living with Liz, and Matthew does not want to change this, but he is concerned about being increasingly excluded from Tom and Jack's lives.

Matthew seeks your advice as to his position.

Commentary

Here you are asked to advise the divorced father of two young boys on his position in relation to a number of problems which have arisen since the mother formed a new relationship. You should note that Matthew is happy for the boys to continue to live with their mother, i.e. residence is not in dispute. The main issues are contact and removal from the jurisdiction, which will be decided on the basis of the welfare principle (**s. 1 CA 1989**) and the welfare checklist (**s. 1(3)**).

Answer plan

- Parental responsibility.
- **S. 8**—contact order.
- The welfare principle.
- Statutory checklist.
- Leaving the jurisdiction—PSO, **s. 8**.

Examiner's tip

There is no evidence to suggest that Liz will take the children to New Zealand without obtaining the appropriate consent—your answer should not therefore focus on child abduction.

Suggested answer

At the time of their divorce 18 months ago, Matthew and Liz were able to settle things amicably. However, since Liz acquired a new partner, problems have arisen in relation to contact and there is a possibility of the boys being taken to New Zealand. Ideally

Matthew should try to talk to Liz about the children and to see whether these matters can be sorted out on an amicable basis. But if Liz will not discuss the boys with him, then he may feel that he needs to take some formal steps to safeguard his position. As a married father, Matthew shares parental responsibility for Tom and Jack with Liz (**s. 2 Children Act (CA) 1989**) and this has not been affected by their separation or divorce (or by the arrival of Bruce). No **s. 8** orders have been made to date so that when Matthew has Tom and Jack with him he may exercise his parental responsibility as he sees fit and may act independently, in the best interests of the boys (**s. 2(7)**). Liz may do the same. As the non-resident parent Matthew retains the right to be involved in, and to have opinions on, the boys' upbringing. In a situation where one parent is unhappy with what the other parent is doing (as here), then it may be necessary to make application to the court. Matthew does not wish to change the residence arrangements as he believes that it is in Tom and Jack's best interests to stay with Liz; he simply wants to ensure that he is not in practice replaced as the boys' father by Bruce. However, if Liz and Bruce were to marry then it would be possible for Bruce to acquire parental responsibility (PR) by way of agreement to that effect with everyone who has PR for the child. If Matthew were to refuse to consent, then Bruce could acquire PR by a court order (under **s. 4A CA 1989** inserted by **s. 112 of the Adoption and Children Act 2002**). Matthew, of course, would not lose his PR, he would share it with Liz and Bruce and, should Matthew marry again, his spouse could acquire PR too.

The first problem relates to contact which cannot be agreed between Matthew and Liz. As a parent, Matthew may apply as of right (**s. 10(4)(a) CA 1989**) for a contact order (**s. 8**). An order for reasonable contact would include staying contact, and leave the specific arrangements to Liz and Matthew. This type of order is to be preferred but if agreement cannot be reached, then the court may define contact in terms of duration and frequency. Defined orders tend to be restrictive and do little to encourage ordinary, natural relationships between parents and children. When deciding whether and, if so, what order to make, the court will be influenced by the non-intervention principle (**s. 1(5) CA 1989**) and the welfare principle (**s. 1**). The checklist (**s. 1(3)**) applies in the event of a dispute and it is likely that the court will attach weight to the wishes and feelings of Tom and Jack on the matter (*Re P (A Minor) (Education: Child's Wishes)* [1992] 1 FCR 145). On the facts given, there seem to be no reasons why Matthew should not have regular contact; there is nothing to indicate that he is no longer a fit and proper person to have contact with his sons and no apparent reasons why physical contact would be considered undesirable. It is clear from both *Re L (A Child) (Contact: Domestic Violence)* [2000] 2 FLR 334 and **Art. 9(3) of the United Nations Convention on the Rights of the Child 1989** that parental contact is appropriate except where it is not in the child's interests. The boys are 8 and 10, and obviously have a well-established relationship with their father which should be preserved. Tom and Jack's best interests will be served by having continued contact with their natural father. But what if Liz still makes it difficult for Matthew to see Tom and Jack or even tries to stop contact altogether? If the original order is for reasonable contact, then Matthew would have to return to the court to have contact defined and, if there are still problems, consider taking steps to enforce the order. Since the implementation of the **Children and Adoption Act 2006** in-court conciliation may preclude the need for enforcement. In addition, the court can now attach a contact activity direction to the order (**s. 11C**) which would require Liz to attend programmes or counselling to encourage her to facilitate contact. The court may also make a family assistance order (**s. 16 CA 1989**) in the hope that a CAFCASS or local authority officer can produce a solution. If none of these options work, Matthew could take court action to enforce the order. Liz could be fined for non-compliance with a contact order or as a last resort, and to encourage compliance, she could actually be imprisoned for contempt. Such a draconian step is usually only considered for persistent failures and in *Re F (Contact: Enforcement: Representation of Child)* [1999] 1 FLR 810, the Court of Appeal noted that treatment rather than imprisonment is better where contact orders are disobeyed. Nonetheless, failure to enforce contact decisions may violate the **European Convention on Human Rights** (see *Hokkanen v Finland* [1996] 1 FLR 289 and *Re K (Contact: Committal Order)* [2003] 1 FLR 277). In intractable contact disputes the court may transfer residence (*V v V (Children) (Contact: Implacable Hostility)* [2004] EWCA Civ 1215 and *Re C (A Child)* [2007] EWCA Civ 866), or even transfer residence and make a supervision order in favour of the local authority (*Re M (Intractable Contact Dispute: Interim Care Order)* [2003] 2 FLR 636). In *Re E (Residence Order)* [2009] EWCA Civ 1141 the Court of Appeal indicated that transferring residence should (like imprisonment) be a last resort. In cases such as this the court may wish to utilize the powers of enforcement acquired under the **Children and Adoption Act 2006**, for example imposing an unpaid work required (**s. 11J**). This can be done if a warning was attached to the original (or amended) order (**s. 11I**) and the resident parent has no reasonable excuse for failing to comply with the order.

The second area of concern is that Liz has a new partner (Bruce, a New Zealander) and there is 'talk of marriage'. We are told that he is living in the UK, but we do not know whether this is a permanent or temporary arrangement. Matthew is obviously not very happy at the prospect of his sons going on a trip to New Zealand with Bruce but, even in the absence of a residence order in her favour, it is possible that Liz may take the boys out of the country with impunity. A residence order in Liz's favour would be subject to the automatic condition that Liz could remove the boys from the jurisdiction for up to one month only, without Matthew's written consent or leave of the court (**s. 13(2)**). In the absence of any residence order, Liz *might* be open to prosecution under the **Child Abduction Act 1984**. She could, however, claim (**s. 1(5)(c)**) that Matthew is unreasonably refusing to consent. If there is 'sufficient evidence' of that, then the onus switches to the prosecution (**s. 1(6)**). If Matthew does not want Tom and Jack to leave the UK at all, he should apply for a prohibited steps order (**s. 8 CA 1989**) which will specify that before the boys can be taken out of the UK, the issue must be referred to the court.

It may be that Matthew would not object to Tom and Jack merely having a holiday in New Zealand, but that his fear is that Liz and Bruce may decide to live permanently in New Zealand. A prohibited steps order would ensure that the matter would have to be referred to the court. Would the court give leave for Tom and Jack to leave the jurisdiction permanently? In the past the courts had indicated that leave would be refused only if it could be clearly shown that the move would be contrary to the child's interests (see *Re T (Removal from Jurisdiction)* [1996] 2 FLR 352). But in *Payne v Payne* [2001] 1 FLR 1052 (the first case in which the impact of the **European Convention for the Protection of Fundamental Rights and Fundamental Freedoms 1950** (European Convention) on relocation cases was considered by the Court of Appeal in a substantive appeal), Thorpe LJ warned against the danger of elevating the reasonable proposals of the primary carer into a legal presumption that leave will be granted. Then, there would be an obvious risk of breaching the respondent's rights, not only under **Art. 8** (right to respect for private and family life) but also under **Art. 6** (right to a fair trial). The need to retain paternal links, the planned emigration being ill-thought out, the views of competent children, the motives of the emigrating parent have all come to the father's aid and justified refusing leave. For example, in *Re B (Leave to Remove)* [2008] EWCA Civ 1034 the German mother was refused leave to return to Germany with her three children (despite the fact that it would exacerbate her depression) as it was clear that she would use the relocation as an opportunity to sever contact with the father. But if the proposed relocation is realistic (i.e. well researched and practical) and is not designed to sever contact with the other parent, leave is likely to be granted due to the adverse impact that a refusal would have on the primary carer, which was emphasized in *Payne v Payne*. *Re H (Children)* [2011] EWCA Civ 529 and *Re C (A Child)* [2011] EWCA Civ 72 are recent examples. In cases where the care of the children is shared, the *Payne* approach is not appropriate (see e.g. *Re K (Children)* [2011] EWCA Civ 793), but this does not apply to Liz and Matthew. In this particular case, relocating to New Zealand seems reasonable as Bruce is from New Zealand, but the mother's motivation for moving may be called into question given that she is obstructing contact between the children and their father. It is thus possible that leave would be refused, as in *Re B (Leave to Remove)* [2008] (see earlier).

Further reading

Bond, G. (2011) 'Shared Residence: The Norm—A Panacea—A Mistake'. Fam Law 1066.

District Judge Andrew Grand (2011) 'Disputes Between Parents: Time for a New Order'. Fam Law 74.

Eaton, D. and Reardon, M. (2011) 'Relocation after *K v K*'. Fam Law 1093.

George, R.H. (2011) 'Practitioners' Views on Children's Welfare in Relocation Disputes: Comparing Approaches in England and New Zealand'. 23(2) CFLQ 178.

Gilmore, S. (2011) 'The *Payne* Saga: Precedent and Family Law Cases'. Fam Law 970.

Hayes, M. (2006) 'Relocation Cases: Is the Court of Appeal Applying the Correct Principles?' 19 CFLQ 351.

Kaganas, F. (2011) 'Regulating Emotion: Judging Contact Disputes'. 23(1) CFLQ 63.

Ministry of Justice (2011) *Family Justice Review Final Report*.

Ministry of Justice (2012) *Government Response to the Family Justice Review: A System with Children and Families at its Heart*.

Nickols, D. (2012) 'A Presumption of Shared Parenting: Long Awaited or Misguided?' Fam Law 573.

Swan, Z. (2011) 'Moving on from *Payne*. . . .?' 64 Student Law Rev 36.

Trim, H. (2011) 'Residence and Contact Orders: As You Were—For Now'. Fam Law 756.

Websites

www.cafcass.gov.uk

www.nfm.org.uk

10

Children and the local authority

Introduction

This chapter deals with **Parts III, IV and V of the Children Act (CA) 1989** which contain the public law relating to children. In 2011, 29,494 children were involved in public law applications made by local authorities, which was a 13 per cent increase compared with 2010 (Judicial and Court Statistics, 2012). In terms of disposals, the courts made 10,884 care (and substitute supervision for care) orders, 5,063 supervision orders, 1,181 emergency protection orders and 227 education supervision orders in 2011, which emphasizes the importance of local authority intervention. The three problem questions in this chapter consider these key orders. The number of children looked after by local authorities is also increasing: in England the figure has reached 65,250 (Department of Education, *Looked After Children Statistics*, Sept 2011) whilst in Wales a further 5,419 children are being looked after by the local authority (www.assemblywales.org). Many of these children are being looked after under a voluntary arrangement made between parents and the local authority. Voluntary arrangements form the basis of the second question in this chapter.

Students should also be aware that private law orders, such as residence and contact, can be made during an application for a care or supervision order: in 2011 the courts made approximately 8,000 s. 8 orders during public law proceedings (Judicial and Court Statistics, 2012, Table 2.4). In addition, candidates must be prepared to discuss the general principles of the **CA 1989**, for example the welfare principle, when answering questions on the public law. The final question in this chapter focuses on the child's wishes which, of course, appears on the welfare checklist.

Question 1

Les, a trainee local authority social worker, would be grateful for your advice on one of his current cases.

Molly, who is 21 and unmarried, has two children, Norman aged 5 and Oscar aged 1. Six months ago Peter, aged 18 years, moved in with them and Molly is expecting their child. Staff at the local health centre are concerned that Oscar is underweight and failing to thrive. Norman's teacher, Miss Quinn, is concerned that he has become rather withdrawn in the last few months. Her view, when he started school a year ago, was that he was small for his age and not very clean. When she attempted to discuss the matter with Molly she was told cheerfully 'All kids hate washing, don't they?' Les thinks that Molly loves her children and cares for them, albeit in a rather haphazard manner, and although she has serious learning difficulties she has managed to cope until recently. Molly no longer attends the clinic at the health centre and when the health visitor called recently Peter refused to let her into the house. Neighbours have contacted the social services department reporting that the children were out in the garden late at night in cold weather wearing thin clothes and no shoes.

Miss Quinn has informed Les that as a result of talks with Norman she suspects he is being sexually abused by Peter. Molly screamed at her to 'keep out of it' when Miss Quinn suggested that Norman should have a medical examination.

Les thinks that the time has come to take immediate action.

 Commentary

This problem question requires you to consider the powers given to a local authority for the emergency protection of children. As Les wishes to take 'immediate action' to protect Oscar and Norman you should discuss local authority investigations, emergency protection orders, exclusion requirements and child assessment orders, but it is not necessary to consider long-term options, such as a care order or a supervision order. Nor is it necessary to consider removal by the police under **s. 46(1)** as this is only required in exceptional cases where there is insufficient time to apply for an emergency protection order. You should, however, explore the steps that can be taken (if any) to protect Molly's baby, once it is born.

 Answer plan

- Local authority duty to investigate, **s. 47 CA 1989**.
- Protection of children—**Part V CA 1989**.
- Child assessment order, **s. 43**.
- Emergency protection order, **s. 44**.
- Exclusion requirements, **ss. 38A and 44A**.

Examiner's tip

Child assessment orders and emergency protection orders are not 'family proceedings' and so the court hearing the application cannot make a **s. 8** order in lieu.

Suggested answer

Les is aware of the concern that has been expressed about the welfare of the children by staff at the health centre, the health visitor, Molly's neighbours and Miss Quinn and so, understandably, wishes to do something. Where a local authority has reasonable cause to suspect that a child is suffering, or is likely to suffer significant harm, it must investigate before it decides what action to take (**s. 47 Children Act (CA) 1989**, see *Re S (Sexual Abuse Allegations: Local Authority Response)* [2001] 2 FLR 776). Action under **s. 47** is normally the first step to be taken when a question of child protection arises. Les should attempt to work in partnership with the family and, except in emergencies, case conferences (which are multi-disciplinary, interagency meetings designed to create an action plan for protecting the child and helping the family), should be held before anyone contemplates removing a child. The early involvement of the local authority lawyer would allow evaluation of the evidence and consideration of the options available. Any intervention by the local authority must be looked at from the child's point of view, i.e. is it going to do more harm than good? If Les acts on insufficient information the children may be removed from a home where they are not in danger, or removed and returned to a home where they are in danger. The questions that must be asked are: is this an emergency situation where immediate action must be taken, is there enough evidence to initiate proceedings and if not, how can such evidence be obtained?

A child assessment order (CAO) using **s. 43 CA 1989** may be able to provide the evidence that Les requires and is suitable for non-emergency situations. As Munby J explained in *X Council v B (Emergency Protection Order)* [2004] EWHC 2015 (Fam), if the objective is to assess a child, rather than to protect him or her from immediate harm, a CAO may be more effective and less intrusive than an emergency protection order. Only the local authority or the National Society for the Prevention of Cruelty to Children (NSPCC) can apply for a CAO and in 2011 only nine orders were made (Judicial and Court Statistics, 2012, Table 2.4). This order may be granted by the court if the applicant has reasonable cause to suspect that the child is suffering or is likely to suffer significant harm, an assessment is necessary to determine this and is unlikely to be made without such an order (**s. 43(1)**). The court must be satisfied with the reasonableness of the applicant's belief.

If the local authority decides that a CAO is appropriate it must take reasonably practicable steps to give notice of the application to Molly; the children's father; Peter (if he has parental responsibility, or is regarded as another person caring for the child); and

Norman and Oscar (**s. 43(11)**). As the notice period is seven days, this order is not suitable where there is a need for urgent action. A CAO imposes a duty to produce the child to the person named in the order for assessment (**s. 43(6)**). The local authority does not acquire parental responsibility on the granting of a CAO. As a CAO can last for no longer than seven days and cannot be extended, Les should ensure that arrangements for the assessment have been carefully planned so that the time available is not wasted. A CAO does not allow a child to be removed from home unless the court makes a direction to that effect (**s. 43(9)**) and the child must be returned home as soon as possible. The results of the assessment should give enough information for the authority to decide whether or not to apply for an emergency protection order, or a care or supervision order. It may be that the fears were unfounded or it may be that the problem, if there is one, could be dealt with in another way, for example with local authority support for Molly and the provision of child care classes. That may seem somewhat naive and optimistic in view of the fact that as Molly is carrying Peter's child he is likely to be around for the foreseeable future, even though the chances of a long-term relationship may seem unlikely.

Les may be concerned to hear that if Molly were to fail to comply with a CAO there is nothing that can be done to enforce it. However, the local authority would be unlikely to allow the matter to rest there and would almost certainly apply for, and get, an EPO. Indeed, if, during **s. 47 CA 1989** enquiries, access to a child is refused, the local authority has a *duty* to apply for an EPO if the child's welfare demands it (**s. 44(1)(b)**).

The court must not make a CAO if there are grounds for making an EPO (**s. 43(4)**) and may treat a CAO application as an EPO application (**s. 43(3)**). It may be that a thorough and complete assessment could not be carried out in seven days, so Les may think it necessary to apply for EPOs, which can be for up to eight days (**s. 45(2)(a)**) but can be extended for up to another seven days using **s. 45(4) and (5)**. By then there should be enough evidence to allow the authority to decide whether or not to proceed with a care application. The local authority may take the view that applying for a CAO is an appropriate course of action in relation to Oscar; however, Norman appears to be in immediate danger and as a consequence, an EPO (**s. 44**), rather than a CAO is likely to be sought by the local authority. The court will only make an EPO under **s. 44 CA 1989** if it is satisfied that there is reasonable cause to believe the child is likely to suffer significant harm if he is not removed from, or does not remain in, his present accommodation (**s. 44(1)(a)**). Unlike child assessment orders, anyone can apply for an EPO and, in 2011, 1,181 EPOs were made (Judicial and Court Statistics, 2012, Table 2.4). An EPO application (unlike an application for a child assessment order) can be made on a without notice basis. In the case of an application by a local authority, the court may only make an order if it is satisfied that enquiries in respect of the child are being made under **s. 47(1)(b)** and that those enquiries are being frustrated by access to the child being unreasonably refused to a person authorized to seek access and that the applicant has reasonable cause to believe that access to the child is required as a matter of urgency (**s. 44(1)(b)**). This lowers the hurdle considerably in many cases, as where **s. 44(1)(b)** is satisfied, no other threshold test applies. The local authority will not have to prove that the removal must be immediate for an EPO to be granted. Peter may promise to leave the home, the power to remove the child who is the subject of the order would continue for the duration of the order and if Peter were to return, the child could be removed.

Powers are given to the court to exclude an alleged abuser when making an interim care order (s. 38A) or an EPO (s. 44A). The exclusion requirement can be made where the grounds for an interim care order or an EPO have been made out and there is reasonable cause to believe that if Peter is excluded from the home, the child will cease to suffer or cease to be likely to suffer significant harm and that Molly is able and willing to give the child the care it would be reasonable to expect a parent to give him. Additionally, and here lies the problem, Molly must consent to the inclusion of the exclusion requirement. A power of arrest may be attached to the exclusion requirement (s. 38A(5)) or the court may accept an undertaking from Peter, instead of making an exclusion requirement. Molly could apply under **Part IV of the Family Law Act 1996** for a non-molestation or occupation order against Peter, to protect Norman from abuse, but this seems unlikely in the circumstances and the local authority cannot apply for such orders (see **Chapter 5**). If the local authority wants contact to be restricted and/or the child to be medically examined, it should ensure that the application requests such conditions.

Even if the conditions for making an EPO or a CAO are satisfied, the court is not bound to make an order. The child's welfare must be the court's paramount consideration (s. 1(1)) and the court must be satisfied that it would be better to make an order than no order at all (s. 1(5)). Applications for a CAO or an EPO do not come within family proceedings and, as a consequence, the court has no power to make s. 8 orders even where an EPO or a CAO is refused.

If the local authority successfully applies for an EPO, it acquires parental responsibility for the child but must allow reasonable contact between the child who is the subject of the order and Molly. The court could give directions for assessment and prohibit contact between the children and Peter, or allow supervised contact so that neither Molly nor Peter are allowed to put pressure on the children to persuade them to withdraw any allegations.

Prior to the **Children and Young Persons Act 2008**, an application could be made to discharge the order only after 72 hours had expired. The **2008 Act** removed this requirement and so Molly or Peter, as a person with whom the child was living prior to the order, could apply to discharge the order immediately.

If Les is concerned about the care a newborn baby would receive from Molly and Peter, he could advise the local authority to make an application for a care order (s. 31), or an EPO, immediately after the birth of the baby, on the basis that the child is likely to suffer significant harm. A baby certainly should not be removed from its mother without the sanction of the court, unless it is an emergency situation. In *R (G) v Nottingham City Council* [2008] EWHC 152 (**Admin**) an interagency child protection conference that took place prior to the child's birth recommended that the local authority apply for an interim care order once the baby was born. The child was removed from its mother two hours after the birth but no interim care order had been made. The removal was therefore unlawful as the child was not in immediate danger. However, following the European Court of Human Rights decision in *P, C and S v UK* [2002] 2 FLR 631 even the removal of a baby under an EPO may breach the parents' right to respect for family life under **Art. 8 of the European Convention for the Protection of Human Rights and Fundamental Freedoms 1950.** Local authorities should, when managing a perceived risk, try to find a way to allow mother and child to remain together in order to prevent a challenge under **Art. 8.** For example, in *Re J (Residential Assessment: Rights of Audience)* [2009] EWCA Civ 1210 the mother and child were taken into residential care to assess the mother's parenting abilities. In this instance her ability was thought to be inadequate and the local authority initiated care proceedings. However the case demonstrates that local authorities can protect a child and assess the risk to it without infringing the mother's rights under **Art. 8.** In the case of Molly's unborn child, the need to take action will depend upon whether Peter is part of her life and whether the care given to Norman and Oscar has improved by the time the baby is born.

 Question 2

During the course of their turbulent marriage, Stan has left his wife Rose and their three children (aged 14, 12 and 9) on numerous occasions. Last year, on one of these occasions, it all became too much for Rose and she attempted suicide. She was admitted to hospital and voluntary arrangements were made for the children with the local authority. The children were looked after for almost a year by Mr and Mrs Taylor who are experienced foster parents. Contact between the children and their mother was maintained by visits and letters.

Rose and the children returned to the family home three months ago, Stan joined them a month later. Last week Stan walked out 'never to return' and Rose has become extremely depressed fearing that she cannot cope on her own. The hospital is willing to take her as a voluntary patient. Rose contacted the local authority with a view to making a voluntary arrangement for the children and much to her relief was told that Mr and Mrs Taylor were able and willing to look after the children again. The children are distressed about their mother's health but feel reassured that they will be able to be accommodated in familiar surroundings with people they know and like.

Rose was due to go into hospital tomorrow, but yesterday Stan telephoned her, stating that he did not think that she should abandon the children in this way and that he intended to oppose the arrangement. Stan has a job as a long distance lorry driver making deliveries around Europe, which involves him being out of the country for three weeks in every month. Rose is concerned that even if the children go to Mr and Mrs Taylor's home, Stan will remove them when he returns to the UK.

Can the other parties involved ensure that their plans will not be disrupted by Stan?

Commentary

The main area that you are required to consider in this answer is local authority support for children and families under **Part III of the CA 1989**. As yet, there is no general test for competency in parenting; Stan has parental responsibility but does not appear to be behaving very responsibly. Nothing short of adoption can take away his parental responsibility, but as this question and answer illustrate, parental responsibility may have to be shared or, it could be argued, restricted.

Answer plan

- Local authority support for children and families—**Part III CA 1989**.
- Local authority duty to children in need, **s. 17 CA 1989**.
- Parental responsibility, **s. 2, s. 3**.
- Provision of accommodation, **s. 20**.
- Removal from jurisdiction, **s. 13(1)(b) CA 1989**. **Child Abduction Act 1984**.
- Wardship.
- Residence order—**s. 8**.
- Local authority intervention.

Examiner's tip

Although this question focuses on local authority support for families in need, students require knowledge of the law on parental responsibility and residence in order to answer it fully.

Suggested answer

Rose wishes to make a voluntary arrangement with the local authority so that her children can be accommodated by them while she is in hospital. Every local authority has a general duty to safeguard and promote the welfare of children in its area who are in need and, so far as is consistent with that duty, to promote the upbringing of such children by their families (**s. 17(1) Children Act (CA) 1989**). It appears that the local authority was supportive the last time Rose went into hospital and that there was a successful voluntary partnership which safeguarded the welfare of the children. Rose and Stan each have parental responsibility as they are the natural and legal parents of the children and they are married to each other (**s. 2(1)**). 'Parental responsibility' means all the rights, duties, powers, responsibilities and authority which by law a parent of a child has in relation to the child and his property (s. 3(1)). Rose and Stan will have the responsibility for raising their children, but the local authority has a duty to accommodate children in need in its area when the person caring for them is prevented from looking after them. Where there is a voluntary arrangement, the local authority does not acquire parental responsibility. Even where children are taken into care and a local authority acquires parental responsibility (s. 33(3)), the parents do not lose parental responsibility, they share it with the local authority (s. 2(6)). However, the role of the local authority should not be underestimated. As the House of Lords pointed out in *R (M) v Hammersmith and Fulham London Borough Council* [2008] UKHL 14, local authorities 'are nevertheless replacing to some extent the role played by the parent in a child's life' (para. 20).

Before providing accommodation under s. 20 the local authority must, so far as is reasonably practicable and consistent with the child's welfare, ascertain the child's wishes regarding the provision of accommodation and give due consideration (having regard to his age and understanding) to such wishes. As far as these three children are concerned, living with the Taylors appears to be the next best thing to living with their mother when she is well.

Where there is more than one person with parental responsibility for a child, each of them may act alone and without the other in meeting that responsibility (s. 2(7)). Therefore Rose may make arrangements with the local authority without waiting to consult Stan. Nevertheless, the Act acknowledges the continuing nature of parental responsibility and allows Stan, as a person with parental responsibility, to object to the local authority providing accommodation. Stan must be able to show that he is willing and able to provide or arrange alternative accommodation for the children (s. 20(7)). It seems unlikely that Stan can provide accommodation if he continues with his present job, and as he made no arrangements the last time the children were accommodated by the local authority, this may suggest that he may not be able to do so on this occasion. If Rose were to apply for and be granted residence orders in respect of the children, this would prevent Stan objecting to the voluntary arrangement (s. 20(9)(a)). Before making a residence order, which is an order settling the arrangements to be made as to where the child is to live (s. 8(1)), the court would need to be satisfied that doing so would be better than making no order at all (s. 1(5)). When considering whether to make a residence order, the child's welfare must be the court's paramount consideration (s. 1(1)), and where the making of the order is opposed by any party to the proceedings, the court must have regard to the welfare checklist (s. 1(3)), which includes a consideration of the capability each of the child's parents has in relation to meeting that child's needs. Although Rose has problems of her own, her children appear to be her first concern whereas Stan, from the most benevolent viewpoint, could at best be described as feckless or, more realistically, uncaring for his wife and children and totally selfish. Stan may argue that a residence order would take away his right to object to the children being accommodated; so in his view it should not be granted. He does not appear to have been a responsible parent when times were hard and in the final analysis it is not Stan's 'rights' which are important but the welfare of the children.

However, Stan could wait until the children are living with the Taylors and then, without notice, remove them (**s. 20(8)**) provided no person with a residence order objects. Unlike **s. 20(7)**, there is no requirement in **s. 20(8)** for the parent to be able to accommodate the child. Stan may not remove the children if Rose has a residence order (**s. 20(9)**). Where a residence order is in force with respect to a child, no person may remove him from the UK without either the written consent of every person who has parental responsibility for the child or the leave of the court (**s. 13(1)(b)**). Stan should be warned that the **Child Abduction Act 1984** makes it a criminal offence for anyone with parental responsibility for a child under 16 to take the child out of the UK, without the consent of all those with parental responsibility, or leave of the court.

If the Taylors are concerned about Stan taking the children away, they could apply for wardship under the inherent jurisdiction of the High Court (see **Chapter 6**). This may be getting more involved than they contemplated when they agreed to foster children for the local authority. As the children lived with them for less than one year, the Taylors cannot apply for leave to apply for a residence order unless they have the consent of the local authority (**s. 9(3)**). If the court were to grant the Taylors a residence order, then they would have parental responsibility while the order was in force (**s. 12(2)**). Parental responsibility would be shared with Rose and Stan. Even if the Taylors do not acquire parental responsibility, they, as persons with care of the children, may (subject to the provisions of the **CA 1989**) do what is reasonable in all the circumstances of the case for the purpose of safeguarding or promoting the child's welfare (**s. 3(5)**).

The children could apply to court for leave to make applications for residence orders, if they did not wish to go with their father (**s. 10(8)**). The court may only grant leave if it is satisfied that a child has sufficient understanding to make the proposed application for the residence order (*Re C (Residence: Child's Application for Leave)* [1995] 1 FLR 927 and *Re H (Residence Order: Child, Application for Leave)* [2001] 1 FLR 780). The court could make residence orders stating that the children are to remain with their foster parents.

If no one has residence orders in respect of the children, the local authority could apply for an emergency protection order (EPO) or for a care or supervision order. An EPO would appear to be an extreme reaction to the situation and would require the local authority to satisfy the court that there is reasonable cause to believe that the children are likely to suffer significant harm if they do not remain with the Taylors (**s. 44(1)(a)**). For a care or supervision order to be granted the court would have to be satisfied that the children would suffer significant harm if they were to be taken away from the Taylors by Stan and that the harm is attributable to some deficiency in parental care (**s. 31(2)**). Any **s. 8** orders would be discharged automatically by the making of a care order (**s. 91(2)**) and any non-parent would lose parental responsibility. Rose could apply for a discharge of the order (**s. 39**) when she returns home. With local authority support providing a range and level of services appropriate to the children's needs (**s. 17(1)**), she should be able to cope without Stan.

It is up to the local authority, considering its own circumstances and resources, to determine how to respond to the needs of children in its area (*R (G) v Barnet London Borough Council; R (W) v Lambeth London Borough Council; R (A) v Lambeth London Borough Council* [2003] 3 WLR 1194). In *Re T (Judicial Review: Local Authority Decisions Concerning Children in Need)* [2004] 1 FLR 590, it was said that although the court could direct the local authority to reconsider the services it should provide for the claimant, it could not direct the local authority to take a particular course.

If the local authority is concerned that the children may be in and out of accommodation, and is of the view that this would be unsettling for the children, it should clarify the legal position to the parents and explain that it, the local authority, may decide to instigate care proceedings. The *Practice Direction Public Law Proceedings Guide to Case Management 2010* indicates that local authorities should notify parents of their intention to apply for a care or supervision order in a 'letter before proceedings'. This may make Stan come to his senses and stop him using the children to punish Rose for their failing marriage. One of the main aims of the Act is to make decisions about children more child-centred and in the best interests of the children. Hopefully, Stan may be brought round to this point of view before more drastic action needs to be taken by the local authority.

 Question 3

Adam, aged 12, was found by the police yesterday after his mother, Barbara, had reported him missing. He was found at the railway station attempting to board a train to where his father lives with his new family. Adam has run away from home on numerous occasions since his mother married Clive a year ago. Barbara and Clive are partners in a very successful interior design consultancy.

Diane, a local authority social worker was allocated to Adam's case six months ago but does not feel she has made much progress. Barbara and Clive always listen politely and benignly to the advice that Diane offers but do nothing about putting her advice into practice. Diane is finding their attitude rather patronizing.

The headmaster of Adam's school is very concerned about Adam's persistent absenteeism.

Diane feels that anything that money can buy is lavished on Adam but that he lacks time and attention from Barbara and Clive. Diane is convinced that Adam should be taken into care.

Advise Diane.

Commentary

This question requires students to consider the course of action that Diane, a local authority social worker, should take in relation to Adam who has run away from home on a number of occasions and regularly misses school. Students should discuss the possibility of an educational supervision order but also whether a care order or supervision order should be sought. In relation to the latter two orders, the problem for Diane is for her to satisfy the court that the threshold criteria for an order have been satisfied under **s. 31 CA 1989**.

Answer plan

- Removal and accommodation of children by police in cases of emergency, **s. 46 CA 1989**.
- Education supervision order, **s. 36**.
- Welfare of the child, **s. 1**.
- Application for care order—threshold criteria, **s. 31**.
- Beyond parental control.
- Guardian, **s. 41**.
- Effects of care/supervision orders.

Examiner's tip

Do not assume that in such an affluent family a child could not suffer harm—the **CA 1989** recognizes that a child's emotional development can be impaired by lack of emotional care and education.

Suggested answer

If the police had reasonable cause to believe that Adam would be likely to suffer significant harm, they could have removed him to suitable accommodation and kept him there for up to 72 hours (**Children Act (CA) 1989, s. 46**). The police do not acquire parental responsibility but are given the power to apply on behalf of the appropriate authority for an emergency protection order under **s. 44**. Diane should note that it would appear that the police did not regard any of the incidents as an emergency as they returned Adam to his home rather than taking him into police protection.

Diane should consider an education supervision order (ESO) as a first step to ensure Adam's attendance at school. If the local education authority is considering applying for an ESO to deal with Adam's truancy, it must consult the social services committee (s. 36(8)). On the application of the local education authority, the court may make an ESO (s. 36(1)) where it is satisfied that the child is of compulsory school age and is not being properly educated (s. 36(3)). A child requires efficient full-time education suitable to his age, ability and aptitude and any special educational needs he may have. Where he is a pupil at a school which he is not attending regularly, it will be assumed that he is not being properly educated unless it is proved otherwise (s. 36(5)). Adam's welfare must be the court's paramount consideration (s. 1(1)) and the court must have regard to the statutory checklist (s. 1(3)) and the no order principle (s. 1(5)). A care order could be made if everything that could have been done under an ESO had already been tried (*Re O (A Minor) (Care Order: Education: Procedure)* [1992] 2 FLR 7).

An ESO is intended to transfer the primary obligation to ensure that the child is educated from the parent to the local education authority. While the ESO is in force it is the duty of the supervisor to advise, assist, befriend and give directions to the child, his parents and any person with parental responsibility for him, in order that the child is properly educated. Initially, an ESO will be for one year although the court may extend the order. Adam, his parents, anyone with parental responsibility and the local education authority may apply to discharge the ESO. Clive, on his marriage to Barbara, will not have automatically acquired parental responsibility for Adam, although he would acquire it if he is granted a residence order in respect of Adam. In addition, as Adam's stepfather he could acquire parental responsibility under **s. 4A CA 1989** by agreement with Barbara (and Adam's father if he has parental responsibility) or by court order.

Truancy alone is not a ground for a care order, although if the truancy is a symptom of a wider problem a care order could be available. Application for a care order can be made only by the local authority or the NSPCC. Before the local authority makes a decision with respect to Adam it has a duty under **s. 22** to ascertain his wishes, the wishes of his parents and anyone else with parental responsibility.

In any application for a care or supervision order, the court should appoint a children's guardian unless satisfied that it is not necessary to do so in order to safeguard the child's interests (s. 41(1)). The children's guardian will wish to establish the grounds for the local authority's application. The children's guardian will meet Adam and establish what he wants to happen; see Adam's father and hopefully discuss Adam's feelings of rejection and the need for contact in the future; and meet Barbara and Clive and Adam's headmaster and hear their views. A solicitor will be appointed and instructed to act for Adam by the children's guardian.

The only way that a local authority can take a child into care is by going to court and satisfying the threshold criteria set out in **s. 31**. It must be established that the child is suffering or is likely to suffer significant harm (s. 31(2)(a)). The words 'is suffering' refer to the period immediately before the process of protecting the child is first put in motion (*Re G (Children) (Care Order: Evidence of Threshold Conditions)* [2001] 2 FLR 1111). The burden of proof of showing to the court's satisfaction that the child is likely to suffer significant harm lies on the applicant and the standard of proof is the ordinary civil standard, i.e. the balance of probabilities. In the past, it was thought that the more serious or improbable the allegation of abuse, the more convincing is the evidence required to prove the allegation. However, in *Re B (Care Proceedings: Standard of Proof)* [2008] UKHL 35 the House of Lords declared that this was not the case as there was 'no logical or necessary connection between seriousness and probability' (para. 72). A conclusion that the child is suffering, or is likely to suffer harm has to be based on facts, not just suspicion (*Re H and others (Minors) (Sexual Abuse: Standard of Proof)* [1996] 1 All ER 1). 'Harm' means ill treatment or the impairment of health or development (s. 31(9)). There is no definition of 'significant' in the Act but in *Humberside CC v B* [1993] 1 FLR 257 the court indicated that it should not be equated with 'substantial' but means 'considerable', 'noteworthy' or 'important'. Impairment of health or development will cover cases of neglect of emotional care and in such circumstances the court is directed to compare the child's health or development with that which could reasonably be expected of a similar child. In the case of a truant of average intelligence, 'similar child' was held to be a child of equivalent intellectual and social development who has gone to school and not merely an average child who may or may not be at school (*Re O (A Minor) (Care Order: Education: Procedure)* [1992] 2 FLR 7). To assess if Adam's development has been impaired, he will be compared with an average 12-year-old who does attend school regularly. Where truancy caused the child's intellectual and social development to suffer, she was thereby suffering significant harm (*Re O (A Minor) (Care Order: Education: Procedure)* (see earlier)).

Section 31(2)(b) requires the harm or likelihood of harm to be attributable to the lack of reasonable care by the parent, or to the child being beyond parental control (*Lancashire County Council and Another v B and Another* [2000] 2 AC 147; *North Yorkshire County Council v SA* [2003] 2 FLR 849). In addition to a finding of significant harm, the court must evaluate the care given to Adam and then ask itself whether that care meets the required standard or whether Adam is beyond parental control. The lack of parental control could be the fault of the parents or the child. In addition, truancy may occur because the child is beyond parental control or because the care given to the child does not meet the required standard. In *Re O (A Minor) (Care Order: Education: Procedure)* (see earlier) the court stated that if 'a child is suffering harm in not going to school and is living at home it will follow that the child is beyond her parents' control *or* that they are not giving the child the care that it would be reasonable for a parent to give.' Most care orders are based on the care or lack of care given to the child: a care-profiling study conducted by the Ministry of Justice in 2008 showed that only five out of 386 cases examined were based upon the child being beyond parental control (*Care Profiling Study* (Ministry of Justice, 2008), p. 36).

Even if the s. 31 threshold is crossed, the court has a discretion whether to grant a care or a supervision order or not, and if it decides not to do so it may either make a s. 8 order or it may decide to make no order; Adam's welfare is the paramount consideration (s. 1(1)). The court will consider the welfare checklist which includes a duty to listen and ascertain the wishes and feelings of the child. The weight placed on Adam's wishes will depend on his age and understanding; the court will be guided by the children's guardian. While the court has a duty to listen to Adam's wishes, it will not be constricted by those wishes and will disregard them if his future welfare appears to diverge from them. It is the decision of the court and not the child (*Re P (A Minor) (Education)* [1992] 1 FLR 316).

An assessment of what the local authority has done before instigating proceedings will have been carried out by the children's guardian, followed by an exploration of the possibility of an agreement between the local authority and Adam's parents to avoid court proceedings. It may be that the children's guardian will be more successful than Diane in persuading the parties to face their responsibilities when they realize the potential consequences of their thoughtlessness. Hopefully, Adam's mother and father will make an arrangement, taking into consideration Adam's wishes, as to where he should live, with sufficient contact with the non-residential parent. If the matter proceeds to court the children's guardian will advise whether any order is necessary to protect the child's interests.

The court will need to be satisfied that the making of an order is better for Adam than making no order (**s. 1(5)**). The court may make a **s. 8** order as an alternative to a care or supervision order, whether or not the threshold criteria are proved.

On the granting of a care order the local authority acquires parental responsibility, which is shared with the parents. Where a care order is made the responsibility for the child's care is with the authority rather than the court. The court retains no supervisory role monitoring the authority's discharge of its responsibilities (*Re S (Minors) (Care Order: Implementation of Care Plan); Re W (Minors) (Care Order: Adequacy of Care Plan)* [2002] 1 FLR 815).

It should be noted that the making of a care order does not necessarily mean that the child will be removed from his or her parents. Amendments to the **CA 1989** made by the **Children and Young Persons Act 2008** require a local authority to make arrangements for the child to live with a parent, or a person with parental responsibility or a person in whose favour a residence order had been made prior to the care order, unless to do so would be inconsistent with the child's welfare or would not be reasonably practicable (**s. 22C(3) and (4)**). If this is not possible, the authority should attempt to accommodate the child with other relatives or friends (**s. 22C(6)(a) and (7)(a)**). The latter need to be approved as local authority foster parents.

After care proceedings have come to an end and the local authority is implementing the care plan, the requirements of **Art. 8** of the **European Convention** still apply. Parents must be involved in the decision-making process, even when proceedings have come to an end and the care plan is being implemented (*Re G (Care: Challenge to Local Authority's Decision)* [2003] 2 FLR 42). Following the **Adoption and Children Act 2002** the local authority must appoint an independent reviewing officer to oversee the implementation of the care plan.

If a supervision order were to be made, Adam would be placed under the supervision of the local authority (**s. 31(1)**). Neither the supervisor nor the local authority would acquire parental responsibility. It is the duty of the supervisor to advise, assist and befriend the child. This may seem more appropriate than a care order because if any child needs assisting or befriending it would appear to be Adam (*Re O (Supervision Order)* [2001] 1 FLR 923).

Question 4

Are the wishes and feelings of the child presented to the court satisfactorily in care proceedings?

 Commentary

This essay question instructs students to consider whether the 'voice of the child' is heard satisfactorily in the context of care proceedings. You are required to evaluate the provisions of the **CA 1989** which allow a child's voice to be heard in care proceedings, namely the statutory checklist and the role of the children's guardian. It should be noted that the **CA 1989** contains further provisions that enable children who are subject to a care order to have their views taken into account, for example **s. 34** (application for contact or for contact to be refused) and **s. 39** (application to vary or discharge a care order), however, these are post-order issues and so have not been included in the suggested answer.

 Answer plan

Issues/areas to include	Application to the question
Gillick v West Norfolk and Wisbech AHA [1986]	Recognizes the rights of mature children to make decisions.
S. 1 CA 1989—the welfare principle	In care proceedings, the child's welfare is paramount (not his views)
S. 1(3)—the welfare checklist	The ascertainable wishes and feelings of the child should be considered in the light of his age and understanding. It does not have priority over other factors in the checklist.
Appointment of a children's guardian—**s. 41**	The guardian represents the child's interests and will ascertain his views. The guardian may recommend that the court does not follow the child's wishes.
Duties of the guardian	Will communicate the child's views to the court if the child does not attend.
Appointment of a solicitor	Separation representation can ensure that the child's voice is heard.
The court hearing—**Re W** [2010]	No presumption against the child giving evidence.

Examiner's tip

Avoid a detailed description of the aspects of care proceedings that do not address the question set.

 Suggested answer

After the decision in *Gillick v West Norfolk and Wisbech AHA* [1986] 1 FLR 224, there was a recognition that children should have more influence over decisions which affect them and in the Cleveland Report it was said that 'the child is a person and not an object of concern' (*Report of the Inquiry into Child Abuse in Cleveland 1987* (Cm 412, 1988)).

In response, the **Children Act (CA) 1989** recognizes that the views of a child should be taken into account and in the checklist contained in the Act the court is directed to have regard, amongst other matters, in particular to the ascertainable wishes and feelings of the child concerned, considered in the light of his age and understanding (**s. 1(3)(a)**). The statutory checklist is designed to assist the court in operating the welfare principle which must be applied in certain specified proceedings.

In care proceedings, once the court is satisfied that the grounds for an order exist, the principle that 'the child's welfare shall be the court's paramount consideration' will be applied (**s. 1(1)**) and the court will consider the welfare checklist. Although the wishes and feelings of the child are first on the checklist of factors to be taken into account, that does not give them priority over other items on the checklist, including any harm the child is suffering or is at risk of suffering (*Re J (A Minor)*[1992] 2 FCR 785). Nonetheless, there has become an increasing awareness of the importance of listening to the views of older children and taking into account what they say, not necessarily agreeing with what they want nor doing what they want, but paying proper respect to older children who are of an age and maturity to make up their minds as to what they think is best for them. It should be borne in mind that older children very often have an appreciation of their own situation which is worthy of consideration by, and the respect of, adults and the courts (*Re S (Contact: Children's Views)* [2002] 1 FLR 1156, children of 16, 14, and 12).

In care proceedings the court must appoint a children's guardian for the child concerned, unless it is satisfied that it is not necessary to do so in order to safeguard his interests (**s. 41(1)**). The Children and Family Court Advisory and Support Service (CAFCASS) has a duty to ensure that there are sufficient officers of the service for appointment as guardian to meet fully the requirements imposed by statute. However, in *R v Children and Family Court Advisory and Support Service* [2003] 1 FLR 953, the court took the view that CAFCASS was not under a duty to provide a guardian immediately. The 'no delay' principle in **s. 1(2) CA 1989** did not, of itself, found a conclusion that all steps had to be taken immediately or that CAFCASS had to make an officer available immediately on request.

The independence of the guardian is important. A local authority cannot interfere with the manner in which children's guardians consider it necessary to carry out their duties (*R v Cornwall County Council, ex p G* [1992] 1 FLR 270). The children's guardian does not represent the local authority, rather, his or her primary duty is to safeguard the interests of the child (**s. 41(2)(b)**). The children's guardian will wish to establish the grounds for the local authority application for a care order and examine and take copies of local authority records in relation to the child (**s. 42**) (*Re T (A Minor) (Guardian ad Litem: Case Record)* [1994] 1 FLR 632). The child's wishes and feelings should be ascertained by the children's guardian and it should be ensured that the child understands that, although his views will be communicated to the court, the children's guardian may recommend that the court does not follow his wishes.

Parents, anyone with parental responsibility and anyone who is felt to be important to the child, for example teachers, doctors or relatives or anyone whose information can assist in safeguarding the interests of the child, must be seen by the children's guardian. After these investigations, the children's guardian produces a written report which advises on the interests of the child. The report should be filed with the court seven days before the hearing and copies are served, by the court, on the parties.

A solicitor will be appointed and instructed by the children's guardian to act for the child. Where a solicitor is satisfied that the child wishes and is able to give instructions which conflict with the children's guardian, then instructions are to be taken solely from the child (*Re H (A Minor) (Care Proceedings: Child's Wishes)* [1993] 1 FLR 440). Separation representation can ensure that the child's voice is heard, but this does not mean that the child will actually attend the hearing and present oral evidence (see later).

The framework within which the children's guardian has to operate is set out in the **Family Proceedings Rules 1991**. The children's guardian will have a duty to advise and work with the court in regard to timetabling in the child's best interests. There is a general principle that any delay in determining the question is likely to prejudice the welfare of the child (**s. 1(2)**). It may be that the child could benefit from a constructive delay, but what should not happen is that the proceedings be allowed to drift without control. If the delay is purposeful it should be encouraged (*C v Solihull Metropolitan Borough Council and Others* [1993] 1 FLR 290). The court will also look to the children's guardian to advise on the appropriate court to deal with an application.

At each hearing the children's guardian has to advise the court of the options available from the range of orders, and their suitability. The wishes of the child and the weight to be given to those wishes must be conveyed to the court and the court should be advised on whether the child should attend each hearing. In *Re O (Care Proceedings: Evidence)* [2004] 1 FLR 161 the court refused to hear oral evidence from the child. The courts have thus been sensitive to the potentially harmful impact of court attendance on a child (*Re W (Secure Accommodation Order: Attendance at Court)* [1994] 2 FLR 1092). They have had to balance the rights of children to participate and be heard against their need to be protected from exposure to material that might be damaging (*Re A (Care: Discharge Application by Child)* [1995] 1 FLR 599). In *LM (By her Guardian) v Medway Council, RM and YM* [2007] EWCA Civ 9 the Court of Appeal upheld a decision that it was appropriate for a 10-year-old girl to give evidence to the court by videolink. However, the court indicated that the starting point is that it is undesirable for a child to give evidence in care proceedings. But in *Re W (Children)* [2010] UKSC 12 the Supreme Court confirmed that there is no presumption against a child giving evidence in care proceedings. There will, however, be circumstances when it is inappropriate for the child to do so. In *Re J (Child Giving Evidence)* [2010] EWHC 962 a teenage boy who was the subject of care proceedings was permitted to give evidence, because he particularly wished to do so and would feel a sense of injustice if his request was refused. This demonstrates that the child's voice can be heard in public law proceedings. If a child is not permitted to attend a hearing, his or her views will have to be presented by the children's guardian. The report of the children's guardian is not binding on the court, but it has a considerable influence on the court's decision and the court should give reasons if the recommendations are not to be followed (*S v Oxfordshire County Council* [1993] Fam Law 74).

The **CA 1989** has recognized that children's wishes and feelings should command serious attention and provides a structure and personnel (the children's guardian in care proceedings) to allow that voice to be heard. It is nevertheless acknowledged that children are vulnerable and impressionable, lacking the maturity to weigh the longer term against the shorter (*Re S (A Minor) (Representation: Child's Wishes)* [1993] Fam Law 244). The duty of the children's guardian is to safeguard the interests of the child; that is achieved not only by ascertaining the wishes of the child but also taking into account the wider issues and recognizing that a child can be manipulated by adults and is not necessarily mature enough to appreciate what is in his own best interest. The court has a duty to listen to and ascertain the wishes and feelings of the child, but the court will not be constricted by those wishes and should disregard them if the child's future welfare appears to diverge from his expressed wishes. It has to be the decision of the court and not the child (*Re P (A Minor) (Education)* [1992] 1 FLR 316).

Therefore the wishes of the child will be presented to the court but not necessarily followed by the court. This may not satisfy the child but the wishes of the child are *not* the most important factor. The court's decision will be consistent with one of the main aims of the Act which is that the welfare of the child is paramount.

Further reading

Brophy, J. and Cover, M. (2012) 'Children, the Recession and Family Courts'. Fam Law 526.

Davis, L. (2011) 'Baby P's Serious Case Reviews: Some Legal Lessons'. Fam Law 43.

Department for Children, Schools and Families (2010) *Working Together to Safeguard Children—A Guide to Inter-Agency Working to Safeguard and Promote the Welfare of Children.*

Jones, M. (2012) 'Placing a Child Within the Family: Section 20 v Private Fostering'. Fam Law 558.

Keating, H. (2011) '*Re MA*: The Significance of Harm'. 23(1) CFLQ 115.

Ministry of Justice (2011) *Family Justice Review Final Report*.

Schofield, G. and Simmonds, J. (2011) 'Contact for Infants Subject to Care Proceedings'. Fam Law 617.

Websites

www.cafcass.gov.uk

www.carelaw.org.uk

www.education.gov.uk

www.open.justice.gov.uk/courts/care-proceedings/

11 International child abduction

Introduction

International parental child abduction has become a widespread problem owing to the growth in international relationships, the increase in family breakdown and cheaper and easier travel (e.g. free movement of persons within the EU). In January 2012 'Reunite', a UK-based charity specializing in international parental child abduction, recorded a 47 per cent increase in the number of cases reported to its advice line (www.reunite.org). In addition, the International Child Abduction and Contact Unit (which operates the **Hague Convention**) dealt with 444 new cases in 2011, whilst the Foreign and Commonwealth Office handled 161 new cases in the financial year 2010/11.

Article 11 of the United Nations Convention on the Rights of the Child 1989 requires those states which are parties to the Convention to take measures to combat the illicit transfer and non-return of children. Many of the signatories to the UN Convention have ratified the **Hague Convention on the Civil Aspects of International Child Abduction 1980** which governs the wrongful removal or retention of a child. Eighty-seven countries have ratified the Convention, including the UK. The first question in this chapter involves the removal of a child from the USA (which has also ratified the Convention) to the UK.

The Council of Europe has also adopted a convention that tackles child abduction, namely the **European Convention on Recognition and Enforcement of Decisions Concerning the Custody of Children 1980**, which was implemented by **Part II of Child Abduction and Custody Act (CACA) 1985**. If both conventions apply to a particular case, **s. 16(4)(c) of CACA** provides that the **Hague Convention** application takes precedence over the European Convention application. To complicate matters further, cases concerning two EU member states will be regulated by the provisions of **Brussels II** (**Council Regulation (EC) 2201/2003**) which modify the **Hague Convention**. **Brussels II** was implemented in the UK by the **European Communities (Jurisdiction and Judgments in Matrimonial and**

Parental Responsibility Matters) Regulations 2005 and in *JRG v EB* [2012] EWHC 1863 (**Fam**) the High Court refused to make an order under the **Hague Convention** because the father should have applied for registration of the French custody order under **Brussels II**. It is therefore essential that the correct application is made. Of course, many children are taken to or from countries that have not ratified any of these international agreements. The second question in this chapter considers how the courts in England and Wales should tackle cases of international child abduction from non-Convention countries.

 Question 1

Rhett, born in the USA, met and married Sylvia in North Carolina, USA, ten years ago. Their son Tod was born there a year later. Six months ago Sylvia brought Tod to England for a two-month visit to her parents' (and her childhood) home. At the end of the holiday she decided to remain in England and eventually to divorce Rhett. She informed Rhett and her parents of her decision. Tod is attending the local junior school. He is flourishing there, away from his domineering father. The severe facial twitch which Tod suffered when he lived in the USA has disappeared in England. Rhett agreed to his wife's and son's two-month trip, although he did not wish to join them as it coincided with his local hunting season. Rhett is president of the local Guns in Hunting Club.

Rhett has consulted lawyers in the USA and he has told Sylvia that there will be court proceedings unless she brings Tod home 'pronto'. Rhett is concerned that Tod is becoming an English 'cissy'. Tod is a vegetarian, as are his mother and grandparents.

Sylvia seeks your advice.

 Commentary

Obviously, the USA is not a signatory to the **European Convention on Recognition of Decisions Concerning the Custody of Children 1980** and is not a member of the European Union. It is therefore unnecessary to discuss the European Convention or **Brussels II**. In your answer you are expected to apply the **Hague Convention** to the facts set out in the question. Sylvia needs to know whether she is likely to be ordered to return Tod to the USA under the **Hague Convention**. Therefore, the key elements of habitual residence, wrongful removal or retention and the grounds for refusing an order to return must be considered.

 Answer plan

If the answer to the following questions is YES, the UK courts must order the return of Tod:

- Have both states ratified the **Hague Convention**?

- Is Tod under 16?

- Is Tod's habitual residence in the USA?
- Has Tod been retained in breach of 'rights of custody'?
- Was Tod unlawfully 'retained' less than one year ago?

BUT if the answer to any of the following questions is YES, the courts might not order the return of Tod:

- Had Rhett ceased to exercise custody rights?
- Did Rhett consent to or acquiesce the retention?
- Is there a grave risk of harm to Tod if he is returned?

Examiner's tip

Do not attempt a problem question regarding child abduction unless you are sure that you know whether the country in question has ratified the **Hague Convention**.

Suggested answer

Sylvia should be alerted to the fact that the **Hague Convention on the Civil Aspects of International Child Abduction 1980** (incorporated into UK law by **Part I of the Child Abduction and Custody Act (CACA) 1985**) may be used to secure the prompt return of Tod to the USA. The whole purpose of the Convention is to ensure that parties 'do not gain advantage by either removing a child from the country of its usual residence, or having taken the child, with the agreement of any other party who has custodial rights, to another jurisdiction, then wrongfully to retain that child' (*Re E (A Minor) (Abduction)*[1989] 1 FLR 135).

Every Convention country has a Central Authority, which deals with the administrative action required to operate the remedies under the Convention. The International Child Abduction and Contact Unit acts as the Central Authority for England and Wales. Central Authorities must cooperate with each other to promote the objects of the **Hague Convention**, one of which is to secure the prompt return of children wrongfully removed to, or retained in, any contracting state (**Art. 1**).

Rhett may contact the Central Authority in the USA which, in turn, would deal with the Central Authority in the UK, in an attempt to secure a voluntary return of Tod to the USA. However, if Sylvia will not agree to a voluntary return then the Central Authority will initiate proceedings. Again, Sylvia must be warned that, should the Convention apply to Tod's circumstances, the courts cannot investigate the merits of the case and must order his return unless one of the grounds in **Art. 12 or 13** apply (see later). 'The courts of the country of habitual residence should determine their future...The interests of the child in each individual case are not paramount since it is presumed under the Convention that the welfare of children is best met by return to their habitual residence' (*Re M (A Minor) (Child Abduction)* [1994] 1 FLR 390).

The **Hague Convention** applies where a child under 16 who is habitually resident in one contracting state is wrongfully removed to, or retained in, another (**Art. 4**). Clearly, Tod is under 16, but where is his habitual residence? Nowhere in the Convention is the term defined. However, in *Re J (A Minor) (Abduction: Custody Rights)* [1990] 2 AC 562, it was said by Lord Brandon (at 578–9) that the expression is not to be treated as a term of art, it is a question of fact to be determined by all the circumstances of the case. Lord Brandon went on to say that it is possible for habitual residence in a country to end in a single day, by leaving with an intention not to return, but it is only acquired after an appreciable time with a settled intention to remain. However, in *Re H-K (Children)* [2011] EWCA Civ 1100 a family had agreed to move to England for one year and the court held that the father's intention to return to Australia and the mother's agreement to do so, did not prevent a change of habitual residence. When a child lives with his parents, the child's habitual residence will normally be that of his parents (*Re A (Wardship: Jurisdiction)* [1995] 1 FLR 767). In *Re A (Abduction: Habitual Residence)* [1998] 1 FLR 497 it was held that a short visit to a country (in this case a three-week visit to Greece) does not initiate a period of habitual residence. It seems likely that, immediately before his retention, Tod was habitually resident in the USA. Where both parents have parental responsibility neither can unilaterally change the child's habitual residence (*Re B (Minors) (Abduction) (No. 2)* [1993] 1 FLR 993).

Rhett agreed to a two-month visit to England but, after that time elapsed, Tod was being retained against Rhett's wishes. Removal or retention of a child is wrongful where it is in breach of 'rights of custody' attributed to a person or any other body under the law of the state in which the child was habitually resident before the removal or retention (**Art. 3**). 'Rights of custody' include rights relating to the care of the person of the child and, in particular, the right to determine the child's place of residence (**Art. 5**). The law of the country of the child's habitual residence determines the existence of rights of custody, which includes rights which would have been exercised but for the retention (**Art. 3**). The quality of the parent's relationship with the child is not relevant (*Re D (Abduction: Custody Rights)* [2006] UKHL 51). By her retention of Tod in England, Sylvia frustrated Rhett's equal and separate rights of custody.

Where a child has been wrongfully removed or retained for less than a year, the court must order the return of the child (**Art. 12**). Even where a year has elapsed, such return is mandatory unless it is demonstrated that the child is 'settled in its new environment' (**Art. 12**). However, **Art. 13** gives the court a discretion whether to order return if the person who opposes the return can establish that the applicant, at the time of the removal or retention, was not exercising custody rights or consented to it, or subsequently acquiesced in it, or there is a grave risk of physical or psychological harm if the child is returned, or a mature child objects. As the House of Lords explained in *Re M (Abduction: Zimbabwe)* [2007] UKHL 55, a child might not be returned if the 'limited and precise circumstances' set out in **Art. 13** apply (para. 12). However, the House of

Lords made it clear that the circumstances do not need to be exceptional as previous case law had suggested (e.g. *Klentzeris v Klentzeris* [2007] EWCA Civ 533).

Consent and acquiescence are questions of fact and the weight to be attached to the evidence is a matter for the judge's discretion (*Re H (Abduction: Acquiescence)* [1997] 1 FLR 872). In *D v S (Abduction: Acquiescence)* [2008] EWHC 2807 (Fam) the High Court made it clear that consent or acquiescence must not be based on a misrepresentation or non-disclosure. In *A v T* [2011] EWHC 3882 (Fam) a return order was refused because the Swedish father had agreed in writing to the relocation before the children were born and had since affirmed his consent. Rhett has made it clear that he does not consent to, or acquiesce in, the wrongful retention of Tod. Sylvia may claim that there is a grave risk that return would expose Tod to physical or psychological harm or place him in an intolerable position. In *N v N (Abduction: Article 13 Defence)* [1995] 1 FLR 107 the court ordered that three children should be returned to Australia even though there was some evidence that the father had sexually interfered with one of the children. The court was entitled to weigh the risk of psychological harm of return against the psychological harm of refusing return. However, in exercising its discretion the court must give due weight to the primary purpose of the Convention. A less stringent approach would undermine the spirit and purpose of the Convention, which is the speedy return of children so that a court in the country of their habitual residence can decide what is best for the child. Similarly, in *Re E (Children)* [2011] UKSC 84 the Supreme Court ordered the return of the children to Norway despite the fact that the father was violent, domineering and controlling and that the mother suffered from a mental disorder which would deteriorate if she were required to return. This was because it was in the children's interests for their future to be decided in Norway and **Art. 12** requires the child to be returned to the state of its habitual residence and not to the other parent (*B v K (Child Abduction)* [1993] FCR 382). But in *Re S (A Child)* [2012] UKSC 10 the Supreme Court refused to order the return of a child because the mother's mental state would be affected by her return to Australia, which could diminish her attachment to the child. In this case, the father was a former heroin addict whom the mother accused of relapsing, the mother had obtained a non-molestation order against him and she feared his mental state and impulsive actions.

Under **Art. 13** it is possible to consider the objections of the child to returning to the parent and not to the state (*Re M (A Minor) (Child Abduction)* [1994] 1 FLR 390). In *S v S (Child Abduction) (Child's Views)* [1992] 2 FLR 492, the court refused to order the return of a 10-year-old girl to France as there was a grave risk that return would result in physical or psychological harm. She objected to being returned and had reached the age and degree of maturity where it was appropriate to take account of her views. The girl had a severe stammer and behavioural problems in France but these had disappeared (like Tod's facial twitch) in England. A CAFCASS officer or children and family court reporter would assess whether Tod is of sufficient maturity to object to being returned; if so, he would then convey Tod's views to the court. However, *W v W* [2010] EWHC 332 (Fam) demonstrates that the courts will take into account the views of very young children. In this case a CAFCASS officer interviewed two children aged 8 and 5 to establish if they objected to being returned to Ireland. The officer reported that the 8-year-old boy became very fidgety and his 5-year-old sister started to cry when asked whether they wanted to return to Ireland. Black J pointed out that the **Hague Convention** does not stipulate an age at which a child's views should be taken into account. The decision of the High Court was later upheld in the Court of Appeal. It is therefore likely that Tod, aged 9, will, at the very least, be interviewed to establish his views.

In exercising their discretion, the courts have been influenced by the fact that a child returned to the country of habitual residence would be more than likely to be allowed to leave again by a court of that country (*Re K (Abduction: Consent)* [1997] 2 FLR 212). In *Re T (Abduction: Child's Objections to Return)* [2000] 2 FLR 193, the court heeded the objections of an 11-year-old to being returned to Spain, to a mother with drink problems. However, the court is not obliged to respond to the child's wishes as *Zaffino v Zaffino (Abduction: Children's Views)* [2005] EWCA Civ 1012 demonstrates. Here, a 13-year-old girl was returned to Canada, despite her objections. But in *Re C (Abduction: Application to Set Aside Return Order)* [2012] EWCA (11 July 2012) a 15-year-old girl successfully appealed a return order as she had changed her mind as to where she wished to live.

This case may appear to be on the borderline, bearing in mind that we have not heard Tod's views. A two-stage process is required under **Art. 13**. The establishment of one of the **Art. 13** 'defences' gives a court a discretion whether or not to order the child's speedy return and in *H v H (Abduction: Acquiescence)* [1996] 2 FLR 570 it was held that the court must consider, for example, the extent to which refusal would frustrate the purpose of the **Hague Convention**. If the court decides that this is not a case where it should exercise its discretion, which seems likely, then Sylvia must return Tod. If Sylvia wishes Tod to live with her in England, she must apply for an order for custody, in a court in the USA, and an order that Tod should be allowed to leave that country with her. In the event of parental disagreement about his diet etc., a court of the appropriate country could decide the issue.

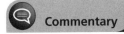

Question 2

In cases of international child abduction from a 'non-Hague Convention' country, which principle should the court apply—welfare or comity?

Commentary

This question requires to students to consider the approach that the English courts should adopt when hearing cases that involve abductions from non-Hague Convention countries. Your answer should focus on the development of case law following the incorporation of the **Hague Convention** by the **CACA 1985** through to the House of Lords', decision in *Re J (Child Returned Abroad: Convention Rights)* [2005] UKHL 40.

Answer plan

- Abduction to and from non-Convention countries.
- The **Hague Convention**—once the model.
- Re-assertion of the welfare principle.
- Attitude of other country's courts.
- The House of Lords decision in **Re J (Child Returned Abroad: Convention Rights)**.

 Examiner's tip

It would be a grave mistake to attempt this question if you do not understand the word 'comity', which means extending courtesies to other nations, particularly through the recognition and enforcement of executive, legislative and judicial acts.

 Suggested answer

Applications for the return of children from England and Wales to a country which is not a signatory to the **Hague Convention on the Civil Aspects of International Child Abduction** are usually decided by the High Court in wardship, where the welfare of the child is paramount. The court has a duty to promote and protect the interests of the child and in *McKee v McKee* **[1951] AC 352** the Privy Council explained that the court has a complete discretion to select from options which range from a peremptory return order to, itself, undertaking a full consideration of the merits of the case. It is possible that the welfare of a child may require that the dispute be settled in a foreign court. However, abduction cases, under the wardship jurisdiction, raise no presumption of prompt return: all the circumstances of each case must be considered. It is also possible for such cases to be decided under the **Children Act (CA) 1989**. For example, in *Re J (Child Returned Abroad: Convention Rights)* **[2005] UKHL 40** the mother brought the children to the UK and applied for a residence order and, in response, the father requested a specific issue order for the return of his child to Saudi Arabia. Whichever jurisdiction is used, the decision will be based on the principle that the welfare of the child is the court's paramount consideration (**s. 1(1) CA 1989**).

The **Hague Convention** was incorporated into English law by the **Child Abduction and Custody Act (CACA) 1985**, following which the courts appeared to have felt constrained to apply **Hague Convention** principles to non-Convention cases. The objects of the Convention are to secure the prompt return of children wrongfully removed or retained in any contracting state and to ensure that rights of custody under the law of one contracting state are effectively respected in the other contracting states. 'The courts of the country of habitual residence should determine their future...The interests of the child in each individual case are not paramount since it is presumed under the Convention that the welfare of children is best met by return to their habitual residence' (*Re M (A Minor) (Child Abduction)* [1994] 1 FLR 390).

Such a presumption of prompt return and comity between nations is supportable in Convention cases, because the preamble to the **Hague Convention** confirms that the signatories are 'firmly convinced that the interests of children are of paramount importance in matters relating to their custody.' However, it cannot be assumed that the safeguards which are built into the system between contracting states, will be applied in non-Convention countries. In the non-Convention cases of *Re F (A Minor) (Abduction: Jurisdiction)* [1991] 1 FLR 1 and *G v G (Minors) (Abduction)* [1991] 2 FLR 506, the Court of Appeal took the view that Parliament was not departing from the welfare principle when it incorporated the **Hague Convention** into English law in the **CACA 1985**. Rather, it was giving effect to a belief that in normal circumstances it is in the interests of children that parents should not abduct them from one jurisdiction to another and that any decision relating to the custody of children is best decided in the jurisdiction in which they hitherto have normally been resident. Immediate return to non-Convention countries was ordered in each case. Following this, *Re S (Minors) (Abduction)* [1994] 1 FLR 297 suggested that international comity had become a legal principle, as the Court of Appeal declared that the philosophy of the **Hague Convention** should be applied to non-Convention cases (in this instance the abduction of a child from Pakistan). As Hayes and Williams explained, the Court of Appeal was 'preserving comity between nations' by ordering the return of children to a 'system which would take account of matters which an English court would regard as incompatible with the welfare principle' (*Family Law—Principles, Policy and Practice*, 2nd edn (Butterworths, 1999), p. 404). The approach taken in *Re S* was endorsed in *Re M (Abduction: Peremptory Return Order)* [1996] 1 FLR 478 where the Court of Appeal declared that very exceptional circumstances would be needed to justify departure from the general principle of peremptory return.

The welfare principle was reasserted by the Court of Appeal in *Re P (Abduction: Non-Convention Country)* [1997] 1 FLR 780. Allowing the appeal against a peremptory return order, it was said that the judge had misdirected himself and had wrongly considered himself bound by the authorities to apply the spirit of the **Hague Convention** in a non-Convention case. The child's welfare should have been the paramount consideration. Further support to the welfare principle was given in *Re JA (Child Abduction: Non-Convention Country)* [1998] 1 FLR 231 where the mother had abducted the child from their country of habitual residence, the United Arab Emirates, which was not a party to the **Hague Convention**. The Court of Appeal said that the authorities before the advent of the **CACA 1985** seemed clearly to establish that it was an abdication of the responsibility of the court to surrender the determination of its ward's future to a foreign court whose regime might be inimical to the child's welfare. Of course, returning a child to its country of residence will not always be inimical to the child's best interests. For example, in *Re Z (Non-Convention Country)* [1999] 1 FLR

1270 the court returned the child to Malta because it was satisfied that the Maltese courts would apply the welfare principle when determining issues relating to the child. It should be noted that in 2003 the President of the Family Division and the Chief Justice of Pakistan agreed the UK–Pakistan Protocol which provides that in normal circumstances the welfare of the child is best determined by the courts of the child's habitual residence.

In 2005, the House of Lords finally determined the approach to be taken by the courts when considering abductions from non-Convention countries. In *Re J (Child Returned Abroad: Convention Rights)* [2005] **UKHL 40** Baroness Hale indicated that there 'is no warrant either in statute or in authority for the principles of the **Hague Convention** to be extended to countries which are not parties to it' (para. 22). The court must decide what is in the best interests of the child and there is no presumption that returning the child to the country from where it came will be in the child's best interests. Baroness Hale declared that the most one can say is 'that it is likely to be better for a child to return to his home country for any disputes about his future to be decided there' and that a case must be made for not returning him or her (para. 32). The court indicated that the following factors should be considered when deciding whether a child should be returned to his home country: the degree of connection with each country; the length of time spent in each country; the approach taken to determining issues in the foreign country; and the effect of the decision on the primary carer. In this particular case, the House of Lords upheld the decision of the High Court not to return the child to Saudi Arabia. The father had made allegations about the mother's association with another man and there was concern as to how she would be treated in Saudi Arabia. In addition, there was no jurisdiction in the home country that would enable the mother to apply to the court for permission to relocate to England. It was not, therefore, possible for the relocation issue to be resolved by a court in Saudi Arabia. In contrast, the court in *Re U (Abduction: Nigeria)* [2010] **EWHC 1179** was satisfied that the matter could be fairly determined in the home country of Nigeria where the courts would treat the mother and father equally and apply the welfare principle. The situation in Nigeria was therefore quite different from the situation in Saudi Arabia.

It thus seems that following the **CACA 1985**, which incorporated the **Hague Convention** into UK law, the courts felt bound to apply the philosophy of the **Hague Convention** to non-Convention cases and therefore upheld the principle of comity. However, the House of Lords in *Re J* (see previous paragraph) made it clear that such cases should be determined on the basis of the welfare principle. In some cases, this will require the child to be returned to his or her home country but in other instances, the child's welfare will require a refusal to make a return order.

Further reading

Farell, F. (2011) 'Back to Basics: Waking up to Child Abduction'. Fam Law 1274.

Honeyman, G. and Mellor, J. (2011) 'Representation of Children in Hague Proceedings: A Welfare Perspective'. Fam Law 613.

Lowe, N. and Stephens, V. (2011) 'Operating the 1980 Hague Abduction Convention. The 2008 Statistics'. Fam Law 1216.

Websites

www.hcch.net

www.justice.gov.uk/protecting-the-vulnerable/official-solicitor/international-child-abduction-and-contact-unit

www.pact-online.org/

www.reunite.org

12

Property rights

Introduction

Questions on property rights tend to focus on ownership of the family home, which is usually the parties' most significant asset. If a married couple divorce or civil partners dissolve the partnership, the court has a discretion to reallocate property under the **Matrimonial Causes Act (MCA) 1973** and the **Civil Partnership Act 2004** (see **Chapter 13**). However, if an unmarried or unregistered couple separate, the division of property is based on ownership, which is determined by the application of general principles of property law. Ownership of assets is also important if a spouse, civil partner or a person in a cohabiting relationship becomes insolvent or dies. The most significant development since the sixth edition of this book is the decision of the Supreme Court in *Jones (Appellant) v Kernott (Respondent)* [2011] UKSC 53, which concerned the calculation of beneficial interests in property where the legal title is in joint names, but there is no express declaration as to how it is to be shared.

 Question 1

You have been asked to advise Tony, who has recently separated from Mei. Tony and Mei became a couple six years ago and shortly afterwards they bought a house, which Tony 'thinks' was registered 'in his own name'. The house cost £75,000 of which Tony paid £25,000 which he had won in the National Lottery. He raised the rest on a mortgage. The couple moved into the house, having agreed that they would take equal responsibility for household expenses (excluding the mortgage payments which Tony paid) and maintenance costs. Two years ago they made equal contributions towards a £10,000 extension. Mei has always done the cooking and cleaning as well as looking after the garden and performing do-it-yourself jobs around the house. There are no children. Mei is claiming that Tony owes her half the net value of the house, in which the equity is now £100,000.

(a)   Advise Tony, eliciting from him any further information you may require. [20 marks]

(b)   If Tony and Mei were husband and wife, in what circumstances would the court be required to apply declaratory, rather than adjustive, principles? [5 marks]

Commentary

The advantage of this style of question is that it does a lot of the analysis for you; it may take a little longer to absorb, but it tells you what to do more clearly than a simple 'Advise' or 'Discuss'. The question requires students to discuss the acquisition of a legal interest in property through the creation of a trust and the circumstances in which the courts apply declaratory principles in relation to married couples. As the facts indicate that 'there are no children' you do not need to consider child maintenance under the **Child Support Act 1991** (as amended) or **s. 15 of and Sch. 1 to the Children Act 1989**, which empower the court to make property adjustment orders in favour of non-marital children.

Answer plan

- Property ownership. Formalities. Legal ownership.
- Beneficial ownership. Trusts—implied/resulting/constructive.
- Common intention, Detrimental reliance.
- Relevance of declaratory principles to spouses, e.g. death, third party rights, remarriage.

Examiner's tip

Do not ignore the 'eliciting any further information you may require' instruction in part (a). It puts you in the position of an actual adviser, whose skill will be to know what questions to ask after the client has told you what he thinks you need to know.

Suggested answer

(a)   Before we can advise Tony it is necessary to obtain further information from him. First, you will need to ask Tony whether he and Mei are married. It is assumed that they are not as there is no mention of a wedding and part (b) of the question seems to suggest that they are cohabitants. Secondly, it is essential to discover, from the actual document, whether Mei is registered as the legal and beneficial owner of the property. **Section 52 of the Law of Property Act (LPA) 1925** requires a deed for the conveyance or creation of any legal estate in land. So if the house was indeed taken in Tony's name only, it follows that Mei will have no claim to the legal estate. On the other hand, if what 'he tells you' proves inaccurate to the extent that Mei's name is also on the title, then it is necessary to examine the conveyance to determine the proportions in which the beneficial entitlements are held. Since 1998, when two or more persons are registered as joint owners they are asked to complete a declaration as to their beneficial interests, but this does not always happen. Furthermore, the courts are required to deal with cases involving property acquired before 1998 as *Stack v Dowden* [2007] UKHL 17 demonstrates. In that case, the property in question was registered in joint names but the beneficial interests were not specified. The House of Lords declared that in domestic cases, the starting point is joint beneficial interest. The burden of proving that the beneficial interests are different from the legal interest falls on the person making this claim. In *Jones v Kernott (Respondent)* [2011] UKSC 53 the Supreme Court confirmed the decision in *Stack v Dowden* and explained that the presumption of joint beneficial interest may be rebutted by evidence that it was not or *ceased to be* the common intention of the parties. In this particular case the court held that initially there was no evidence to rebut the presumption, but the parties' intentions changed after Mr Kernott moved out and ceased to contribute to the property and the couple cashed in an insurance policy which enabled Mr Kernott to purchase a property of his own. Once the presumption of joint beneficial interests has been rebutted, the question of shares will need to be considered. If there is no evidence of an actual agreement as to how the beneficial interest should be shared and it is not possible to infer a common intention from the parties' behaviour, the court will have to impute an intention, which the court considers fair having regard to the whole course of dealing between them in relation to the property. The financial contributions that each has made will be one, but not the only, factor.

If the property is registered in Tony's sole name, he may have declared an express trust in favour of Mei, which would mean that she has a beneficial interest in the property. **Section 53 of the LPA 1925** requires a signed written document in order to create an express trust. As a consequence, the wife in *Gissing v Gissing* [1971] AC 886 could not claim that an express trust had been created when her husband told her that the house was hers. Tony should also be aware that **s. 53(2) LPA 1925** states that **s. 53** does not affect the 'creation or operation of resulting, implied or constructive trusts'. It is therefore possible that Mei could acquire a beneficial interest in the property if a resulting, implied or constructive trust can be established. A resulting trust is created if one party provides all or some of the purchase price for a property that is registered in the name of the other party. Mei has not contributed to the purchase price and so could not claim that a resulting trust exists. In any event, the House of Lords in *Stack v Dowden* [2007] indicated that the flexible constructive trust is more appropriate for matrimonial or quasi-matrimonial cases. To establish a constructive trust, Mei would need to show a common intention that they should both be beneficial owners and that she relied on this to her detriment. A common intention will be found if the parties expressly discussed sharing the property or if intention can be inferred from the parties' conduct. In *Grant v Edwards* [1987] 1 FLR 87 the claimant was told that her name was not going on the title deeds because if it did there might be problems in her then pending divorce proceedings. This express discussion was sufficient to establish a common intention. If

Tony and Mei had a similar conversation, Mei will have established the required common intention. Inferring intention from conduct is more difficult. In *Lloyds Bank v Rosset* [1991] AC 107 Lord Bridge stated that it was extremely doubtful whether anything other than a direct contribution to the purchase price would suffice. It is thus clear that intention can be inferred from a direct contribution to the purchase price, and previous authorities also suggest that making mortgage payments will be sufficient (*Re Gorman (A Bankrupt)* [1990] 2 FLR 284). This will not assist Mei as she did not contribute to the purchase price and Tony took exclusive responsibility for the mortgage. Intention can also be inferred from indirect financial contributions. In *Le Foe v Le Foe* [2001] 2 FLR 97 FD the wife paid for day-to-day domestic expenditure while the husband made the mortgage payments. The wife acquired a beneficial interest because the husband would not have been able to pay the mortgage if the wife did not take responsibility for household expenses. In *Stack v Dowden* the House of Lords stated that the approach adopted in *Lloyds Bank v Rosset* was too restrictive and Probert suggests that the approach taken in *Le Foe* 'is to be preferred as a matter of authority and as a matter of policy' (*Cretney and Probert's Family Law* (2009), p. 98). However, it is unclear whether Mei's financial contribution to household expenses would be considered equivalent to Mrs Le Foe's contribution. In addition, Mei's non-financial contributions to the household, i.e. cooking, cleaning, gardening and DIY, will not be sufficient to generate a beneficial interest. In *Burns v Burns* [1984] FLR 216 a couple had lived together for 19 years, the woman giving up her job to look after the man and (their) two children; she had put her earnings into the housekeeping, bought goods for the house, laid a patio and had done decorating work. She did not, however, show the 'necessary intention'. In contrast, the non-financial contribution made by the female cohabitant in *Eves v Eves* [1975] 1 WLR 1338 was sufficient to demonstrate the necessary intention because the work was considered out of the ordinary. She had used a 14lb sledgehammer to break up concrete and demolish a shed and carried out expensive decorations, which according to the Court of Appeal would only have been done in pursuance of an express or implied agreement. In *Stack v Dowden* the House of Lords suggested that making improvements to property that add significant value may be sufficient to establish common intention. However, in *James v Thomas* [2007] EWCA Civ 1212, which was decided after *Stack v Dowden*, renovation work undertaken by the female party was deemed insufficient. It is unclear whether Mei's £5,000 contribution to the extension would constitute an improvement that adds significant value to the property.

If Mei does satisfy a court of 'common intention', she then has to demonstrate the further requirement of 'detrimental reliance'. In *Hyett v Stanley* [2004] 1 FLR 394 the property was in the man's sole name. The woman agreed to execute a legal charge in the bank's favour and the couple gave a joint and several covenant to discharge their liabilities to the bank, secured against the property. It was held that the woman became entitled to an immediate and absolute beneficial interest in the property by way of a constructive trust. The Court of Appeal concluded that the couple could only reasonably have intended that they should each take a half share in the beneficial interest in the property. Also, she had acted to her detriment in reliance on that understanding by assuming the risk of joint liability on the mortgage. Indirect financial contributions may constitute detrimental reliance on an express agreement but non-financial contributions, such as Mei's cooking, cleaning, gardening and DIY will not. Even if Mei does establish a common intention and detrimental reliance, it is unlikely that her claim for half of the equity will be successful as there is no automatic entitlement to equal shares (*Stack v Dowden* [2007]). Finally, there seems to be no evidence to sustain a claim based on either contract (*Tanner v Tanner* [1975] 1 WLR 1341) or proprietary estoppel (*Pascoe v Turner* [1979] 1 WLR 431). Mei might, therefore, have to settle for the return of her £5,000 contribution to the extension.

(b) Normally, if a marital relationship has deteriorated to the extent of litigation over home ownership, divorce (or a separation order or annulment) is likely, in which case the discretionary, adjustive jurisdiction of the divorce court under **Part 2 of the Matrimonial Causes Act (MCA) 1973** will apply. There are still a number of circumstances, however, where the question of beneficial ownership may be relevant. First, the parties to a marriage may not seek divorce, or any other matrimonial cause, or the ground(s) may not be available. Secondly, the divorce court's powers may no longer be exercisable: a former spouse loses the right to apply for a property adjustment on remarriage (**MCA 1973, s. 28(3)**).

In addition, the courts may be required to make a declaration as to ownership if a third party is involved. For example, a creditor may seek to enforce a judgment against a spouse's share in property by way of a charging order against the debtor's interest in the family home. A spouse's creditor will not be able to attack property beneficially owned by the other spouse, unless the latter has made herself liable; *Lloyds Bank plc v Rosset* [1990] (mentioned earlier) was concerned with this situation. The bankruptcy of one spouse naturally brings this issue into sharp relief. The property of the debtor, but not his or her spouse, will vest in the trustee in bankruptcy. It is, therefore, essential to determine the beneficial ownership of family property. Another possibility is illustrated by *Harwood v Harwood* [1991] 2 FLR 274. The firm in which the husband was a partner contributed to the cost of the matrimonial home, and the court could not resolve matters (it wanted to order a sale under **s. 24A MCA 1973**) until the extent of the other partner's interest had been established. Furthermore, the legal and equitable interests might be relevant in the actual exercise by the divorce court of its discretion as, after all, the existing position is the necessary starting point (*Tebbutt v Haynes* [1981] 2 All ER 238).

Death, of course, terminates more marriages than does divorce and only the deceased's property passes by will or the intestacy rules. If the deceased left his or her property to someone other than the surviving spouse, the latter may claim that he or she actually owned the property and as a consequence his or her share cannot pass by will.

 Question 2

Consider the property interests generated by the activities of Harry and Wendy, a married couple, in each of the following situations. How far would your answers differ if they were unmarried?

(a) Harry and Wendy keep a cache of gold under their mattress. It all comes from H, who receives the metal by way of income payments. One day, with H's knowledge, W has some of it made into a necklace for her to wear.

(b) One Christmas, Wendy, a businesswoman, buys two sports cars, one red and one green, with her own money and gives Harry a set of keys to the green one. Wendy nearly always drives the red one, and Harry the green one, although both cars are insured in her name. Now, some years later, Wendy is bankrupt.

(c) One of them gives the other a monthly housekeeping allowance from which the recipient manages to save £2,000 which the latter spends on clothes before dying in a road accident.

NB: the parts of this question are equally weighted.

Commentary

This is another multi-part question, but this time with segregated data. The examiners have taken three issues of property rights, i.e. common funds, gifts and housekeeping allowances, and woven a separate story around each. Candidates will note that the parties are married, but the question also requires an explanation of the legal position if the parties were unmarried. In some cases there is little difference, but in others notable distinctions exists between spouses and cohabitants. The suggested answer contains reference to **Part 15 of the Equality Act 2010**, which contains provisions on the presumption of advancement and housekeeping payments. Students should be aware that at the time of writing **Part 15** was not in force.

Answer plan

Issue	Relevant law if the couple are married	Relevant law if the couple are unmarried
(a) The gold	Common fund—joint interest if intended for common use	Common fund—as for married couples
	Presumption of advancement (will be abolished by **Equality Act 2010**)	No presumption of advancement
(b) The sports cars	Gift of a chattel—intention and deed or delivery	The same as for married couples
	Insolvency—**Insolvency Act 1986**	
(c) The housekeeping allowance	**MWPA 1964**—if H gives it to W it belongs to both equally (but not if W gives it to H)	**MWPA 1964** does not apply
	Equality Act will apply the rule to payments made by W	Common law rules apply

Candidates should note that the parts of the question are equally weighted and as a result equal time should be devoted to each.

Suggested answer

The theme which runs through this question is partnership 'rights' over property other than the family home. The various aspects are, respectively: the 'common fund'; gifts between the partners; and housekeeping allowances. Normally the declaratory position between spouses will not be decisive because of the divorce court's discretionary adjustive powers. There is, however, still scope for proceedings under **s. 17 of the Married Women's Property Act (MWPA) 1882**, and the declaratory position may still be determinative where third parties are involved (insolvency and death). In *Pettit v Pettit* **[1970] AC 777**, the House of Lords held that **s. 17** did not give the court the power to vary existing interests.

(a) The question here is who owns the gold, both under the mattress and around W's neck. Prima facie, the income of either spouse remains his/hers, as in *Heseltine v Heseltine* **[1971] 1 All ER 952** where the wife received income from her own investments. Where there is a 'common fund', however, the couple may be taken as acquiring a joint interest in it. This arose in *Jones v Maynard* **[1951] Ch 572** where the husband authorized his wife to draw on his bank account, after which they both paid in and both drew out. Occasionally he used such withdrawals to pay for investments in his own name. It was held that the wife was entitled to a half share in the account and in her husband's investments, even though his inputs had exceeded hers and they had made no express arrangements about the matter.

It thus seems that where both spouses contribute, however unequally, such an intention will be imputed in the absence of contrary agreement. Here, of course, H is the sole contributor; however, if W can establish that it is nonetheless a common fund intended for the use of both spouses, then the property will be jointly owned. We are told that 'H and W' keep the gold under 'their' mattress and that W took some of it with H's knowledge. Furthermore, there is nothing to suggest that H objected to W taking the gold. This may be sufficient to establish the intention required to create a common purse. In the past, the rebuttable presumption of advancement may have come into play in circumstances such as these. The presumption provided that a transfer from husband to wife was presumed to be a gift. In a case such as this, W might claim that H had transferred some of the gold to her and that the presumption of advancement made it a gift. As the presumption was based on the fact that wives were financially dependent on their husbands who had a duty to maintain them, the presumption has weakened as spouses have greater financial equality. The **Equality Act 2010** finally abolishes the presumption of advancement (**s. 199**) and the common law duty of a husband to maintain his wife (**s. 198**) although these provisions are not yet in force.

If the cache of gold is considered a common fund, either party can withdraw from it and items purchased from it for personal use belong to that individual. The necklace is, of course, an item of personal use and so, even if the cache is held to be a common purse and therefore jointly owned, the necklace might be taken as being hers alone. If the cache of gold is not considered a common purse, the necklace will belong to W if it is a properly executed gift (see the answer to part (b)). Establishing that the necklace has been properly gifted is likely to be more straightforward than proving that the car was properly gifted in the following problem.

Were H and W cohabitants, the same reasoning would apply because the idea of the common purse is based on the purpose for which it was formed, and not on the nature of the parties' relationship (*Paul v Constance* [1977] 1 All ER 195). But the presumption of advancement would not apply.

(b) The issue in this part of the question is whether ownership of the green car, as well as the red one, will vest in W's trustee in bankruptcy. Has W managed to make an earlier, binding, gift of it to H? It should be acknowledged at the outset that there is no presumption of undue influence as between husband and wife (*Howes v Bishop* [1909] 2 KB 390) and nothing in the question suggests actual undue influence.

In order to perfect the gift of a chattel, there must be intent on the donor's part plus either a deed (not in issue here) or delivery. It may be that the giving of the keys (at Christmas, a time for presents) will be sufficiently symbolic, as in *Lock v Heath* (1892) 8 TLR 295 where the husband's delivery of one chair to his wife was held to cover all his furniture. Thus, there may be enough evidence here to overcome the twin difficulties which bedevil the proof of delivery as between spouses, i.e. the fact that spouses frequently use each other's property and that the goods in question may already have been used by both parties before the gift.

A further difficulty may be less easily overcome. English law is reluctant to infer delivery where to do so would be a vehicle for the deprivation of the 'donor's' creditors. *Re Cole* [1964] Ch 175 has dangerous parallels to the present case. There the husband completely furnished a new house before his wife ever set foot in it. 'It's all yours' said he, after she had completed her tour, which began when he took his hands from her eyes after she had entered the first room. Nonetheless, the furniture (which he used, as here) remained insured in his name (again, as here). It was held that the gift was not perfected and the trustee was held entitled to the goods. Further, it is at least arguable that as it is the wife, and not the husband, who is the alleged donor, there was (still) a presumption of resulting trust in her favour, as in *Mercier v Mercier* [1903] 2 Ch 98.

Finally, **s. 423 of the Insolvency Act 1986** must not be overlooked. It enables any transaction at an undervalue (e.g. a gift) to be avoided by the trustee in bankruptcy, if it was made with the intention of defeating the claims of creditors. Given that there was a gap of 'some years', this is clearly unlikely here. Overall, however, it seems likely that the green car will join the red one in the hands of W's trustee in bankruptcy.

It is suggested that there would be little, if any, change in the position were the couple not married to one another, as the 'delivery' difficulty would be equally applicable. In addition, **s. 423 of the Insolvency Act 1986** applies to an insolvent cohabitant as to any bankrupt.

(c) This part of the question concerns savings made from housekeeping allowances and purchases made from such savings. **Section 1 of the MWPA 1964** provides that money or property derived from the housekeeping allowance made by the husband to the wife 'shall, in the absence of any agreement between them to the contrary, be treated as belonging to the husband and wife in equal shares.' If the 'giver' of the money is H, **s. 1** would apply as there appears to be no contrary agreement. However, if H is the recipient, **s. 1** does not apply. Early case law indicated that if the wife gave money to her husband for housekeeping purposes, the money belonged to him as head of the household (**Edward v Cheyne (No. 2) (1888) 13 App Cas 385 (HL)**). However, Lowe and Douglas suggest that the courts would not take such a view today and that the money or property would remain the wife's (*Bromley's Family Law*, 10th edn (2006), p. 136). **Section 200 of the Equality Act 2010** amends **s. 1 MWPA 1964** so that money or property derived from a housekeeping allowance made by the husband *or wife* will belong to husband and wife equally. Furthermore, money or property derived from a housekeeping allowance made by one civil partner to the other will belong to the partners equally as a result of **s. 201**. At the time of writing, these provisions had not come into force.

In this particular case, the recipient of the housekeeping allowance has died suddenly. If **s. 1 MWPA 1964** applies, the property is owned in equal shares, which means the deceased's share passes to his or her personal representatives, rather than automatically passing to the survivor as the 'common purse' does. So there is the danger that half the value of the clothing could end up elsewhere, perhaps under a residuary bequest. However, if the recipient of the allowance is H, **s. 1 MWPA 1964** does not currently apply and it is therefore assumed that the property belongs to W. The clothing would not, therefore, pass to H's personal representatives. In both cases, it could be argued that there was a tacit agreement (were the other to have known of it) that the items belong wholly to the buyer, because of their personal nature, in which case the personal representatives could end up with the lot.

If the couple are cohabitants, the **MWPA 1964** is inapplicable and on the face of it the common law rules will apply. Whichever partner was the supplier, any unspent balance, here represented by the clothes, would belong to that partner. On the other hand, one might be able to argue that there was an agreement that property should belong to them equally or that such personal items belong to the buyer (see earlier). The truth is that we await a decision.

Further reading

Clarke, S. and Greer, S. (2012) *Land Law Directions*, 3rd edn (Oxford: Oxford University Press).

Fretwell, K. (2011) 'Fairness is What Justice Really Is: *Kernott v Jones* in the Supreme Court'. Fam Law 753.

Fretwell, K. (2012) 'The Cautionary Tale of *Jones v Kernott*'. Fam Law 69.

Haynes, M. (2012) 'TR1s and Keeping Up with the Jones's: *Kernott v Jones*'. Fam Law 585.

Pawlowski, M. and Brown, J. (2012) 'Orders for Sale: The Creditor and the Family Home—Part 1'. Fam Law 64.

Pawlowski, M. and Brown, J. (2012) 'Orders for Sale: The Creditor and the Family Home—Part 2'. Fam Law 180.

Websites

www.landregistry.gov.uk

13

Ancillary financial relief for adults

Introduction

On most family law courses, a fair amount of time is spent looking at financial relief for adults. Applications for financial relief during marriage can be made under the **Domestic Proceedings and Magistrates' Courts Act 1978** or under **s. 27 of the Matrimonial Causes Act (MCA) 1973**. Both forms of application are used if the parties do not wish to divorce and in practice both are rare. Consequently, family law courses focus on financial provision and property adjustment ancillary to divorce, nullity and (judicial) separation under the **MCA 1973** and now the **Civil Partnership Act 2004**. In practice these ancillary matters, and the children's future, are where attention is now focused and although disputes relating to such issues will increasingly be referred to mediation, it is necessary to understand the powers of the courts.

Students who choose to tackle financial relief questions must be aware of the range of orders available to the court, the criteria for the court's exercise of discretion contained in **s. 25 MCA 1973** and key case law in relation to the latter, for example *Miller; McFarlane* [2006] 1 FLR 1186 and *Radmacher (formerly Granatino) (Respondent) v Granatino (Appellant)* [2010] UKSC 42. There are three questions in this chapter: two problems questions and one essay. The problem questions concern financial relief ancillary to divorce and in line with common practice in examination questions, the couples do not have children, as child support is segregated from spousal provision.

 Question 1

Richard is divorcing his wife, Hyacinth. When they married three years ago Richard, a successful businessman, was 45 and Hyacinth 25. Hyacinth insisted at the time of their marriage that Richard should sell his bachelor flat and buy a house in their joint names, which he duly did. The house is now valued at £1 million and there is no mortgage.

Richard earns £110,000 a year, and has further assets worth some £2 million. Hyacinth, a secretary and part-time model, has not worked since the marriage but was always happy to spend Richard's money. There are no children.

Last year Richard was diagnosed as having multiple sclerosis. Hyacinth's reaction was to tell him that she had no intention of spending her life looking after an invalid and that she was leaving him to go to live with Justin, with whom she had been having an affair for two years. When Richard said he did not know how he would carry on without her, Hyacinth said it would probably be best all round if he killed himself and then at least she could have the house.

Richard has now received a letter from Hyacinth's solicitor with a proposed financial settlement. Hyacinth wants half the value of the house, £3,000 a month maintenance and a lump sum of £50,000. Justin is a 'mature' student with no income and cannot support her.

Advise Richard as to whether he should accept this offer.

 Commentary

In your answer to this question you are required to advise Richard who is considering accepting an offer to settle made by his wife Hyacinth. In order to do so properly, you need to know your way around the relevant provisions of the **MCA 1973** and, using the information provided in the question itself, hazard a guess as to how a court would be likely to exercise the wide discretion vested in it in such circumstances. Richard would need to know this, even if the couple utilize mediation, rather than the courts, to resolve the issue, in order to avoid agreeing to an unfair settlement.

 Answer plan

- Ancillary financial relief—**Part II MCA 1973**.
- Periodical payments and lump sums.
- Property adjustment.
- 'All the circumstances'.
- *White*: not half.
- *Miller; McFarlane*: a clean break?

 Examiner's tip

Follow the instructions contained in the question, i.e. 'Advise Richard as to whether he should accept this offer'—you will gain no marks for discussing the ground for divorce.

Suggested answer

In order to advise Richard as to whether to accept Hyacinth's offer, it is necessary to determine whether the offer is reasonable by examining the relevant provisions of the **Matrimonial Causes Act (MCA) 1973** and considering what the likely outcome would be if the court was asked to resolve the ancillary matters in the given circumstances.

Hyacinth is asking for half the value of the house (£500,000); £3,000 a month maintenance; and a £50,000 lump sum. But would the court actually award this? The **MCA 1973** gives the court very wide powers of financial provision and property adjustment, so that it is usually possible to achieve a fair, just and reasonable result (**ss. 21–6**). Financial provision orders available include periodical payments (secured or unsecured) and a lump sum order (LSO), whilst a property adjustment order can involve a transfer, settlement or variation of settlement. It is also possible for the court to order a sale (under **s. 24A**) or make a pension-sharing order (under **s. 24B**).

Richard is presumably living in the matrimonial home which, at Hyacinth's insistence, is in both their names. Hyacinth is asking for half the value, a sum to which as a joint tenant she is technically entitled. Courts with divorce jurisdiction, however, have wide property adjustment powers and are not constrained by existing beneficial ownership. How, then, will the court decide what is a fair and just settlement for Richard and Hyacinth? In *White v White* [2000] 1 AC 596 (HL) the House of Lords indicated that any award made must be measured against the 'yardstick of equality' whilst in *Miller v Miller; McFarlane v McFarlane* [2006] UKHL 24 the House of Lords emphasized the importance of sharing (as well as needs and compensation). However, this does not mean that property must always be divided equally between the spouses. In many cases, there will be insufficient assets to divide property equally *and* meet the needs of the parties. As the latter prevails, equal division will not be possible in such cases. But if there are surplus assets (as in this case), the court will need to explain why it is not ordering equal division. The decision of the court will be based on the statutory guidelines contained in **s. 25 MCA 1973**.

Section 25(1) requires the court to consider 'all the circumstances of the case' and to give first consideration to the welfare of any minor children of the family who has not attained 18. The latter is clearly inapplicable. The court is then directed to consider the specific matters listed in **s. 25(2)**, which create no hierarchy (*Piglowska v Piglowski* [1999] 2 FLR 763). **Section 25(2)(a) and (b)** are always very relevant, i.e. the present and future income and other financial resources of both parties, including any increase in capacity it would be reasonable to expect a party to take steps to acquire, and the present and future needs, obligations and responsibilities of each. Here, Richard is a successful businessman with an annual salary of £110,000, he has substantial savings and may well have a pension (future resource). The good news for him is that, as Baroness Hale said of Mr Miller, these key assets were 'assets generated solely by the husband during a short marriage'. Similarly in *B v B (Ancillary Relief)* [2008] EWCA Civ 284 the court did not divide the assets equally because they had been brought to the marriage primarily by the wife. Hyacinth has not worked since the marriage, preferring to spend Richard's money, though she is apparently a secretary and part-time model. Should she be expected to work? It is not enough to make general assertions about earning capacity, evidence is required that Hyacinth can in fact become self-supporting. Hyacinth is only 28, she has no young children to look after, has not been out of the job market for too long and would seem to have earning potential either as a secretary or model.

The fact that the marriage has been short (three years) is also relevant (**s. 25(2)(d)**), as is the standard of living enjoyed by the parties before the breakdown of the marriage (**s. 25(2)(c)**). But Hyacinth cannot expect to be enabled to maintain the same standard forever, particularly now that the court need no longer attempt to keep the parties in the financial position they would have been in had the marriage not broken down. Again, the House of Lords was adamant that the high standard of living provided by Mr Miller for two years and nine months did not entitle his 33-year-old former wife to expect it to continue unabated post-divorce for the rest of her life. This approach was also taken in the high-profile case of *McCartney v Mills McCartney* [2008] EWHC 401 (Fam).

Section 25(2)(e) MCA 1973 directs the court to have regard to any physical or mental disability of either party; the fact that Richard has multiple sclerosis will be viewed as significant. The court is also required to consider the contribution made by both to the welfare of the family under **s. 25(2)(f)**. Although domestic and non-domestic contributions are equally valuable (*White v White*, see earlier), Hyacinth appears to have made very little contribution to the welfare of the family. In *Miller; McFarlane* (see earlier), Baroness Hale said that big mismatches in their respective contributions to the welfare of the 'family' are relevant and in *Charman v Charman (No. 4)* [2007] EWCA Civ 503 the mismatch justified departing from equal division of assets.

Of particular significance in this case is the conduct of the parties (**s. 25(2)(g)**). Hyacinth's conduct certainly merits examination. First, she had been secretly having an affair with Justin for two years before she left Richard. Secondly, her reaction to Richard's illness was unforgivable. In *K v K (Financial Provision: Conduct)* [1988] 1 FLR 469 a wife helped her depressed husband with his suicide attempts in order to set up home with her lover and to get as much from her husband's estate as possible. The court held that to ignore this conduct would offend right-thinking members of society. The facts are not dissimilar here. Hyacinth saw an opportunity to get the house, presumably for herself and her lover, and what happened to Richard was of no concern to her. In addition, her behaviour at the time of the marriage could be considered suspect; what were her motives for insisting on the flat being sold and a house bought in joint names? Did she never intend to stay long, but wanted to ensure half the house was hers, as in *Cuzner v Underdown* [1974] 2 All ER 351? It would appear that Hyacinth's conduct is such that to ignore it would offend a reasonable person's sense of justice and falls within **s. 25(2)(g)**. In *Clark v Clark* [1999] 2 FLR 498, a wife who had induced her much older husband to buy property in her name had her conduct borne in mind by the divorce court. But Richard should note that her 'bare' adultery will not help him under this head—Mr Miller did not have to pay any more 'just' because he went off with another woman.

Under the **MCA 1973** (as amended) the goal now seems to be to make the parties self-sufficient. The court has a mandatory duty, when deciding whether to make financial provision, to consider whether it would be appropriate to terminate the financial obligations of the parties as soon after the decree as the court thinks just and reasonable (**s. 25A(1)**). The court will consider an immediate clean break or a limited term order.

One option available to the court in this case would be a deferred clean break. If the court considers it appropriate to do so, it may make a periodical payments order (PPO) in Hyacinth's favour for a limited term only, to enable her to adjust without undue hardship to her change of status (**s. 25A(2)**). Here, as we have seen, Hyacinth has real potential for increasing her earning capacity and should be made to make adjustments to her life and attain financial independence as soon as possible. It would seem entirely appropriate to limit any PPO, even though Hyacinth does not have a job at present, particularly as the marriage was short, and childless (***Barrett v Barrett*** [1988] 2 FLR 516). In addition, Hyacinth should be debarred (by an order under **s. 28(1A)**) from applying for an extension of the term: if not, Hyacinth could at any time during its life apply for the period to be lengthened (***Richardson v Richardson (No. 2)*** [1994] 2 FLR 1051). However, in the circumstances it would not seem inappropriate, unjust or unreasonable to effect an immediate clean break (**s. 25A(3)**) with no continuing obligations at all. Once again, the wife's conduct hardly permits her to argue that his earning capacity was a resource to be equitably shared (as noted in ***J v J*** [2004] EWHC 52 (**Fam**)). Property adjustment orders could be made and Hyacinth's claim for periodical payments dismissed. Hyacinth, as a joint tenant, is entitled to half the value of the house, but a court could well decide to reduce her share in the light of her conduct.

One suspects that Richard is likely to want to settle and, knowing what a court is likely to do, it is suggested that Hyacinth is offered a one-off, unreopenable, capital pay-off, representing far less than 50 per cent of his assets. Given that Mrs Miller obtained less than one-sixth of her husband's solely generated £32 million, after a near three-year marriage with no reckonable misconduct, the offer to be made to Hyacinth does not seem unreasonable.

Question 2

Victor and Margaret were married 25 years ago. The matrimonial home was bought in joint names. Victor has been in index-linked pensionable employment in the public sector all his working life. Margaret was a secretary but gave up work early on in the marriage to run the home. She successfully completed a cordon bleu cookery course earlier this year.

Victor and Margaret had a daughter, Sarah, who died last year aged 8. Sarah was born with Down's syndrome and Victor could never cope with the fact that a child of his was disabled. He found her an embarrassment and wanted her to go into a residential home. Margaret would not hear of this and, three years ago, Victor left the matrimonial home. He is living in a comfortable flat owned by his father who is terminally ill. Victor will inherit the flat and a considerable sum of money when his father dies.

Since moving out, Victor has paid maintenance for Margaret (and for Sarah until her death), together with all outgoings on the house. He has some money in a building society account.

Divorce proceedings have now been commenced. Margaret is claiming maintenance and wants to stay in the matrimonial home. Victor says she can have the house if she takes on all the outgoings, but he will not pay maintenance any longer, as he feels that she could now seek employment.

Advise Victor.

 Commentary

As with **Question 1**, it is possible that the parties will resolve this financial dispute using mediation, but it is necessary to understand the powers of the court in order properly to advise the client and ensure that he does not agree to an unfair settlement. You need to discuss the orders available under the **MCA 1973**, the principles that will influence the court's decision and the possible 'package' that the court would create if the matter is not resolved by the parties. As always, take your cue as to which aspects require emphasis from the information provided, for example the length of the marriage.

 Answer plan

- Principles only, not amounts.
- Powers—**ss. 22–4 MCA 1973**.
- Criteria—**s. 25(2) MCA 1973**.
- Property adjustment *and* periodical payments?
- Pension—'attach' or 'share'?

 Examiner's tip

The examiner will have deliberately omitted certain crucial facts, for example the value of the house, because he or she is putting you in the adviser's position and expects you to raise the issue.

Suggested answer

On divorce, the court has very wide powers under the **Matrimonial Causes Act (MCA) 1973** (as amended) to make arrangements which are, in all the circumstances, just and fair. The financial position of both Victor and Margaret will be considered as a whole, and any financial settlement will be a complete package unique to them. On the information provided, it seems likely that at least until Victor's father's death there are insufficient funds to prevent one or both of them from noticing the difference. This is not a *White v White* [2000] 2 FLR 981 situation: the problem is how best to share the loss, not the surplus.

Financial provision orders available under **ss. 23, 24 MCA 1973** include periodical payments orders, secured or unsecured, and lump sum orders. Secured periodical payments would ensure that payments would not cease on Victor's death. If there are sufficient assets, a lump sum order might, even today, be made on the basis of a *Duxbury* ([1987] 1 FLR 7) calculation. This is a computer program which produces 'capitalized maintenance' by taking into account variables, for example inflation, life expectancy and income tax.

In relation to the matrimonial home, the court has a wide discretionary power to adjust property rights (**s. 24**) and to make arrangements which are in all the circumstances just. Possible options here are a transfer of property order (TPO) or a settlement of property order (SPO). We know that Margaret wants to remain in the matrimonial home and that Victor says she can have it, but only on condition that she takes on all the outgoings. The house is in joint names and Victor could sign his half share in the home to Margaret. Indeed, even if Victor did not agree to this, a court could make a TPO to recognize that, although Margaret may not have made any financial contribution to the home, her efforts in the home have supported Victor. However, one must be realistic, and Margaret has not worked for over 20 years and has no income at present. Can she afford to run the house? Almost certainly not, at least not immediately. Margaret would need financial provision orders to enable her to take over the outgoings. Of course, much is dependent on the size and value of the property: it is thus necessary to elicit this information from Victor.

One possibility would be for the court to make a *Martin* order (*Martin v Martin* [1976] 3 All ER 625), allowing Margaret to continue to live in the home (even though there are no relevant children) until she remarries, cohabits, voluntarily removes or dies. The house would then be sold and the proceeds divided. *Martin* orders avoid the disadvantage inherent in a *Mesher* order (*Mesher v Mesher* (1973) [1980] 1 All ER 126) in relation to the wife's ability to rehouse herself when the postponed sale eventually takes place (*Clutton v Clutton* [1991] 1 All ER 340). With such an order, provision could be made for Victor to continue to contribute to the mortgage and other outgoings, or Margaret could be awarded an increased lump sum order (LSO) or periodical payments order (PPO) so that she herself could make the payments.

Margaret is probably not going to be made to leave the house unless it is unrealistically big for her, but the court is going to have to decide on the best way to enable her to remain there. In deciding what provision to make for Margaret, the court will be governed by the legislative guidelines of **s. 25**. **Section 25(1)** directs the court to have regard to 'all the circumstances of the case' and to give first consideration to the welfare of any minor children of the family. Clearly, the latter is not relevant here. The court is then directed to consider the specific matters listed in **s. 25(2)**. First, the income, earning capacity and other financial resources of each party now and in the foreseeable future, including any increase in earning capacity it would be reasonable to expect a party to take steps to acquire (**s. 25(2)(a)**). All Victor's assets will be taken into account. We are told that he has money in a building society account and also that he lives in a flat owned by his father, presumably rent free, thus freeing more of his income for possible maintenance payments. Inheritance expectations are rarely relevant because they are uncertain (***Michael v Michael*** [1986] 2 FLR 389) but the court may take account of the likelihood that Victor will benefit under the will of his father who is terminally ill. We are told that he will inherit the flat and a considerable sum of money (future resources), although we should remember that in ***Miller; McFarlane*** [2006] 1 FLR 1186 it was held that inheritances during the marriage are non-marital/family assets and that this may be taken into account. In ***H v H (Financial Provision)*** [2009] EWHC 494 a husband was not expected to share bonuses earned after the couple had separated. However, Victor and Margaret's situation differs from these cases as there are insufficient resources to meet the parties' needs.

Also relevant under **s. 25(2)(a)** is Margaret's potential earning capacity. Victor thinks she should be self-supporting, particularly now that, tragically, she no longer has a young child to look after. But does Margaret in fact have any earning potential and is it reasonable to expect her to seek employment? Margaret is probably in her late forties, she has not worked for over 20 years and will undoubtedly find it very difficult to find a 'good' job. In ***Leadbeater v Leadbeater*** [1985] FLR 789, in not dissimilar circumstances, the Court of Appeal decided that it was not reasonable to expect the wife to 'familiarize herself with modern office technology'. The court will require evidence to prove earning capacity and will surely take the view, certainly since ***White v White*** (mentioned earlier) and ***Miller; McFarlane*** (mentioned earlier), that after a long marriage (25 years) and having been a good mother and homemaker and also taking into account her age (**s. 25(2)(d)**), Margaret is entitled to more than just being able to survive (***M v M*** [1987] 2 FLR 1). We do not know how useful Margaret's cordon bleu cookery qualification might be. Margaret and Victor's respective needs, obligations and responsibilities are also relevant. The parties' needs are often in practice the main factor and, of course, include accommodation. Here, Victor is living in his father's flat and Margaret is in the matrimonial home and wishes to stay there. Neither party is entitled to expect to maintain the standard of living which he or she enjoyed during the marriage—that would badly damage the other—but adequate recognition should be given to it and after a long marriage, as here, the vulnerable party is entitled to the security of a reasonably decent standard of living.

The court will acknowledge the contribution made by Margaret to the welfare of the family by looking after the home and caring for Sarah (**s. 25(2)(f)**). She has a real value as a housewife and her contribution may be relevant in assessing a lump sum order that may be made in her favour. In addition, **s. 25B(2) MCA 1973** (as inserted by the **Pensions Act 1995**) requires the court to consider whether to make a financial provision order when a spouse has a pension scheme. **Section 25B(4)–(6)** allows for 'attachment' whereby the pension fund manager could be ordered to divert some of the eventual payments from the pensioner to his divorced wife. Alternatively, the court could make a 'pension sharing order' under **s. 24B** (inserted by the **Welfare Reform and Pensions Act 1999**) which directs the scheme's trustees to transfer a specified amount of one spouse's entitlement to the other on divorce.

It is unlikely that conduct will influence the outcome. Victor's attitude towards Sarah was not exactly exemplary, but he does not appear to have done anything that the court has so far thought inequitable to disregard within **s. 25(2)(g)**.

Section 25A directs the court to the desirability of promoting severance of financial obligations between the parties. In all cases where a court is deciding whether to make financial provision, there is a mandatory duty to consider a clean break or impose a time limit on financial obligations (**s. 25A(1)**). If the court decides that no continuing obligations should be imposed, it may effect an immediate clean break (**s. 25A(3)**). This would involve making property adjustment orders and dismissing any claim for periodical payments with a direction that no further application be made. But there is no presumption that a clean break must be ordered (*SRJ v DWJ* [1999] 2 FLR 176). A clean break appears unlikely in the circumstances and as a consequence, the court may make a PPO. When contemplating making a PPO, the court must consider whether it is appropriate to make the order for a limited term, sufficient to enable Margaret to adjust without undue hardship to ending her dependence on Victor. Can and should Margaret find a way of adjusting her life to attain financial independence? In *Barrett v Barrett* [1988] 2 FLR 516, Butler Sloss LJ said that limiting an order was not appropriate in a situation where the wife had no job and where it could not be predicted whether she would ever have one. It would seem, therefore, that to terminate payments to Margaret would cause hardship, and it should be left to Victor to apply to have the PPO varied if and when she does become self-sufficient. In *Flavell v Flavell* [1997] 1 FLR 353, the Court of Appeal suggested that the termination of a PPO in favour of a former wife in her fifties would normally only be appropriate if she had a lot of capital and a good earning capacity. In *Miller; McFarlane* it was held that PPOs can be used to 'compensate' the recipient (e.g. where a wife looks after the children and reduces her earning capacity), as well as to maintain him or her. Unlike property orders and lump sum orders, PPOs can be varied by the court under **s. 31 MCA 1973**. Margaret might therefore apply for the PPO to be increased in the future (an upward variation), as Mrs McFarlane did recently (*McFarlane v McFarlane* [2009] EWHC 891 (Fam)). Alternatively, Victor might apply to capitalize the PPO when he inherits his father's estate (**s. 31(7A)**; see *Lauder v Lauder* [2007] EWHC 1227 (Fam)).

Most likely, a PPO would be made whether or not the house is actually transferred over to her by Victor, but particularly in the event of a *Martin* order, in which case she may also receive a lump sum to ensure the equitable redistribution of the available assets. Such measures could take appropriate account of Victor's testamentary and pensionary expectations. Let us hope that (perhaps with the help of mediation) the parties will be successfully encouraged to reach a settlement at, or before, a Financial Dispute Resolution appointment.

 Question 3

To what extent will agreements concerning financial arrangements reached by the parties to a marriage be recognized by the courts on divorce?

 Commentary

This question instructs students to consider the extent to which agreements concerning financial arrangements are recognized by the courts in the event of divorce. It therefore requires candidates to discuss the enforceability of pre-nuptial, post-nuptial and post-separation contracts and the role of consent orders. Students should consider relevant provisions of the **MCA 1973** and recent case law such as ***Radmacher (formerly Granatino) (Respondent) v Granatino (Appellant) [2010] UKSC 42.*** If the question had asked students to consider the extent to which couples can determine the financial consequences of separation (as opposed to spouses) it would have been necessary to examine the validity of cohabitation contracts also (***Sutton v Mischon de Reya* [2003] EWHC 3166 (Ch)**).

 Answer plan

Type of agreement	Relevant law
Pre-nuptial agreements—made before the marriage	Cannot oust the jurisdiction of the court under **MCA 1973**
	S. 25(1) MCA 1973—must be considered as one of the relevant circumstances
	***Radmacher v Granatino* [2010]**—criteria to apply when determining the weight to accord
	Law Commission provisional recommendations

Type of agreement	Relevant law
Post-nuptial agreements—made after the marriage but before separation	*MacLeod v MacLeod* [2008]—distinguished from pre-nuptial contracts
	Considered enforceable subject to **s. 35 MCA**—power to vary
	Radmacher and *Kremen v Agrest* suggest they should be treated in the same way
Post-separation agreements	Usually upheld **s. 35 MCA 1973**—power to vary
	Advisable to encapsulate into a consent order

 Examiner's tip

Impress the examiner by referring to the provisional proposals made by the Law Commission in relation to pre-nuptial contracts.

 Suggested answer

The courts have wide-ranging powers to make financial and property orders on divorce under the **Matrimonial Causes Act (MCA) 1973**. But will the court exercise those powers if the spouses have made an agreement relating to financial arrangements after divorce? Such agreements might be concluded before the couple marry (pre-nuptial or pre-marriage or ante-nuptial agreements), after the couple have married but before they have separated (post-nuptial agreements) or after the relationship has broken down and the couple have decided to separate (post-separation agreements). These three types of agreement will now be considered in turn.

Pre-nuptial agreements

A pre-nuptial contract is not strictly binding on the courts in England and Wales because it is not possible to deprive the courts of their power to make financial orders under the MCA 1973. Initially, such contracts were also considered unenforceable on the ground of public policy, because they envisage divorce before the marriage has even begun. However, in *M v M (Pre-Nuptial Agreement)* [2002] 1 FLR 654 the court indicated that this objection was not as significant as it used to be, given the high rates of divorce. If one spouse applies for financial relief, the court is not obliged to enforce the pre-nuptial agreement, but must not disregard it completely as s. 25(1) directs the court to take into account *all* the circumstances of the case when deciding whether and how to exercise its powers. This includes the existence of, the terms of and the circumstances surrounding the conclusion of a pre-nuptial agreement. In *N v N (Jurisdiction: Pre-Nuptial Agreement)* [1999] 2 FLR 745 the court held that the weight to be attached to such an agreement is a matter for the divorce court in exercising its financial relief discretion under s. 25 MCA 1973. Initially, the judiciary was hostile towards ante-nuptial agreements. For example, in *F v F (Ancillary Relief: Substantial Assets)* [1995] 2 FLR 45, Thorpe J held that they were of 'very limited significance' but, since then, support for such contracts has grown and in *K v K (Ancillary Relief: Prenuptial Agreements)* [2003] 1 FLR 120 the court held that injustice would be done to the husband if the agreement was ignored completely. In that particular case, the couple had entered into a pre-marriage contract that limited the wife's claim to the husband's capital in the event of divorce. When the marriage broke down shortly after, the wife applied for financial relief for herself and her child. She was awarded periodical payments in recognition of her child-caring duties and her husband had to provide a home for the child (although it would revert to him, when the child's full-time education was completed). But the agreement was decisive in terms of capital as the wife did not receive any. It should be noted that both spouses had received independent legal advice before signing the pre-nuptial contract. If the parties had not done so, the court might not have taken the agreement into account. Other factors, such as non-disclosure by one party and signing the contract on the eve of the wedding, have also affected the court's perception of the agreement (*J v V (Disclosure: Offshore Corporations)* [2003] EWHC 3110 (Fam)).

In 2010, the Supreme Court clarified the status of pre-nuptial contracts in *Radmacher (formerly Granatino) (Respondent) v Granatino (Appellant)* [2010] UKSC 42. Prior to marrying in England, the German heiress and her French fiancé signed a pre-nuptial agreement which was subject to German law and restricted the parties' rights to make a financial claim against one another in the event of divorce. When the couple separated the husband petitioned for financial relief and was awarded over £5.5 million in the High Court. However, the Court of Appeal reduced this to approximately £1 million because due weight had not been given to the pre-nuptial contract. The husband appealed to the Supreme Court which indicated that three issues arose for consideration. First, were there circumstances surrounding the formation of the contract which should detract from the weight accorded to it (e.g. undue pressure, lack of information or lack of advice)? Secondly, did the foreign element enhance the weight to be accorded to it? Finally, did the circumstances prevailing at the time of the court order make it fair or just to depart from the agreement? For example, did the agreement prejudice the requirements of any children or had the applicant's needs changed? The Supreme Court indicated that in this case there were no circumstances surrounding the formation of the contract which should detract from its weight as the husband was aware of the contents and declined the opportunity to take legal advice. The fact that it was binding under German law demonstrated that the parties intended to be bound by it and there were no circumstances prevailing at the time of the court order which would make it just to depart from the agreement. The Supreme Court thus agreed with the Court of Appeal that the husband should be granted provision for his role as father of the two children, but not for his long-term needs. In relation to the latter, the agreement was decisive.

The family courts have had the opportunity apply the ruling in *Radmacher* on a number of occasions. In *Z v Z* [2011] EWHC 2878 the High Court held that the agreement had been freely formed by the French couple concerned and there were no circumstances rendering it unfair. It was thus appropriate to depart from equal sharing, which the court would have ordered in the absence of the contract and as the agreement did not exclude the possibility of a maintenance claim, the wife was awarded periodical payments, which were capitalized.

The Law Commission Consultation on Marital Property Agreements (Law Com No. 198) opened in January 2011 and ended in April 2011. The Law Commission has provisionally recommended that for an agreement to be enforceable: it should be in writing and signed by both parties; there should be full and frank disclosure; there should be no vitiating factors; and legal advice should be a requirement. Provided that an agreement meets these requirements, it should be enforceable unless it fails to provide for children or leaves one spouse reliant on state benefits. In February 2012, the Law Commission announced that the consultation would be extended to review the extent to which one spouse should be obliged to meet the other's needs after divorce and the treatment of non-marital property. A supplementary consultation paper is to be issued in autumn 2012 and a full report is expected in 2013.

Post-nuptial agreements

In the past, post-nuptial contracts have been distinguished from pre-nuptial contracts as they are formed after the couple has married rather than before. As Baroness Hale pointed out in *MacLeod v MacLeod* [2008] UKPC 68, a pre-nuptial contract may be the price that one party extracts from the other in return for his or her willingness to marry, but in the case of post-nuptial contracts the couple have already undertaken responsibilities towards one another and so this risk does not exist. *MacLeod v MacLeod* [2008] concerned a deed made eight years after the couple had married, that confirmed but also significantly amended a contract signed prior to the marriage. When the couple separated, the husband fulfilled his obligations under the contract but, despite this, the wife took action for financial relief. At first instance the court awarded the wife an additional lump sum to reflect her housing needs and made financial orders for the benefit of the five children. However, the Privy Council overturned the lump sum award on the basis that the post-nuptial agreement that the parties had signed should be enforced. The Privy Council thus held that post-nuptial agreements are capable of being enforced, provided that no vitiating factors are present, such as undue influence as in *NA v MA* [2006] EWHC 2900 (Fam). The court also pointed out that they are capable of being varied in the same way that a post-separation agreement can be varied but, as explained later, the courts are reluctant to alter a properly concluded contract. In *Radmacher v Granatino* [2010] UKSC 42 the Supreme Court indicated (*obiter dicta*) that the factors that a court must consider when determining the weight to be accorded to a pre-nuptial agreement should apply to post-nuptial contracts (although Lady Hale disagreed). In *Kremen v Agrest* [2012] EWHC 45 the High Court did so and concluded that no weight should be attached to the agreement as it was highly disadvantageous to the wife, she had not received independent legal advice, she did not appreciate the implications of the agreement and the husband had failed to disclose the extent of his wealth. The Law Commission's provisional recommendations apply to pre-nuptial and post-nuptial agreements, which suggest that they should, indeed, be treated in the same way.

Post-separation agreements

A post-separation contract is an agreement reached between spouses after the relationship has broken down. Because mediation and the private settlement of disputes are encouraged, agreements relating to financial arrangements should be enforceable as *Soulsbury v Soulsbury* [2007] EWCA Civ 967 demonstrates. **Section 34(1) MCA 1973** provides that maintenance agreements are enforceable, but any provision in such contracts purporting to restrict any right to apply to a court for an order shall be void. Post-separation contracts are thus capable of being enforced, but both parties have the right to apply to the court for the agreement to be varied. **Section 35** empowers the court to vary an agreement on the basis of 'a change in the circumstances' or if 'the agreement does not contain proper financial arrangements with respect to any child of the family.' In *Edgar v Edgar* [1980] 1 WLR 1410 (CA) the Court of Appeal indicated that other circumstances will be relevant, such as 'undue pressure by one side' and the 'exploitation of a dominant position to secure an unreasonable advantage'. The court also emphasized that 'formal agreements, properly and fairly arrived at with competent legal advice, should not be displaced unless there are good and substantial grounds for concluding that an injustice will be done by holding the parties to the terms of their agreement' (p. 1417). The Law Commission provisional recommendations referred to earlier, also apply to post-separation agreements, which suggest that all three forms of agreement should be treated in the same way.

Finally, it should be noted that the parties may present to the court an agreement that has been reached and ask the court to make a consent order under **s. 33A MCA 1973**. The court will examine the terms of the agreement in order to ensure that it is fair and equitable but it does not scrutinize it in detail. A consent order may be made following Financial Dispute Resolution appointments which were introduced in 2000 to encourage divorcing couples to reach an agreement. If a consent order is made it can be challenged in the same way that any other court order can be challenged, i.e. there must be a flaw in the trial process (e.g. non-disclosure) or a fundamental unforeseen change of circumstances (*Barder v Calouri* [1988] AC 20 (HL)). It is thus more difficult to reopen an agreement embodied in a consent order than it is to vary a separation agreement under **s. 35 MCA 1973**.

This answer has demonstrated that spouses are able to reach an agreement relating to financial provision on divorce and in many cases they will be upheld. However, it is not yet clear whether pre-nuptial, post-nuptial and post-separation contracts should be treated in the same way. Hopefully, after the Law Commission has issued a report in 2013, legislation will be introduced to clarify the issue.

Further reading

Burrows, D. (2012) 'Supervening Events: Barder Appeals and the Set Aside Jurisdictions: Part I'. Fam Law 452.

Clark, B. (2011) 'Ante-Nuptial Contracts after *Radmacher*: An Impermissible Gloss?' 33(1) JSWFL 15–24.

Cooke, E. (2012) 'Pre-Nups and Beyond: What is the Law Commission up to Now?' Fam Law 323.

Scherpe, J. M. (2011) 'Fairness, Freedom and Foreign Elements—Marital Agreements in England and Wales after *Radmacher v Granatino*'. 23(4) CFLQ 513–27.

Scott, T. (2012) 'The First Post-*Radmacher* Decision: *Z v Z (No. 2)*'. Fam Law 73.

Websites

www.nfm.org.uk

www.resolution.org

14

Child support: the state and the court

Introduction

Until the **Child Support Act (CSA) 1991** came into force, child maintenance was determined by the courts on a case-by-case basis. The **CSA 1991** replaced this system with a formulaic approach and created the Child Support Agency (CSA) to administer it. Although the **CSA 1991** has been amended on a number of occasions (as discussed in **Question 1**), the basic premise of the original **CSA 1991** remains. The parent with care will identify the non-resident parent, the administrative body uses a fixed formula to determine his or her liability and will punish him if her if he or she does not pay. Under the **Child Maintenance and Other Payments Act 2008**, the CSA became one of two delivery bodies of the Child Maintenance and Enforcement Commission (CMEC), with the other being 'Child Maintenance Options' which provides information and support. For example, Child Maintenance Options has developed a 'Child Maintenance Private Agreement Form' to help parents formulate their own family-based arrangements. In July 2012, CMEC was disbanded and the CSA and Child Maintenance Options now fall under the remit of the Department for Work and Pensions.

Although most maintenance applications are dealt with by the CSA, the courts have retained a residual role. The second question in this chapter considers such applications.

 Question 1

How far have the shortcomings of the Child Support Act 1991 been ameliorated by subsequent reforms?

Commentary

This question requires students to discuss the shortcomings of the **CSA 1991** and to examine the changes made to the **1991 Act** by the **CSA 1995**, the **Child Support, Pensions and Social Security Act 2000** and, most recently, the **Child Maintenance and Other Payments Act 2008** which is not fully in force. Ensure that you do not merely explain the changes that have taken place but you discuss whether the shortcomings of the **1991 Act** have been ameliorated.

Answer plan

Reform	Impact
CSA 1995	Enabled a parent to apply for a departure direction—helped to remedy the unfairness of the system BUT made it more complicated
Child Support, Pensions and Social Security Act 2000	Simplified the formula—made the calculation quicker and reduced costs
	Introduced reductions for other relevant children—enables the non-resident parent better to provide for children living with him BUT the non-resident children receive less
	Introduced reductions for shared care—designed to encourage shared parenting
	Introduced tougher sanctions
Child Maintenance and Other Payments Act 2008	Introduction of the gross income scheme—will speed up the calculation and allow for regular reviews
	Increased the flat rate—minimal impact on the recipient
	Abolished the duty on parents in receipt of benefits to apply to the CSA and enabled those who did to keep all maintenance—improves the standard of living for many children
	Improved enforcement mechanisms

Examiner's tip

Bring your answer up to date by referring to further proposals for change, for example *Supporting Separated Families: Securing Children's Futures, Strengthening Families, Promoting Responsibility* (DWP, 2012).

Suggested answer

Prior to the implementation of the **Child Support Act (CSA) 1991**, the courts could award child maintenance under the **Matrimonial Causes Act (MCA) 1973**, the **Domestic Proceedings and Magistrates' Courts Act (DPMCA) 1978** and the **Children Act (CA) 1989**. Their activation was dependent upon a private initiative, taken normally by the other parent and the powers of the court under each statute were governed by (similar) discretionary codes. It became extremely clear that these methods left many children in one-parent families poorly supported by the non-resident parent (in most cases the father) and that, in so far as the shortfall was being met, it was by the taxpayer, mainly through the medium of social security benefits. Furthermore, there was evidence of a wide variety in the orders actually made by the courts and problems concerning the enforcement of court orders.

The White Paper *Children Come First* (Cm 1264, 1990) set out the case for change and the proposals for reform, which were incorporated into the **CSA 1991**. The basic principles of the Act were (and still are) that a non-resident parent (which does not include a step-parent) should have to pay child support based on a formula. That maintenance is collected by an administrative body (the CSA) and paid to the parent with care.

Post-implementation, a number of well-publicized objections arose concerning the formula used to determine the maintenance liability, injustices caused by the lack of flexibility and the administrative shortcomings of the CSA.

The original formula was extremely complex because it was based on how much maintenance was required and how much the non-resident parent should be left with to live on. This meant that the CSA was slow to make assessments and mistakes were made, both of which were costly. In addition, there was a lack of flexibility in the system. The **CSA 1995** attempted to deal with the latter by enabling either parent to apply for a 'departure direction' in three 'cases'. The first involved 'special expenses' and covered costs incurred in travelling to work, maintaining child contact and certain debts incurred for the benefit of the family before the marriage breakdown. The second 'case' concerned 'property or capital transfers' made before the **1991 Act** came into force. It was an attempt to address the resentment expressed by some fathers (and their new families) that these men would not have entered 'clean break' divorce settlements, under which they may have ceded the family home to their former wives, had they realized that the maintenance assessments subsequently calculated under the Act would be so high. The third 'case' concerned parents awarded no child support or very low levels of child support when the non-resident parent had assets capable of producing income or had a lifestyle inconsistent with the declared income or had deliberately reduced his or her income. The **Child Support, Pensions and Social Security Act 2000** retained this system by allowing either parent to apply for a 'variation' in three situations which are similar to those that justified a departure direction under the **1995 Act**. They are currently contained in **s. 28A CSA 1991**. The introduction of departure directions was welcomed as it alleviated injustice, but it also made child support assessments more complicated and thus contributed to delays and increased costs. The CSA was thus further criticized.

The **Child Support, Pensions and Social Security Act 2000** simplified the formula used to determine child support liability by introducing a system whereby a set percentage of the non-resident parent's income was deducted depending upon how many children he or she had. If the non-resident parent earns over £200 per week net he or she will pay 15 per cent of his or her income for one 'non-resident' child, 20 per cent for two and 25 per cent for three or more. An upper limit of £2,000 net per week was imposed by the legislation, which means that the maximum assessment under the Act is £26,000. If the parent with care wishes to apply for more maintenance, because the non-resident parent is very wealthy, the application needs to be made to the courts under the **CA 1989**. If the non-resident parent's net income is between £100 and £200 per week, he or she will pay a reduced rate. Those with income under £100 pay £5, those with income of less than £5 per week pay nothing, as do certain categories of non-resident parents, for example children under 16. The introduction of a flat rate for low earners and nil liability for certain parents speeds up the assessment process and reduces costs.

The **2008 Act** retains the approach introduced by the **2000 Act** by deducting a set percentage from the non-resident parent's salary. However, the percentages will be based on gross income rather than net income and as a consequence they will be lower. They will be 12 per cent for one child, 16 per cent for two children and 19 per cent for three if the non-resident parent earns under £800. If the non-resident parent earns over £800 he or she will pay the percentages indicated on the first £800 and 9 per cent, 12 per cent and 15 per cent on the income between £800 and £3,000. The advantage of using gross rather than net income is that the CSA does not need to wait for the non-resident parent to supply the information, as details of gross income can be obtained from Her Majesty's Revenue and Customs. The amount payable will be based on the latest available tax year information and will therefore be automatically reviewed on a regular basis. This system, which is due to begin to come into effect in October 2012, should speed up the assessment process, which as explained earlier was one of the major shortcomings of the CSA. The Act also increased the flat rate for low earners to £7 (**s. 4(1) of and Sch. 1 to the CSA 1991**) but the Government has recently announced that it will be increased to £10 (*Supporting Separated Families: Securing Children's Futures, Strengthening Families, Promoting Responsibility* (DWP, 2012)).

The original **CSA 1991** was also criticized because the formula failed to take into account the fact that the non-resident parent might be providing for children living with him or her. The **Child Support, Pensions and Social Security Act 2000** amended the system so that 15 per cent, 20 per cent or 25 per cent of the non-resident parent's income will be ignored (if he or she has one, two or three or more children living with him or her) before calculating the amount payable for the qualifying child or children in question. The **Child Maintenance and Other Payments Act 2008** retains this system but will reduce the amounts ignored to 12 per cent, 16 per cent and 19 per cent because of the introduction of the gross income system.

As explained earlier, the **CSA 1995** created a system whereby a non-resident parent with special expenses could apply for a departure direction. Special expenses might be incurred if the non-resident parent lived some distance from the child and had to pay for flights etc. to maintain contact, but the everyday cost of maintaining contact with a child was not taken into account. The **Child Support, Pensions and Social Security Act 2000** introduced a system whereby the amount payable would be reduced if the qualifying child stayed overnight with the non-resident parent at least 52 times a year. Under the 2000 and 2008 schemes the amount is reduced by one-seventh if the child stays 52 nights and two-sevenths if the child stays between 104 and 155 nights etc. The purpose of this is to encourage contact between the non-resident parent and his or her child and demonstrates a shift away from the original purpose of the Act (namely, to reduce the burden on the taxpayer) towards placing more emphasis on the welfare of the child.

One of the most significant reforms made by the **Child Maintenance and Other Payments Act 2008** relates to applications by parents with care in receipt of social security benefits. **Section 6 CSA 1991** required a parent on certain income-related benefits, such as income support, to allow the CSA to pursue the non-resident parent for child support, unless there was a risk of harm or undue distress to the parent with care or the child. If the parent with care did not cooperate, his or her benefits could be reduced. Furthermore, if the CSA successfully recovered child support, the benefits would be reduced and so the child and the parent with care were not advantaged in any way. The **Child Support, Pensions and Social Security Act 2000** introduced a 'child maintenance premium' whereby the first £10 of child support recovered would be ignored when calculating benefits. This was increased to £20 from October 2008. **Section 6** reflected the rationale of the original legislation, namely to ensure that parents support their children, rather than the taxpayer. The Paper produced by the Department for Work and Pensions, *A New System of Child Maintenance* (Cm 6979, 2006), which preceded the **2008 Act**, made it clear that the purpose of the new system is to reduce child poverty. As a consequence, the **2008 Act** repealed **s. 6** and if the parent with care chooses to apply to the CSA from April 2010 all child support payments will be disregarded when calculating out of work benefits for the parent with care.

The original **CSA 1991** provided the CSA with various enforcement powers, i.e. the power to make a deduction from earnings order and the power to apply to a magistrates' court for a liability order which could ultimately lead to committal to prison. Yet, despite this, billions of pounds of child support remained uncollected. The **2000 Act** provided tougher sanctions such as late payment penalties and disqualification from driving orders, although the latter are rarely imposed. The **2008 Act** added further enforcement powers, for example curfew orders and disqualification from holding or obtaining travel authorization.

This answer has demonstrated that the original **Child Support Act** had various shortcomings as the system it introduced was slow, inflexible, overly complicated, costly and caused injustice. The reforms enacted in 1995, 2000 and 2008 have tackled some of these issues but problems remain, for example relating to enforcement. In 2011 and 2012 two further consultations were launched by the DWP: *Strengthening Families,*

Promoting Responsibility: The Future of Child Maintenance (2011) and *Supporting Separated Families: Securing Children's Futures, Strengthening Families, Promoting Responsibility* (2012). Proposals include charging parents to utilize the child maintenance service in order to encourage couples to make their own arrangements (and to reduce the cost of the state service). Such proposals have been subject to criticism, and so it remains to be seen whether they will be implemented and, if so, whether they will improve matters.

 Question 2

Critically consider the extent to which the child support legislation has affected the family lawyer.

 Commentary

This short essay question asks students critically to consider the extent to which child support legislation has affected the family lawyer. In order to do this, you need to explain when court action may be initiated (i.e. the **MCA 1973**, the **DPMCA 1978** and the **CA 1989**) as the family lawyer will be involved in such claims, but also to explain when the **Child Support Act** applies as this will emphasize the extent to which the family lawyer is *not* involved in maintenance claims. Furthermore, the 'critically consider' element of the question requires you to consider whether the involvement or lack of involvement of the family lawyer in child maintenance cases actually matters.

 Answer plan

- Involvement in **Child Support Act** cases.
- Situations when the **Child Support Act** does not apply: non-UK residents, stepchildren, children over 16.
- 'Top-ups'.
- Claiming lump sums, property adjustment etc.
- Agreements and consent orders.

 Examiner's tip

It is useful to cite some statistics to demonstrate the extent to which the courts and the CSA determine maintenance.

Suggested answer

The **Child Support Act (CSA) 1991** largely transferred the assessment and collection of child maintenance from the courts to an administrative body, i.e. the Child Support Agency. As a consequence, the role of the family lawyer in terms of making applications for maintenance has been greatly reduced. But the family lawyer will be need to be able to advise clients on the **Child Support Acts** and may occasionally become involved in such claims. First, a family lawyer who is advising a client on separation or divorce needs to be able to understand how the **Child Support Act** system works in order to be able to calculate the amount due, so that he or she can consider the impact on the remainder of the financial package that is being negotiated or applied for on divorce. The amount payable through the CSA will be viewed as a 'responsibility' for one party (**s. 25(1)(b) Matrimonial Causes Act (MCA) 1973**) and a 'resource' for the other (**s. 25(1)(a) MCA 1973**) when financial relief applications are heard by the court. Secondly, a client may require advice on applying for a variation under the **Child Support Act (CSA) 1991** or there may be a dispute as to parentage, which the family lawyer is required to assist on. Furthermore, the family lawyer may become involved in child support proceedings if enforcement action is taken in the courts against his or her client. But it should be noted that neither a child support applicant nor a child who suffered due to non-payment can engage a family lawyer to pursue enforcement of an award made by the CSA (*Kehoe v UK* [2008] 2 FLR 1014 (ECtHR) and *Treharne v Secretary of State for Work and Pensions* [2008] EWHC 3222 (QB) respectively). This is a serious issue due to the numbers of non-resident parents who do not pay the amount required of them. On 31 March 2012 non-resident parents were meeting their obligations in 80 per cent of cases, which means that they were failing to do so in 20 per cent of cases (CMEC, *Annual Report and Accounts* (2011–12), p. 5). The family lawyer may become involved in appeals and judicial review cases, although these are relatively rare.

There are also a number of circumstances where the court's jurisdiction still applies and where the work of the family lawyer continues as before. First, the CSA may lack jurisdiction under the **Child Support Act** because one or more of: the person with care; the non-resident parent; and the qualifying child, is not 'habitually resident' in the UK. Indeed, what constitutes 'habitual residence' may itself require legal advice. Secondly, step-parents are not liable under the **Child Support Act** and, as a consequence, an application must be made to the courts if the parent with care wishes to claim financial support from the step-parent. Thirdly, the **Child Support Act** does not apply to children between 16 and 19 years of age who are not in full-time, non-advanced education, or to 'children' over 19 (**s. 55**). As a result, if 'maintenance' is sought for such children it will be necessary to make an application to the courts. Most are made under the **Children Act (CA) 1989** but if the parents are, or have been, married to each other then proceedings may also be possible under the **MCA 1973**, or under the **Domestic Proceedings and Magistrates' Courts Act (DPMCA) 1978**. Each of these routes is based on private legal initiative and usually involves the applicant engaging a family lawyer to act for them. In addition, all three types of claim require the courts to use their discretion, which inevitably means that a family lawyer is required to advise the client as to the likely outcome.

Furthermore, it will be necessary to make an application to the court if the parent with care wishes to seek more maintenance than the maximum possible under the **Child Support Act** system (currently £15,600 for one child and £26,000 for three or more children). **Section 8 CSA** permits the court to make orders to meet expenses in respect of disabled children, which will often exceed the CSA limits. In addition, s. 8(6) recognizes the power of the courts to 'top up' payments after the maximum assessment has already been made under the **CSA**. In *Re P (A Child: Financial Provisions)* [2003] **EWCA Civ 837** the mother made a claim for financial support under **s. 15 of and Sch. 1 to the CA 1989** against the child's father who was extremely wealthy. She was awarded £70,000 per annum in periodical payments, when the maximum payment from the CSA for claims made after March 2003 for one child would have been £15,600. Lawyers have certainly retained the lucrative end of the market, but such claims are relatively rare. In 2008, the courts in England and Wales heard 1,110 financial applications under the **CA 1989** (Judicial and Court Statistics, 2008). By 2011, the number of applications had fallen to 728 with only 614 orders made (Judicial and Court Statistics, 2012, Tables 2.3 and 2.4). In comparison, in the financial year 2011–12, 899,000 children were benefiting from maintenance under the **CSA 1991** (CMEC, *Annual Report and Accounts* (2011–12), p. 5).

It should also be noted that the CSA can only make awards for child maintenance. If the parent with care seeks some other type of order, for example a lump sum or property transfer, it is necessary to initiate court proceedings. Lump sums and property adjustment orders can be made in respect of a child under **s. 24(1) MCA 1973** on divorce or separation. In 2011, 4,616 lump sum orders and 3,650 property adjustment orders were made in respect of children during ancillary relief proceedings (Judicial and Court Statistics, 2012, Table 2.7). It is also possible for the court to make a lump sum order under **s. 27 MCA 1973** and the **DPMCA 1978** for the benefit of a child while the marriage subsists. Applications while the marriage subsists are rare and thus provide little work for the family lawyer. However, lump sum orders and property settlements made under the **CA 1989** are more common. Such claims are often brought by the mother of a child born outside marriage, against the child's father who is particularly wealthy. For example, in *Re P* (see the previous paragraph) the court required the father to provide £1 million for a house for the child and its mother to live in until the child reached the age of 18. At this point the property would revert to the father. Family lawyers will also become involved in court-based matters under **s. 8(5) CSA 1991**, which enables the court to make a maintenance order in favour of a child provided it is in terms agreed in writing by the parties. These will normally be part of an overall financial package on divorce. Similarly, such orders may be varied under **s. 8(3A)**. All in all, just under 14,000 ancillary financial relief orders were made for children in 2011 (Judicial and Court Statistics, 2012, Table 2.7). Finally, it should be noted that the most recent child support legislation, the **Child Maintenance and Other Payments Act 2008**, encourages parents to reach voluntary agreements concerning child maintenance, first because it is thought that parents are more likely to pay and, secondly, to relieve the CSA. This may provide family lawyers with additional work as couples may seek advice regarding the contents and enforceability of such agreements. Child Maintenance Options has developed a standard-form agreement to enable parents to reach their own family-based arrangement, but the extent to which they are utilized is unclear. If recent proposals to charge parents for using the state child maintenance service are implemented, the number of private agreements may increase and, at the same time, the family lawyer may receive additional work (See *Strengthening Families, Promoting Responsibility: The Future of Child Maintenance* (2011) and *Supporting Separated Families: Securing Children's Futures, Strengthening Families, Promoting Responsibility* (2012).

This essay has demonstrated that the role of the family lawyer in relation to child support issues has grown in terms of the variety of issues he or she may asked to advise upon, but has diminished in terms of the quantity of cases that family lawyers will bring to the courts. Whether this change matters depends, of course, upon from whose perspective it is examined. The family lawyer would have regretted the loss of such a large quantity of cases, but would have been pleased that he retained the lucrative end of the market. From the client's perspective, the introduction of an administrative system should have improved matters as far as the client was concerned, but we know that this has not always been the case.

Further reading

DWP (2011) *Strengthening Families, Promoting Responsibility: The Future of Child Maintenance*. Consultation document.

DWP (2011) *Government's Response to the Consultation on Strengthening Families, Promoting Responsibility: The Future of Child Maintenance*.

DWP (2012) *Supporting Separated Families: Securing Children's Futures, Strengthening Families, Promoting Responsibility*. Consultation document.

Ellman, I.M. and Braver, S.L. (2011) 'Lay Intuitions about Child Support and Marital Status'. 23(4) CFLQ 465.

Websites

www.childmaintenance.org

www.cmoptions.org

www.dwp.gov.uk/policy/child-maintenance/

Putting it all together

Introduction

In practice, the person who seeks your advice often wishes a number of issues to be considered, for example divorce, financial matters and children. This chapter provides six examples. As the questions may cover many areas of family law, you will not be able to cover each topic in the same way that you would a single topic question, but you should be able to display a command of a wide area of knowledge, not superficially, but incisively and with depth in the relevant area.

The following table indicates the topics covered by each question in this chapter.

Question	Topics covered
1	**Divorce**: the ground for divorce—fact (b), behaviour, and fact (d), two years' separation
	Children Act 1989: parental responsibility, **s. 8** orders, welfare principle, welfare checklist
2	**Nullity**: voidable marriage—**s. 12(c)** mistake, **s. 12(f)** pregnancy by another, bars
	Paternity: presumptions and testing
	Divorce: the ground for divorce—fact (a), adultery
3	**Children**: parental responsibility, non-marital father, paternity
	International child abduction: Hague Convention, Child Abduction and Custody Act 1985, rights of custody

Question	Topics covered
4	**Domestic violence/harassment: Family Law Act 1996, Protection from Harassment Act 1997**, tort
	Public law relating to children: care order, threshold criteria, contact with a child in care, discharge of care order
	Private law relating to children: residence
5	**Domestic violence:** non-molestation orders and occupation orders
	Nullity: void and voidable marriage, gender reassignment
	Children Act 1989: parental responsibility, **s. 8** orders, residence, change of name, welfare principle, welfare checklist
6	**Financial relief:** on divorce, periodical payments, orders for sale, pension-sharing orders, property adjustment orders
	Family property: claiming a beneficial ownership in the family home, cohabitants

? Question 1

Edgar and Fiona have been married for 12 years. They have two children, George aged 10 years and Harriet aged 8 years. Edgar's work takes him out of the country for six months out of every year. Fiona admits that she finds children 'tedious', and when Edgar is away, George and Harriet are mainly looked after by Edgar's mother.

Fiona has acknowledged that she has a drink problem and has joined Alcoholics Anonymous where she met Ivy who has moved in with Fiona while Edgar is out of the country. Ivy and Fiona are lovers. Ivy occasionally drinks heavily.

When Edgar returned home unexpectedly he found Ivy and her friend Jake staying at the house. Fiona told Edgar that Ivy is bisexual and that Jake and Ivy are lovers. Fiona, Ivy and Jake have decided to move to a commune and intend to take the children with them.

Edgar has confided his unhappiness to Kay, his personal assistant, and with her help and understanding he has accepted that his marriage to Fiona is at an end.

Edgar seeks your advice as he wishes to marry Kay as soon as possible. He has recently gained a promotion and his new job will involve no overseas travel. Edgar is of the view that he will be able to provide a more stable and suitable home for the children and the spouses have agreed that Edgar will buy out Fiona's interest in their house.

Advise Edgar.

Commentary

Divorce and disputes relating to children are a likely area of overlap. This question requires students to consider the ground for divorce under the **Matrimonial Causes Act (MCA) 1973** and **s. 8** orders under the **Children Act (CA) 1989**. However, there is no mention of property or income in the scenario and, as a consequence, students are not expected to discuss ownership of property or ancillary financial relief. Of course, it is quite possible that students will face a problem question that requires discussion of divorce and ancillary relief.

Answer plan

- Divorce—**MCA 1973**. Sole ground—irretrievable breakdown, **s. 1 MCA 1973** proven by one of five facts, **s. 1(2)**.
- Behaviour, **s. 1(2)(b)**. Explain why not adultery, **s. 1(2)(a)**. No-fault fact—**s. 1(2)(d)**.
- Parental responsibility—**CA 1989**.
- Residence order, **s. 8 CA 1989**.
- Welfare principle, **s. 1**. Checklist, **s. 1(3)**.

Examiner's tip

Do not make the mistake of treating Fiona's relationship with Ivy as 'adultery'.

Suggested answer

To begin, it is necessary to advise Edgar that a 'private' resolution of the disagreements between him and Fiona would probably benefit all concerned, save money and best serve his desire to marry Kay 'as soon as possible'. Indeed, the couple will be required to consider mediation before court action can be commenced in relation to the children.

In relation to ending the marriage, the first point to note is that there is nothing to suggest that the marriage between Edgar and Fiona is void (**s. 11 Matrimonial Causes Act (MCA) 1973**) or voidable (**s. 12 MCA 1973**). As a result, Edgar must bring his marriage to an end by divorce. No petition for divorce can be presented within the first year of marriage (**s. 3 MCA 1973**) but as Edgar and Fiona have been married for 12 years this is not a problem. Edgar must present a petition to the divorce county court showing that his marriage has broken down irretrievably, this being the sole ground for divorce (**s. 1(1) MCA 1973**). Irretrievable breakdown must be shown by one or more of five facts, namely: (a) adultery together with intolerability, (b) behaviour, (c) desertion, (d) two years' separation and the respondent consents to a decree being granted and (e) five years' separation (s. 1(2)). As Edgar wishes to marry Kay as soon as possible only the first two 'facts' will be considered at this point as they offer a quicker way out of the marriage than the last three 'facts'.

To petition on the first fact Edgar must prove that Fiona has committed adultery and that he finds it intolerable to live with her (s. 1(2)(a)). Adultery is voluntary sexual intercourse between a man and a woman who are not married to each other, but one of whom at least is married (*Clarkson v Clarkson* (1930) 143 TLR 623). The requirement of one man and one woman will rule out Fiona's relationship with Ivy as the basis for an adultery petition, although it may be considered as 'behaviour' that Edgar cannot be expected to endure.

To petition on the second fact, the petitioner must satisfy the court that the respondent has behaved in such a way that the petitioner cannot reasonably be expected to live with the respondent (s. 1(2)(b)). Behaviour has been defined as 'action or conduct by one spouse which affects the other' (*per* Sir George Baker P in *Katz v Katz* [1972] 1 WLR 955). Evidence of Fiona's relationship with Ivy (*Coffer v Coffer* (1964) 108 SJ 465) and possibly her drink problem may be sufficient behaviour to satisfy the district judge that Edgar is entitled to a decree.

Edgar must show that as a result of Fiona's behaviour he cannot reasonably be expected to live with her. The test is a cross between a subjective and an objective test. 'Would any right thinking person come to the conclusion that this husband has behaved in such a way that this wife cannot be expected to live with him, taking into account the whole of the circumstances and the characters and personalities of the parties?' (*per* Dunn J in *Livingstone-Stallard v Livingstone-Stallard* [1974] 2 All ER 766). The court will look not only at Fiona's behaviour but also at Edgar's behaviour (*Ash v Ash* [1972] Fam 135; *Hadjimilitis (Tsavliris) v Tsavliris (Divorce: Irretrievable Breakdown)* [2003] 1 FLR 81): is he particularly sensitive, is he a drunken petitioner objecting to a drunken respondent? If Edgar can show a disparity in behaviour he should commence divorce proceedings immediately based on the behaviour fact (b).

Even though Edgar may wish to marry Kay as soon as possible, he should at least give some consideration to 'the divorce by consent fact'. **Section 1(2)(d)** provides that irretrievable breakdown can be established if the parties have lived apart for a continuous period of at least two years immediately preceding the presentation of the petition and the respondent consents to a decree being granted. This could allow Edgar and Fiona to bring their marriage to an end with minimum distress to themselves and to their children.

Fiona wishes to take the children to a commune whilst Edgar thinks he can provide a more stable home. As married (or even divorced) parents of these children, they each have parental responsibility for George and Harriet (**s. 2(1) Children Act (CA) 1989**) and each may exercise that responsibility independently (**s. 2(7)**). In the absence of any order, there is nothing Edgar can do to prevent Fiona taking the children to the commune and nothing Fiona can do to prevent Edgar taking the children to his home.

Edgar should apply for a residence order. A 'residence order' means an order settling the arrangements to be made as to the person with whom a child is to live (s. 8(1)). Although Fiona has said that she finds children to be tedious, she has expressed a desire to take the children to the commune, so it would seem highly likely that she will dispute Edgar's application and, presumably, will make an application herself. Where divorcing parents can make their own arrangements as to where the child is to live, then the court will not intervene (s. 1(5) CA 1989). As there is a dispute, the court will need to consider the arrangements for the children. The welfare of George and Harriet will be the court's paramount consideration when deciding where the children should live (s. 1(1)). Where the making of a s. 8 order is opposed, the court is to have regard to the welfare checklist (s. 1(3)). The factors to be taken into account are not given any order of importance, nor is it stated that the factors are to be given equal importance. It is not always necessary for the court to consider all seven items (*H v H (Residence Order: Leave to Remove from Jurisdiction)* [1995] 1 FLR 529).

The court should have regard to the ascertainable wishes and feelings of the children, considered in the light of their age and understanding (s. 1(3)(a)). For young children the court will usually need to rely on the children and family reporter's report. In *Re R (Residence: Shared Care: Children's Views)* [2005] EWCA Civ 42 the views of 7- and 9-year-old siblings, who favoured dividing their time between their parents, were considered by the court. The wishes of George and Harriet, aged 10 and 8, may therefore be taken into account but the court will not be constricted by their wishes and should disregard them if their future welfare appears to diverge from their express wishes. It is the decision of the court and not the child (*Re P (A Minor) (Education: Child's Views)* [1992] 1 FLR 316).

The children's physical, emotional and educational needs will be noted. Their physical needs may be better catered for by Edgar. The welfare officer's report would discuss details of the physical environment in the commune and compare that with the children's present home and the accommodation that Edgar is offering. Fiona does not appear to have made a major contribution to the children's emotional or physical development. Wherever possible, brother and sister should be brought up together so that they are an emotional support to each other (*C v C (Custody of Children)* [1988] 2 FLR 291). Under s. 1(3)(c) the court must have regard to 'the likely effect…of any change in the circumstances'. With Edgar, they would stay in their lifelong home (where his mother may still be available).

Fiona's drink problem (*Re D (A Child) (Residence: Ability to Parent)* [2001] 2 FCR 751 will be taken into account, but what is more likely to cause concern is the fact that Fiona, who has not been a devoted mother, wishes to take the children away from a familiar background into the uncertainty and possible instability of the life of the commune, with what the court may view as unsuitable companions. The capability of the parents and any other person who might care for the children, to meet the children's needs will be considered under s. 1(3)(f). The court may decide that the children would be at risk of suffering harm if they went with Fiona (s. 1(3)(e)) and today there is no presumption that young children (or girls approaching puberty) should live with their mother (*Re G* [2006] UKHL 43).

In the circumstances it would appear unlikely that the court would grant a residence order to Fiona. If Edgar can show that he is capable of providing for the needs of the children, although he cannot show a stable home at this stage, the court may make a residence order in his favour while giving directions as to how the order is to be effected (s. 11(7)).

Question 2

Amanda married Barry over two years ago when she was six months pregnant. She admitted to Barry, before their marriage, that she was not sure whether he, Barry, was the father of the child or whether it was Cliff. Barry, who was jealous of Cliff, had attempted to impress Amanda with stories of his famous and wealthy relatives. The stories were untrue.

Shortly after the child, Desdemona, was born, Amanda resumed her affair with Cliff. Barry knew of the relationship but continued to live with Amanda in the hope that the affair would end.

Last week Amanda told Barry that she was taking Desdemona and going to live with Cliff as he was now free to marry her.

Barry regrets marrying Amanda and has no wish to live with her any more. He has grave doubts as to whether Desdemona is his child, as she bears a striking resemblance to Cliff.

Advise Amanda who states that she wishes to marry Cliff as soon as possible and does not care how the marriage is brought to an end, nor by whom.

Commentary

An overlap of nullity and divorce is something you should expect. In a family law examination, or in practice, it is unlikely that you will be able to consider nullity in isolation without considering divorce, although the reverse situation does not necessarily apply. If you are asked to advise one of the parties you will need to consider not only the availability of the remedies but also the advantages and disadvantages of particular proceedings. In nullity, for example, the parties will normally have to appear in court whereas in an undefended divorce the procedure has become something akin to an administrative process with no necessity for the parties to give evidence in court.

Answer plan

- Nullity—define void/voidable marriages. Void grounds, **s. 11 MCA 1973**. Voidable, **s. 12**.
- Apply voidable grounds to the facts.

- Establishing paternity.
- Bars to voidable marriages, **s. 13**.
- Divorce—**s. 1 MCA 1973**. Sole ground irretrievable breakdown, **s. 1(1)**. Which of the five facts applies to the facts?

 Examiner's tip

Although the court will not annul the marriage on the basis that Amanda did not consent due to mistake, you must nonetheless discuss this ground as the question talks about Barry's untrue stories.

 Suggested answer

Amanda wishes to be free to marry Cliff as soon as possible. If her marriage to Barry were so faulty as never to have existed then she would be free to marry Cliff right away, but nothing in the facts suggests that Amanda's marriage to Barry is void *ab initio*. A void marriage is one that will be regarded as never having taken place and can be so treated by both parties to it without the necessity of any decree annulling it (**s. 11 Matrimonial Causes Act (MCA) 1973**). In contrast, a voidable marriage is one that will be regarded as valid until a decree annulling it has been pronounced (*per* Lord Greene MR in *De Reneville v De Reneville* **[1948] P 100**) (**s. 12 MCA 1973**). A marriage will be void if the parties lack capacity to marry or have not complied with the necessary formalities (**s. 11 MCA 1973**). If the marriage is not void then it must be brought to an end by annulment on a voidable ground, or by dissolution by divorce before Amanda can be free to marry Cliff. In most instances, those wishing to end a void marriage will do so by decree for the avoidance of doubt.

Amanda has said that she does not care how the marriage is brought to an end, nor by whom and Barry has stated that he regrets marrying Amanda, so it would seem that either party would be prepared to initiate nullity or divorce proceedings. It should be noted that nullity will involve a full hearing, whereas divorce can be dealt with simply using the 'special procedure'.

Potentially there appear to be grounds on which the marriage may be voidable (**s. 12**). The non-consummation grounds can be ruled out as can mental disorder, a Gender Recognition Certificate, venereal disease and lack of consent due to duress, as there is no information to suggest that any of these grounds apply. Amanda may claim that she did not validly consent to the marriage due to mistake (**s. 12(c)**). Clearly, she was not mistaken as to the nature of the ceremony; Amanda was aware that she was exchanging marriage vows with Barry (unlike *Mehta v Mehta* **[1945] 2 All ER 690**, where there was a mistaken belief that the ceremony was one of religious conversion). Before the marriage Barry had attempted to impress Amanda with stories of his famous and wealthy relatives and it has now transpired that these stories were untrue. Mistake as to identity will make the marriage voidable only where one party fails to marry the individual whom he or she intended to marry. Mistake as to attributes (*C v C* [1942] **NZLR 356**) or the other party's fortune (*Wakefield v Mackay* (1807) 1 Hag Con 394) will not invalidate the marriage. Therefore Barry's tall stories will not make this marriage voidable.

The marriage might be voidable if at the time of the marriage the respondent was pregnant by some person other than the petitioner (**s. 12(f)**). Desdemona may be Barry's child although she bears a striking resemblance to Cliff. Any child born to a wife is presumed to be the child of the husband although this presumption may be rebutted by evidence which shows on a balance of probabilities the child is not the child of the husband (**s. 26 Family Law Reform Act FLRA) 1969**). The court may direct scientific tests under **s. 20 FLRA 1969** and is allowed to consent to the taking of a sample from a child if it is in the child's best interests (**s. 21(3) FLRA 1969** (as amended by the **Child Support, Pensions and Social Security Act 2000**) see *Re O and J (Children)* [2000] **2 All ER 29**). As Amanda wishes to end the marriage it is to her advantage to undergo DNA testing herself and allow Desdemona to be tested. Barry and Cliff should have no objection to being tested as Barry regrets the marriage and does not believe Desdemona to be his child, while Cliff wishes to marry Amanda and presumably would be delighted if Desdemona were proved to be his child. Were any of the parties to refuse to undergo blood tests the court is empowered under **s. 23(1) FLRA 1969** to draw such inferences as it thinks fit (*Re A (A Minor) (Paternity: Refusal of Blood Test)* [1994] **2 FLR 463** and *Secretary of State for Work and Pensions v Jones* [2004] **1 FLR 282**). If Desdemona is Cliff's child, Amanda would have been pregnant by another at the time of the marriage. Nonetheless, a decree will be refused by the court unless it is satisfied that the petitioner was, at the time of the marriage, ignorant of the facts alleged (**s. 13(3), MCA 1973**). Barry's knowledge that Amanda was pregnant is not in itself a bar; he must also know that she was pregnant by someone other than himself (*Stocker v Stocker* [1966] **1 WLR 190**). Amanda had admitted to Barry that she did not know whether he or Cliff was the father of her child, so there was uncertainty. At the time of the marriage Barry did not *know* that Cliff was the father; if he had such knowledge that would be a bar to a nullity decree, but can it be said that he was ignorant of the facts alleged? Would the court be satisfied?

Amanda is unlikely to raise any bar based on the petitioner's conduct (**s. 13(1)**) as she wishes to end the marriage. Nullity proceedings based on **s. 12(f)** should be brought within three years of the marriage (**s. 13(2)**), although leave may be granted for proceedings to be brought out of time in certain cases of mental disorder (**s. 13(4)**). The marriage took place over two years ago so no time should be wasted in presenting a petition.

If Desdemona is proved to be Barry's child there would be no grounds for nullity proceedings, or the child may be Cliff's but the court may have applied the bar in **s. 13(3)** and not granted a nullity decree. If either situation applies the parties would have to end their marriage by divorce.

Divorce proceedings may not be started within the first year of marriage (**s. 3(1) MCA 1973**). As Amanda and Barry have been married for over two years the bar does not apply. The sole ground for divorce is irretrievable breakdown of the marriage (**s. 1(1) MCA 1973**). However, the court cannot hold that the marriage has irretrievably broken down unless the petitioner satisfies the court of one or more of the five facts set out in **s. 1(2)**. The last three facts were discounted as Amanda wishes to marry Cliff as soon as possible and it would seem that **s. 1(2)(b)** (the respondent has behaved in such a way that the petitioner cannot reasonably be expected to live with the respondent) would not be the most obvious fact to choose as Amanda has committed adultery. For Barry to petition on this fact he must prove that Amanda has committed adultery and he finds it intolerable to live with her (**s. 1(2)(a)**).

Adultery is voluntary sexual intercourse between a man and a woman who are not married to each other, but one of whom at least is a married person (***Clarkson v Clarkson* (1930) 143 TLR 623**). Proof of adultery will be satisfied by Amanda and Cliff admitting adultery in the acknowledgement of service of the petition (***Bradley v Bradley (Queen's Proctor Intervening)* [1986] 1 FLR 128**). In addition, Barry must prove that he finds it intolerable to live with Amanda, although it is not necessary for the adultery to be the cause of the intolerability (***Cleary v Cleary* [1974] 1 All ER 498**). The test for intolerability is a subjective one (***Goodrich v Goodrich* [1971] 2 All ER 1340**). Barry regrets the marriage and does not wish to live with Amanda, this would appear to satisfy the test. If the court accepts that the **s. 1(2)** fact has been proved then, unless it is satisfied on all the evidence that the marriage has not broken down irretrievably, it shall grant a decree of divorce (**s. 1(4)**). It is not necessary for Barry to prove that the irretrievable breakdown was caused by the adultery (***Buffery v Buffery* [1988] FCR 465**). In *Stevens v Stevens* [1979] 1 WLR 885, it was the petitioner's own behaviour that had caused the breakdown.

For the purposes of his divorce petition, Barry cannot rely on adultery committed by Amanda if, after the adultery became known to him, they lived together for a period or periods together exceeding six months (**s. 2(1)**). This is an absolute bar (***Court v Court* [1983] Fam 105**). Where the parties have lived together for periods not exceeding six months, after discovery of the adultery, then this shall be disregarded in determining whether the petitioner finds it intolerable to live with the respondent (**s. 2(2)**). Where the respondent commits adultery on more than one occasion, time does not begin to run until after the petitioner learns of the last act of adultery. Although Barry knew of the relationship he continued living with Amanda and this state of affairs continued throughout their married life. Amanda is living with Cliff; presumably the adultery is continuing therefore **s. 2(1)** will not be a bar. This route out of the marriage would appear to be the most certain and speedy and would not involve the parties in a court appearance.

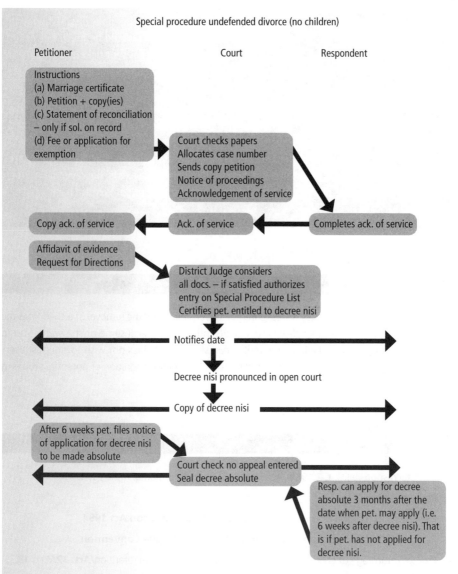

Special procedure undefended divorce (no children)

| Petitioner | Court | Respondent |

Instructions
(a) Marriage certificate
(b) Petition + copy(ies)
(c) Statement of reconciliation
– only if sol. on record
(d) Fee or application for
exemption

Court checks papers
Allocates case number
Sends copy petition
Notice of proceedings
Acknowledgement of service

Copy ack. of service ← Ack. of service ← Completes ack. of service

Affidavit of evidence
Request for Directions

District Judge considers
all docs. – if satisfied authorizes
entry on Special Procedure List
Certifies pet. entitled to decree nisi

Notifies date

Decree nisi pronounced in open court

Copy of decree nisi

After 6 weeks pet. files notice
of application for decree nisi
to be made absolute

Court check no appeal entered
Seal decree absolute

Resp. can apply for decree
absolute 3 months after the
date when pet. may apply (i.e.
6 weeks after decree nisi). That
is if pet. has not applied for
decree nisi.

Figure 2

? Question 3

Ursula, an unmarried mother, has a daughter, Victoria, aged 4. Ted, Victoria's father, spends most weekends with Ursula and his daughter. Ted wishes to marry Ursula but she has told him that she does not wish to 'sign her rights away' either by marriage or by signing documents stating that he is Victoria's father.

William, Ursula's brother, emigrated to Australia five years ago. Ursula is dissatisfied with life in England and believes that schools and career prospects would be much better for them in Australia. Ted does not wish to leave England. William has sent tickets for flights to Australia for Ursula and Victoria; he wishes them to take a holiday to coincide with his birthday in two months' time.

Ted informs you that he wishes to be formally acknowledged as Victoria's father; however, at the moment he admits his relationship with Ursula is 'rocky'. Although he is concerned that Ursula and Victoria may not return to England, he does not wish to prevent them taking a holiday. Ursula says that he is over-reacting and assures him that his concerns are unfounded. Ted does not wish to create a problem where none exists. However, he is worried that once they are out of the country he may not be able to get Victoria back.

Advise Ted.

 Commentary

This question focuses on two key issues: parental responsibility and the removal of a child from the jurisdiction. Often the examiner deliberately omits information because he or she wants you to consider all the options available in different circumstances and does not wish to signpost every step of the way for you; in other words, credit is to be given for recognition of potential problems and solutions.

 Answer plan

- Parental responsibility, **CA 1989**. Acquisition of PR by non-marital father, **s. 4**.
- Proof of paternity.
- Prevention of removal of child from jurisdiction. **Child Abduction Act 1984**.
- Removal—**Child Abduction and Custody Act 1985—Hague Convention**.
- Prompt return/age of child/habitual residence/wrongful removal/retention/**Art. 12/Art. 13**.

 Examiner's tip

In relation to both issues it is impossible to provide a definitive answer unless more information is obtained. It is reasonable to point this out but do not say that there is not enough information in the question for you to be able to answer it.

Suggested answer

There are two main issues of concern to Ted: his parental responsibility for Victoria and international child abduction. Where parents are unmarried, the mother acquires automatic parental responsibility whereas the father must take action to acquire it (**s. 2(2) Children Act (CA) 1989**). Parental responsibility means all the rights, duties, powers, responsibilities and authority which by law a parent of a child has in relation to the child and his property (**s. 3**).

It is possible that Ted acquired parental responsibility by jointly registering the birth of Victoria under **s. 4(1)(a) CA 1989** (as amended by **s. 111 of the Adoption and Children Act 2002**), which came into effect on 1 December 2003. If Ursula and Ted had jointly registered Victoria's birth this will be prima facie evidence that he is the father (**s. 34(2) Births and Deaths Registration Act 1953**; *Brierley v Brierley and Williams* [1918] P 257). Accordingly, the burden would fall on Ursula if she wished to rebut the presumption. It seems unlikely that Ursula would have jointly registered the birth with Ted as the question indicates that she does not wish to sign documents stating that Ted is Victoria's father. As a result of this, it seems that the conclusion of a parental responsibility agreement under **s. 4(1)(b)** is also unlikely. If Ursula changes her mind, a parental responsibility agreement will only take effect if it is made in the form prescribed by the **Parental Responsibility Agreement Regulations 1991 (SI 1991/1478)** and filed with the Principal Registry of the Family Division. It will last until discharged by the court (**s. 4(1)(3)**).

As Victoria's birth was probably registered by Ursula alone and Ursula may be unwilling to enter into a parental responsibility agreement, Ted should apply to court for a parental responsibility order (**s. 4(1)(c)**). It may be necessary to prove paternity by using DNA tests but Ursula may decide to oppose this. Under **s. 20(1) of the Family Law Reform Act (FLRA) 1969** the court has a judicial discretion to direct that tests be taken to seek to determine paternity. The court may refuse to direct a test to be carried out against the will of the parent who has since birth had sole parental responsibility for the child and where the putative father had no relationship with the child (*Re F (A Minor: Blood Tests: Paternity Rights)* [1993] 1 FLR 598). The circumstances are different in this case, as Ted would appear to have established a relationship with Victoria. A test will not be ordered if it is not in the best interests of the child but sought merely to satisfy curiosity (*Hodgkiss v Hodgkiss* [1984] FLR 563). Where the truth as to the child's paternity would be beneficial, a direction should be made (*S v McC, W v W* [1972] AC 24; *Re H (Paternity: Blood Test)* [1996] 2 FLR 65). Increasingly, the courts are taking the view that justice is not served by impeding the establishment of truth. Samples cannot be taken from a person without his consent (**s. 21(1) FLRA 1969**). However, should any of the parties refuse to undergo blood tests the court is empowered to draw such inferences as it thinks fit (**s. 23 FLRA 1969**; *Re A (A Minor) (Paternity: Refusal of Blood Test)* [1994] 2 FLR 463; *Secretary of State for Work and Pensions v Jones* [2004] 1 FLR 282). Furthermore, **s. 21(3) FLRA 1969** (amended by the **Child Support, Pensions and Social Security Act 2000**) enables a court to consent to the taking of a sample in a child's best interests.

If Ted were able to prove paternity he could then apply for a parental responsibility order (**s. 4(1)(a)**). In considering whether to make such an order the welfare of the child will be the paramount consideration (**s. 1(1)**) and the no order principle will apply (**s. 1(5)**). The court will consider the level of commitment to, and involvement with, the child and whether making an order could destabilize a new family unit (which would not apply in this case) and whether it would be justifiable to equate Ted with a married father (*Re P (Parental Responsibility)* [1998] 2 FLR 1996 and *Re J-S (Contact: Parental Responsibility)* [2003] 1 FLR 399). If Ted were to be successful in obtaining a parental responsibility order then he will acquire certain rights and, crucially, Ursula could not remove Victoria from the UK without Ted's consent. Even if Ursula has a residence order in relation to Victoria, no person may remove her from the UK without the written consent of every person who has parental responsibility for her, or the leave of the court (**s. 13(1)**). Section 13(1) does not prevent the removal of a child, for a period of less than one month, by the person in whose favour the residence order is made (**s. 13(2)**). If there is no residence order in force, this does not mean there is no restriction on Ursula taking Victoria out of the country. The **Child Abduction Act 1984** makes it a criminal offence for anyone with parental responsibility for a child under 16 to take the child out of the UK without the consent of all those with parental responsibility, or without the leave of the court. The crime is not committed by a person with a residence order who takes the child out of the UK for less than one month unless it is done so in breach of a court order under **Part II CA 1989**.

As a parent of Victoria, Ted may apply as of right for any **s. 8 order** (*Re C and another (Minors) (Parent: Residence Order)* [1993] 3 All ER 313; s. 10(4)(a)). If Ted feared that Ursula intended Victoria's permanent removal from the UK, he could apply for a specific issue or a prohibited steps order. However, if Ted's fears are merely a product of his over-anxious imagination, with no foundation in reality, then such an application would be inappropriate and may produce an undesired reaction by Ursula.

Ted may find some consolation in that if the worst were to happen, i.e. Ursula and Victoria settling in Australia, then he could invoke **Part I of the Child Abduction and Custody Act 1985** which incorporates the **Hague Convention on the Civil Aspects of International Child Abduction 1980** into UK law. Every Convention country (Australia is a contracting state) has a Central Authority which deals with the administrative action required to operate the remedies under the Convention. Central Authorities must cooperate with each other to promote the objects of the Convention, one of which is to secure the prompt return of children wrongfully removed to or retained in any contracting state (**Art. 1**).

Ted, as a non-marital father, would be disadvantaged, in that his family life is not protected by the **Hague Convention** unless he had taken steps to acquire parental responsibility (see House of Lords in *Re J (A Minor) (Abduction: Custody Rights)* [1990] 2 AC 562, *sub nom C v S (A Minor) (Abduction)* [1990] 2 FLR 442). However, the Court of Appeal has held that terms such as 'rights of custody' have been held to be capable of describing inchoate rights of those who are carrying out duties and enjoying privileges of a custodial or parental character, which may not yet formally be recognized or granted by law (see *Re C (Child Abduction) (Unmarried Father: Rights of Custody)* [2003] 1 FLR 252). The importance to non-marital fathers of having parental responsibility in cases of potential or actual child abduction was emphasized by the Court of Appeal in *Re J-S (Contact: Parental Responsibility)* [2003] 1 FLR 399). This factor provides further incentive to Ted to acquire parental responsibility. Ted may contact the Central Authority in the UK which, in turn, would deal with the Central Authority in Australia, in an attempt to secure a voluntary return of Victoria to the UK. However, if Ursula would not agree to a voluntary return then the Central Authority would initiate proceedings. Should the Convention apply to Victoria's circumstances, the courts could not investigate the merits of the case and must order her return unless one of the grounds in Art. 12 or 13 applied. 'The courts of the country of habitual residence should determine their future…The interests of the child in each individual case are not paramount since it is presumed under the Convention that the welfare of children is best met by return to their habitual residence' (*Re M (A Minor) (Child Abduction)* [1994] 1 FLR 390).

The **Hague Convention** applies where a child under 16 who is habitually resident in one contracting state is wrongfully removed to, or retained in, another (**Art. 4**). The question of a child's habitual residence has been established as one of fact (*Re M (Abduction: Habitual Residence)* [1996] 1 FLR 887). When a child lives with his parents, the child's habitual residence will normally be that of his parents (*Re A (Wardship: Jurisdiction)* [1995] 1 FLR 767). There can be no dispute that, immediately before any retention in Australia, Victoria was habitually resident in the UK. Where both parents have parental responsibility, neither can unilaterally change the child's habitual residence (*Re B (Minors) (Abduction) (No. 2)* [1993] 1 FLR 993). Where a child has been wrongfully removed or retained for less than a year the court must order the return of the child (**Art. 12**). Even where a year has elapsed such return is mandatory unless it is demonstrated that the child is 'settled in its new environment' (**Art. 12**). However, **Art. 13** gives the court a discretion whether to order return if the person who opposes the return can establish that the applicant, at the time of the removal or retention, was not exercising custody rights or consented to it, or subsequently acquiesced, or there is a grave risk of physical or psychological harm if the child is returned, or a mature child objects. There is a heavy burden on a person alleged to have abducted a child if she is to bring herself within the provisions of **Art. 13** (*Re H (Abduction: Grave Risk)* [2003] 2 FLR 141). It would need to be an exceptional case for the child's return to be refused. In exercising its discretion, the court must give due weight to the primary purpose of the Convention. A less stringent approach would undermine the spirit and purpose of the Convention, which is the speedy return of children so that a court in the country of their habitual residence can decide what is best for them. However, in exercising their discretion, the courts have been influenced by the fact that a child returned to the country of habitual residence would be more than likely to be allowed to leave again by a court of that country (*Re A (Minors) (No. 2) (Abduction: Acquiescence)* [1993] 1 FLR 396; *Re K (Abduction: Consent)* [1997] 2 FLR 212).

It is to be hoped that Ursula will relent and enter a parental responsibility agreement with Ted. If not, Ted should apply for a parental responsibility order, as it can be seen that a parental responsibility order provides him with rights in relation to Victoria, notably that his consent must be sought in certain matters and, potentially of importance here, gives him rights under the **Hague Convention.**

Question 4

Ruby, aged 8, was taken into care last year and has settled down well with her foster parents, Simon and Trish. Ruby's parents, Violet and William, were divorced two years ago. Violet's behaviour, which had become increasingly bizarre, culminated in her being committed to a mental hospital last year. By then William had left the area and could not be traced.

As Violet's condition was thought to be improving, six months ago she entered a programme at the hospital, which has the aim of rehabilitating her into the community. Trish told Violet that she was welcome at their home any time. At first the visits went well; Violet would call soon after Ruby returned from school and would take tea with Trish and Ruby, leaving before Simon returned from work. On one occasion, two months ago, Simon returned early and since then Violet has visited the house every evening, waiting for Simon's return. When he insisted that she should limit her visits to seeing Ruby and leave before his return, she declared her undying love for him and has since then pestered him with phone calls during the day at his place of work and throughout the night and weekend at his home. She has delivered letters and presents to his home every day. So far Simon and Trish have been able to shield Ruby from this behaviour.

Last week William called at the house. He wants Ruby to live with him. He has remarried and his wife, Yasmin, has said that she would love to have Ruby come and live with them.

Advise Simon and William.

Commentary

This question illustrates a situation where family law alone cannot provide a remedy. Here the overlap is between family law and the law of tort, i.e. trespass, nuisance and harassment. In terms of the law relating to children, the public *and* private law provisions of the **CA 1989** are relevant.

Answer plan

- Simon and Violet are not associated persons—**Part IV, Family Law Act (FLA) 1996**.
- Tort: Trespass? Nuisance? **Protection from Harassment Act 1997**?
- Injunction appropriate?

- Care order, **s. 31 CA 1989**.

- Contact with child in care, **s. 34**.

- Residence order/discharge of care order/supervision order.

Examiner's tip

Although Simon cannot utilize the provisions of the **FLA 1996**, you must explain why, rather than omitting it completely.

Suggested answer

Although Simon is being pestered in his own home he will be unable to invoke the protection the court can give under **Part IV of the Family Law Act 1996**. The **1996 Act** protects 'associated persons' (**s. 62(3)**) from molestation (**s. 42**). Simon and Violet are not 'associated' therefore Simon must seek a remedy in tort.

It would seem unlikely on the facts that Simon would wish to apply to the county court for a residence order (**s. 8 Children Act (CA) 1989**) so that he could ask for a non-molestation injunction ancillary to those proceedings. Molestation or harassment can be forbidden where the behaviour complained of amounts to an established tort. Simon has limited Violet's visits to his property; if she comes on to his land outside the time allowed she will be a trespasser.

Besetting a person's house, by conduct which seriously interferes with the ordinary use and enjoyment of the house beset, can support an action for nuisance (*J Lyons & Sons Ltd v Wilkins* [1899] 1 Ch 255). The legal owner of property can obtain an injunction on the grounds of private nuisance, to restrain persistent harassment by unwanted telephone calls to his home (*Motherwell v Motherwell* [1976] 73 DLR (3d) 62). Nuisance is not actionable per se, damage has to be proved. If Simon is suffering from 'stress' at this point, the continuation of Violet's campaign could lead to physical or psychiatric illness.

The **Protection from Harassment Act 1997** may provide Simon with an effective remedy against Violet's campaign of adoration. A person must not pursue a course of conduct which the person knows or ought to know amounts to harassment of another (**s. 1**). This involves conduct on at least two occasions, and conduct includes speech (**s. 7**). The court may award damages and it may grant an injunction restraining Violet from any conduct which amounts to harassment (**s. 3**). No power of arrest can be attached to the injunction but a warrant of arrest may be applied for if breach is alleged. It is an offence punishable by up to five years' imprisonment to do anything, without reasonable excuse, prohibited by the injunction (**s. 3(6)**).

The court may take the view that an injunction is an unsuitable remedy against Violet. In *Wookey v Wookey* [1991] 2 FLR 319, the Court of Appeal said that a person who was incapable of understanding an injunction could not be guilty of contempt by diso-beying it. When it appears that a person who is molesting the plaintiff may be suffering from a mental disorder, the Official Solicitor should be notified as soon as possible if an application is to be made to a court for an injunction and the possible need for a guard-ian ad litem should be addressed. If the court has evidence to show that Violet is capa-ble of understanding an injunction, then it should be expressed in words she would be able to understand readily. If she is not capable, then the appropriate way to deal with her would be under mental health legislation.

Simon could not apply for a prohibited steps order while Ruby is in the care of the local authority (**s. 9(1) CA 1989**). Even if Ruby were not in care, a prohibited steps order (**s. 8**) could not be used to prevent contact between Violet and Simon as such contact does not relate to parental responsibility; Ruby is not aware of Violet's pester-ing (***Croydon London Borough Council v A* [1992] 2 FLR 271**).

Ruby was taken into care last year. To make a care order the court must have been satisfied that Ruby was suffering or was likely to suffer significant harm and that such harm was attributable to a deficiency of reasonable parental care, or Ruby being beyond parental control (**s. 31 CA 1989**). The local authority will have acquired parental responsibility on the making of the care order (**s. 33(3)**) and will share that responsibil-ity with Violet and William (**s. 2(6)**).

It is the general duty of every local authority to promote the upbringing of children by their families so far as that is consistent with the duty to safeguard and promote the welfare of children who are in need (**s. 17**). In furtherance of that duty the authority is required to allow Ruby reasonable contact with Violet (**s. 34**). The authority may refuse contact for no more than seven days in an emergency if they are satisfied that it is neces-sary for Ruby's welfare (**s. 34(6)**). Refusal of contact for any longer period must have the court's authorization (**s. 34(4)**). When exercising its power the court must apply the welfare principle (**s. 1(1)**) and will have regard to the welfare checklist (**s. 1(3)**). Would Ruby's welfare benefit by refusal of contact or would it simply be more convenient for Simon? Contact could take place at some place other than Simon's home. The local authority could move Ruby to other foster parents but this would be another disrup-tion for Ruby, particularly since she has settled down well with Simon and Trish. Vio-let's behaviour may cause the local authority to re-evaluate any plans it may have had concerning returning Ruby to her mother's care.

Even though Violet and William are divorced, William will retain parental responsi-bility for Ruby; during the life of the care order the responsibility will be shared not only with Violet but also with the local authority. William could apply for a residence order (**s. 8**) and if that were to be granted the care order would be discharged automati-cally (**s. 91(1)**). William could apply for the care order to be discharged (**s. 39(1)**) and the court may choose to replace the care order with a supervision order (**s. 39(4)**). While a supervision order is in force it is the duty of the supervisor to advise, assist and befriend a supervised child.

In the circumstances, the no order principle should prevail; the court could choose not to discharge the care order. It may be better to allow Ruby to get to know her father again; two years apart is a long gap in the life of an 8-year-old child. In addition, although Yasmin wishes Ruby to live with them, a phased relocation may be preferable to a sudden disruption. This would also allow time for assessment of the new arrangements and a children and family reporter's report. In any proceedings in which any question with respect to the upbringing of the child arises, the court must have regard to the general principle that any delay in determining the question is likely to prejudice the welfare of the child (**s. 1(2)**). Nevertheless, if the delay is purposeful it should be encouraged (*C v Solihull Metropolitan Borough Council and Others* [1993] 1 FLR 290).

Question 5

Mark received a copy of his wife's petition for divorce based on his violent behaviour. On reading the petition and in a fit of temper, he beat Naomi, his wife, causing extensive bruising and a broken rib. Naomi has left the matrimonial home with their children, Olga, aged 6, and Poppy, aged 4.

Mark is due to have a sex change operation next week and he wishes to know whether or not this will make the marriage null and void. He acknowledges that the marriage is over but feels that an annulment would reflect the reality of his situation more than a divorce.

Although Mark no longer wants Naomi and the children to live with him, he does wish the children to continue to regard him as a parent and Naomi to treat him as a sister; Naomi thinks this will be too confusing for Olga and Poppy. She is frightened for her own safety and wishes to bring the marriage to an end and make a new start for herself and the children. The matrimonial home is a rented local housing authority property.

Naomi would like to change her daughters' surname to her own maiden name.

(a) How, if at all, may Mark's behaviour be dealt with if Naomi is not keen on involving the police?

(b) Will the marriage be void after Mark's sex change operation?

(c) Is Naomi free to change the children's surname?

The parts to this question are equally weighted.

Commentary

This question directs students to answer specific questions, so keep to the point. Clearly indicate to the examiner which part of the question you are answering. Do not throw in all the information for the examiner to sort out. You are required to discuss protection from domestic violence, the impact of Mark's sex change operation on the status of the marriage and the possible change of the children's surname.

Answer plan

- Domestic violence—orders—**Part IV FLA 1996**. Power of arrest. Undertakings. Breach.
- Void marriage—**s. 11 MCA 1973**.
- Voidable marriage—**s. 12 MCA 1973**.
- **Gender Recognition Act 2004**.
- Parental responsibility. Residence order. **CA 1989**.
- Change of name—if residence order—**s. 13**—if no residence order then applications under **s. 8**—specific issue or prohibited steps. Welfare principle. Checklist.

 Examiner's tip

If your family module covered aspects of housing law, you could also be asked to consider the local authority's duties in relation to homeless persons.

⇨ **Suggested answer**

(a) Naomi may wish to seek a non-molestation order (**s. 42 Family Law Act (FLA) 1996**) to protect herself from Mark. Although molestation is not defined in the Act, the lack of a statutory definition has not given rise to difficulty in the past. Molestation has been described as 'pestering' in *Vaughan v Vaughan* **[1973] 3 All ER 449**; and in *Horner v Horner* **[1982] 2 All ER 495** included 'any conduct which could be regarded as such a degree of harassment as to call for the intervention of the court' (see *C v C (Non-Molestation Order: Jurisdiction)* **[1998] 2 WLR 599**). There is no question that Mark has molested Naomi. The court may make a non-molestation order where an application has been made by a person associated with the respondent, whether or not other family proceedings have been instituted (**s. 42(2)(a)**); or, of its own motion, in any family proceedings (**s. 42(2)(b)**). Mark is clearly an 'associated person' as he is married to Naomi. Where the court has the power to make a non-molestation order it can accept an undertaking under **s. 46(1)** but **s. 46(3A)** provides that the court should not do so if the respondent has used or threatened violence against the applicant or a relevant child. If the court makes a non-molestation order, breach of this order is automatically an arrestable offence (**s. 42A**) and if prosecuted can be punished with a prison sentence of up to five years (**s. 42A(5)**). Mark will only be guilty of an offence if he is aware of the existence of the order at the time. It is also possible to punish breach of a non-molestation order as contempt of court for which the maximum prison sentence is two years. Mark cannot be guilty of an offence *and* punished for a contempt of court for the same action.

Naomi may also seek an occupation order to gain safe access to the matrimonial home (**s. 33 FLA 1996**). If an occupation order is made and it appears to the court that the respondent has used or threatened violence against the applicant or a relevant child, it must attach a power of arrest to one or more provisions of the order, unless it is satisfied that in all the circumstances of the case the applicant or child will be adequately protected without such a power of arrest (**s. 47(2)**). No power of arrest may be attached to an undertaking (**s. 46(2)**) and consequently the latter should not be accepted by the court if the respondent has used or threatened violence (**s. 46(3A)**). If a power of arrest is attached to an order, a constable may arrest, without a warrant, a person whom he has reasonable cause to suspect is in breach of any such provision (**s. 47(6)**). Breach of an occupation order is contempt of court, punishable by a maximum prison sentence of two years.

(**b**) A marriage is void under **s. 11 of the Matrimonial Causes Act (MCA) 1973** if the parties did not have capacity to marry or the required formalities were not complied with. Under **s. 11(c) MCA 1973** the marriage is void if at the time of the marriage, the parties were not respectively male and female. Mark and Naomi were respectively male and female at the time of the marriage and, consequently, the marriage is not void. The **Gender Recognition Act (GRA) 2004** provides that a person of either gender who is at least 18 may make an application, to a Gender Recognition Panel (GRP), for a gender recognition certificate (GRC). This is on the basis of living in the other gender, or having changed gender under the law of a country or territory outside the UK (**s. 1(1)**). The GRP must grant the application if satisfied that the applicant:

(a) has or has had gender dysphoria (i.e., gender dysphoria, gender identity disorder and transsexualism);

(b) has lived in the acquired gender throughout the period of two years ending with the date on which the application is made; and

(c) intends to continue to live in the acquired gender until death (**s. 2(1)**).

The applicant must provide the information by way of a statutory declaration and medical evidence in support (**s. 3**).

If a GRP grants an application it must issue a GRC to the applicant. Unless the applicant is married, the certificate is to be a full GRC. On the issue of a full GRC, the person will be entitled to a new birth certificate reflecting the acquired gender (provided a UK birth register entry already exists for the person) and will be entitled to marry someone of the opposite gender to his or her acquired gender. A married applicant, such as Mark, would receive an interim GRC, which would make the existing marriage voidable (**s. 12(g) MCA 1973** (as amended by the **GRA 2004**)). A decree would not be granted on the **s. 12(g)** ground unless proceedings were instituted within six months of the issue of the interim GRC (**s. 13(2A) MCA 1973** (as amended by **GRA 2004**)).

The court granting the nullity decree under **s. 12(g)** must issue a full GRC. If the marriage ends for any other reason, i.e. divorce, nullity on any other ground or death, the applicant with an interim GRC may apply, within six months of the end of the marriage, for a full GRC. The fact that a person's gender has become the acquired gender will not affect Mark's status as the father of Olga and Poppy.

(c) Where a residence order is in force with respect to a child, no person may cause the children to be known by a new surname without either the written consent of every person who has parental responsibility for them or the leave of the court (s. 13(1)(a) Children Act 1989). If Naomi has residence orders with respect to Olga and Poppy, she will need Mark's permission, as he has parental responsibility (s. 2(1)), or the leave of the court to change the girls' surname. In view of Mark's stated wish to continue to be regarded as a parent, it would seem unlikely that he would agree to such a change. Where there is no residence order in force, he should apply for a specific issue or a prohibited steps order (s. 8) to prevent a change of name. In *Dawson v Wearmouth* [1999] 1 FLR 1167 the court made it clear that a change of surname is an important matter and that the court should not sanction such a step unless it will improve the child's welfare. In *Re W (A Child) (Illegitimate Child: Change of Surname)* [2001] Fam 1 the court indicated that the factors that should be taken into account include: the welfare of the child; the registered name of the child and reasons for the registration; the reasons for seeking to change the child's name; changes of circumstances since registration; and whether the parents were married. The court held that if the parents were married when the child's birth was registered (as Mark and Naomi were) there would have to be strong reasons to change the child's surname from that of the father. Where an application is made either under s. 13 or s. 8 the court must apply the welfare principle (s. 1(1)). Additionally, in a contested s. 8 application, the court must have regard to the statutory checklist (s. 1(4)). Although it is not mandatory for the court to apply the s. 1(3) welfare checklist in a s. 13 application, it has been acknowledged that it provides a useful *'aide-mémoire'* (*Re B (Change of Surname)* [1996] 1 FLR 791). Are the circumstances sufficiently exceptional or embarrassing to permit a change of name? In *Re W* (see earlier) which involved three separate appeals, one mother was permitted to change her son's surname from that of his father because the latter was a known criminal and the mother feared that the child was at risk of harm. It is unclear whether Mark's sex change operation would be considered in the same light.

 Question 6

H and W have lived together for 25 years. They married each other three years ago after W's previous husband died. There are no children. H has always supported them both from his modest income whilst W has struggled as a writer.

W bought their two-bedroomed house in her sole name 30 years ago for £10,000, all the money coming from an inheritance. When H moved in, they agreed to take equal responsibility for household expenses and maintenance costs. The cooking, cleaning, gardening and such have always been equally shared.

Their relationship began to founder two years ago when W at last wrote a bestseller. She has since neglected H emotionally and financially, had a number of short-lived affairs and she and H's brother (a famous thriller writer) now wish to marry each other as soon as possible. Her latest novel is widely seen as a thinly veiled mockery of H.

The house is now worth £200,000. W is currently generating an annual income of £80,000. H's brother is worth nearly £2 million but H is now on long-term sick leave.

Advise H, who wants as much as he can get by way of financial relief ancillary to divorce. (You do not need to advise him about the divorce itself.) How, if at all, would your answer differ were H and W never to have married?

 Commentary

This question requires students to discuss two topics that may be taught some way apart from one another in a family law module. The first is ancillary financial relief in the divorce court and the second is declaratory property rights, which are relevant when cohabiting couples separate, as the latter cannot apply to the court for ancillary relief.

 Answer plan

- Ancillary financial relief on divorce.
- **MCA 1973**—discretionary adjustment.
- 'All the circumstances'; fairness.
- *White*—not half?
- *Miller; McFarlane*!—compensation by periodical payments.
- Declaratory approach for cohabitant.

 Examiner's tip

It is appropriate and convenient to segregate the two parts of your answer and to deal with the married couple first.

 Suggested answer

This question neatly encapsulates the radically different situations of married and unmarried couples as regards their financial and property positions on relationship breakdown. It is only married couples who may obtain a divorce and thus make applications for ancillary financial relief under **Part II of the Matrimonial Causes Act (MCA) 1973**. Although not unlimited, the divorce court's power of redistribution over the family wealth is enormous. In *Hanlon v The Law Society* [1981] AC 124 Lord Denning MR said that: 'The court hands out ... according to what is the fairest provision for the future ...', an approach confirmed by Lord Nicholls in *White v White* [2000] 3 WLR 1571: the implicit objective must be 'to enable the court to make fair financial arrangements'.

Turning first to H and W as a married couple, the court's powers are to be found in **ss. 21–6 MCA 1973**. These are maintenance pending suit, financial provision (periodical payments secured and unsecured, together with lump sums), property adjustment orders (most notably property transfers), orders for the sale of property and orders relating to pensions. The criteria for the operation of these powers are to be found in **s. 25**. H will be relieved to hear that there is no sex discrimination (*Calderbank v Calderbank* [1976] Fam 93). In *Browne v Browne* [1989] 1 FLR 291 a wife was ordered to pay some £175,000 to her former husband, Butler Sloss LJ remarking that it was 'not in any way an unusual application'. More recently, Lord Nicholls in *White* (see earlier) pointed out that although the traditional division of labour 'is no longer the order of the day, who plays what role should prejudice neither spouse.'

H has 'no money of his own', W has and H should know that under **s. 22 MCA 1973**, on a petition for divorce, the court may make a 'reasonable' order for 'maintenance pending suit'. In *M v M (Maintenance Pending Suit)* [2002] 2 FLR 123 the wife got £330,000 p.a. plus school fees but, more significantly for H, it was held in *A v A (Maintenance Pending Suit: Provision of Legal Fees)* [2001] FLR 377 that the *White* non-discrimination principle permitted a costs element in the award.

So far as the other orders are concerned, the fact that there are no children means that the 'first consideration' specified in **s. 25 MCA 1973** may safely be overlooked, and that the **Child Support Act 1991** is inapplicable. **Section 25** requires the court to consider 'all the circumstances of the case', before specifying a number of them. One unspecified circumstance relevant here is the fact that nearly 90 per cent of their relationship was pre-marital. Now that pre-marital cohabitation is acceptable perhaps greater weight will be attached to it on divorce. This could be crucial to H, whose marriage is child-free and 'worked' only for about a year. In *GW v RW (Financial Provision: Departure from Equality)* [2003] 2 FLR 108 it was held unrealistic to treat the periods differently where a relationship moves 'seamlessly' from cohabitation to marriage. A similar approach was taken in *CO v CO* [2004] EWHC 287, but as part of 'all the circumstances of the case', rather than under the 'duration of the marriage' (**s. 25(2)(d)**).

Section 25(2)(a) and (b) are equally significant. They refer to the parties' past and present resources, needs and liabilities. H has nothing, for the moment at least, whilst W is well paid and about to marry his brother who appears to be very well off. His riches are relevant because they reduce W's needs (*Macey v Macey* [1981] 3 FLR 39). **Section 25(2)(c)** mentions the standard of living enjoyed by the family before the breakdown of the marriage, which is not good news for H, as W's long-awaited success seems to have arrived contemporaneously with the breakdown. We are not told how old they are (**s. 25(2)(d)**), but on the timescale given they must be middle-aged, at least. Should H be over 60 he may fall foul of *A v A (Financial Provision)* **[1998] 2 FLR 180** (20 per cent reduction for reduced expenditure needs) and, if over 70, of *A v A (Elderly Applicant: Lump Sum)* **[1999] 2 FLR 969**, where the husband's low life expectancy ensured that he saw very little of his wife's £1 million assets on their divorce. As already stated, **s. 25(2)(d)** also mentions the duration of the marriage and in *Attar v Attar* **[1985] FLR 649** a single capital payment of £30,000 was thought sufficient after a six-month marriage to a very rich man. The duration of the marriage was also relevant in *Miller; McFarlane* **[2006] 1 FLR (HL) 151** (in relation to the Millers) and in *McCartney v Mills McCartney* **[2008] EWHC 401 (Fam)**.

Section **25(2)(f)** refers to contributions to the welfare of the family, such as looking after the home. This seems to have been a matter of equality here. Section **25(2)(g)**, however, seems particularly significant. It refers to 'conduct…that…would…be inequitable to disregard'. W has had a number of short-lived affairs, neglected H financially and emotionally, has taken up with H's brother and then finally mocked him in a novel. In *Baillie v Tolliday* **[1982] 4 FLR 542** the wife's affair with her father-in-law was held relevant. W's not dissimilar behaviour, coupled with her other actions, may well trigger **s. 25(2)(g)**.

In the absence of an arithmetical approach to financial relief, it is difficult to say exactly what H will receive. It must be remembered that the court must encourage 'self-sufficiency' (**s. 25 MCA 1973**, as amended) by, for example, considering whether any periodical payments order should be for a fixed term. H's strong cards are W's riches, her conduct, his support and the more recent decisions on pre-marital cohabitation. In *Miller; McFarlane* **[2006] 1 FLR (HL) 151** it was necessary to 'compensate' Mrs McFarlane by way of periodical payments because she had supported her high-earning husband as stay-at-home mother and wife. True, H does not seem to have given up the same lucrative work as Mrs McFarlane, a solicitor, but H is clearly older, his relationship was longer and W's conduct has been appalling. He should therefore press for the house (or at least a settlement such as a *Martin* order) and periodical payments of one-third of W's current income until further order. As pointed out in *McFarlane* (where the order was one third), the onus should be on the payer to seek a variation rather than the payee.

If H and W are not married

H as unmarried partner to W epitomizes the value of marriage to the economically weaker party to a broken relationship. With no marriage, there can be no divorce, and no financial relief. There is absolutely no question of tapping in to W's income in which H has no claim under ordinary principles of ownership. The one possible avenue here is to the house, by way of implied, resulting or constructive trust, W having bought it 'in her sole name'. By **s. 53(2) of the Law of Property Act 1925**, the normal requirement of a deed or conveyance for the creation of any legal estate does not affect the creation of such trusts. (Proprietary estoppel, whereby W could be prevented from relying on her rights if H had acted to his detriment on her promise, *Lissimore v Downing* **[2003] 2 FLR 308**, is clearly inapplicable here.)

H did not provide any part of the purchase price, unlike the contributor in *Sekhon v Alissa* [1989] 2 FLR 94 who was subsequently held entitled to an interest in equity in the property by way of resulting trust. (NB: the House of Lords in *Stack v Dowden* [2007] UKHL 17 stated that the flexible constructive trust is more appropriate than the resulting trust for matrimonial or quasi-matrimonial property.) H will, therefore, have to establish a constructive trust if he is to claim a share of the property. To do this it is necessary to show a common intention that both parties should be beneficial owners of the property and that H relied on this to his detriment. A common intention will be found if the parties expressly discussed sharing the property or if intention can be inferred from the parties' conduct. It is possible that H and W discussed sharing the property when they were talking about sharing household expenses and maintenance costs. In the absence of such a discussion, H will have to base the common intention on the parties' conduct. Perhaps there is hope for H in such old-ish cases as *Cooke v Head* [1972] 1 WLR 518 and *Eves v Eves* [1975] 1 WLR 1338, where non-financial contributions went some way towards providing evidence of the necessary intention. But in these cases the claimants, who were women, performed heavy work in order to improve the respective properties. More recently, the woman in *Burns v Burns* [1984] FLR 216 lived with her partner for 19 years, gave up her job to look after him and their two children, bought consumer durables for the house and laid half a patio; however, this was not sufficient to demonstrate a common intention to share the property. In *Lloyds Bank v Rossett* [1990] 2 FLR 155, Lord Bridge was 'extremely doubtful' that anything other than a direct contribution to the purchase price (whether initially or by payment of mortgage instalments) would suffice. However, in *Le Foe v Le Foe* [2001] 2 FLR 97 the court held that a common intention could be inferred from indirect contributions, because the family economy had depended upon them. In *Stack v Dowden* (see earlier) the House of Lords stated that the approach adopted in *Lloyds Bank v Rosset* (see earlier) was too restrictive and Probert suggests that the approach taken in *Le Foe* 'is to be preferred as a matter of authority and as a matter of policy' (*Cretney and Probert's Family Law* (2009), p. 98). H would have to convince the court that his contribution to the family economy was sufficient to amount to a common intention to share. He will then have to demonstrate the further requirement of 'detrimental reliance', which is something H would not have done unless he was expecting a share in the property. Paying bills and household expenses may be enough to establish detrimental reliance but cooking, cleaning and gardening will not be. Perhaps H (as cohabitant) might be better advised to consider a libel action.